MOVABLE TYPES

Movable Types: Roving Creative Printers of the Victorian World

DAVID FINKELSTEIN

OXFORD
UNIVERSITY PRESS

OXFORD
UNIVERSITY PRESS

Great Clarendon Street, Oxford, OX2 6DP,
United Kingdom

Oxford University Press is a department of the University of Oxford.
It furthers the University's objective of excellence in research, scholarship,
and education by publishing worldwide. Oxford is a registered trade mark of
Oxford University Press in the UK and in certain other countries

© David Finkelstein 2018

The moral rights of the author have been asserted

First Edition published in 2018
Impression: 2

Published in the United States of America by Oxford University Press
198 Madison Avenue, New York, NY 10016, United States of America

British Library Cataloguing in Publication Data
Data available

Library of Congress Control Number: 2017962188

ISBN 978–0–19–882602–6

Printed and bound by
CPI Group (UK) Ltd, Croydon, CR0 4YY

Acknowledgements

This book has been long in the making, involving over ten years of research and writing. While writing is often a solitary process, I have been fortunate over the years to have had the support of many colleagues who generously offered their time and their wisdom, pointed me to relevant material, and commented, suggested, and gently corrected where needed. These include Jan Alessandrini, Tom Barron, Iain Beavan, the late Charles Benson, Fiona Black, Kirstie Blair, Laurel Brake, Paul van Capelleveen, John P. Chalmers, Regina Uí Chollatáin, Simon Eliot, Tony Farmar, Simon Frost, Aled Gruffydd Jones, Sheila Kidd, Andrew King, Patrick Leary, Katherine (Kitty) Ledbetter, Alistair McCleery, David Oels, Eve Patten, Robert L. Patten, Sydney Shep, Elizabeth Tilley, Christopher Whatley, Helen Williams, and Bernhard Wirth. Special thanks are reserved for Marion Sinclair, who expertly steered me towards an appropriately concise title for this book.

My thanks go to the SHARP-L electronic bulletin board community, whose comments in response to various queries of mine have materially shaped my thinking on these matters. I also wish to thank my research assistants, Chris Borsing, Greta Golick, Ruth McAdam, Michelle O'Connor, Zsuzsanna Varga, and Helen Williams, whose diggings on my behalf supported my work on relevant Canadian, English, Irish, and Scottish print trade union data.

Over the last ten years I have given papers in progress that have benefited from audience feedback. In this respect I would like to thank in particular Dr Jason McElligott, Prof Eve Patten, Dr Jane Mahoney and Dr Sarah Mitchell for opportunities to feature and discuss early versions of Chapter 2 at conferences and workshops organized at Trinity College Dublin in 2012 and 2015. Also thanks to Elizabeth Tilley for the opportunity to feature work in progress from Chapter 3 at an Irish Research Council funded 'Nineteenth-Century Trade Press' symposium, held at the National University of Ireland, Galway in 2017. Portions of Chapter 1 have appeared in different form as 'Nineteenth-Century Print on the Move: A Perilous Study of Translocal Migration and Print Skills Transfer', in Jason McElligott and Eve Patten, eds. *Theory and Practice in Book, Print and Publishing History* (Palgrave Macmillan, 2014); and as 'The Scottish Printing Diaspora, 1840–1914', in the *Oxford Research Encyclopedia of Literature* (2018). A small section of Chapter 3 has appeared in different form as 'Scottish Compositor Poets and the Typographical Trade Press, 1850–1880' in the special issue, 'Scottish Political Poetry and Song 1832–1918', *Scottish Literary Review* (2018).

I have benefited from access to union records and publications in archives across Britain and Ireland. Special thanks go to the archivists and record holders of the following institutions: Aberdeen University Library Special Collections for access to the Aberdeen Typographical Union records; the British Library; Dundee Central Library; the Marx Memorial Library, London; National Library of Scotland, in particular for access to the Edinburgh Typographical Association records; St Bride's

Library, London; Special Collections, Strathclyde University, for access to the Scottish Typographical Association (Glasgow branch) records; Library of Trinity College, Dublin, for access to their microfilm holdings of the Dublin Typographical Provident Society material.

My thanks also to the British Library, the National Library of Scotland, and St Bride's Library for granting permission to reproduce images from their collections. Front cover image is courtesy of SAPPHIRE (Scottish Archive of Print and Publishing History Records).

Over the years I have been awarded several travel and research grants that have enabled me to visit archival sources and to reflect on my findings. My thanks go to the following for such support: The Bibliographical Society; The British Academy; The Carnegie Trust for the Universities of Scotland; The Gladys Krieble Delmas Foundation; and The Printing Historical Society. I have also benefited from time and space provided by the following fellowships: a Long Room Hub fellowship, Trinity College, Dublin, March 2012; an Institute of Advanced Studies in Humanities Fellowship, University of Edinburgh, 2007.

Last but not least, much love goes to my wife Alison and my children Joseph and Anna, who kept me distracted when I needed to be, and were always there to provide me with hugs and cups of tea at the right moment.

Table of Contents

List of Figures

Except where noted, all images derive from author's private collection.

Introduction

In 1903, twenty-eight-year-old Scots-born Alexander (Sandy) Hossack made a momentous decision. A compositor by trade, he had worked for almost fifteen years alongside his brother James in their father's print shop in Edinburgh, serving his apprenticeship there and helping build up business with the nearby University of Edinburgh community.[1] During that time, he had also become a stalwart member of his union, the Scottish Typographical Association, quietly amassing knowledge and putting together a small amount of savings. It was time to move on, to follow new directions and new opportunities overseas. In May 1903, with help from a union emigration grant, he set sail for South Africa, travelling to Johannesburg, where over the coming decades he would work as a compositor and become heavily involved in trade union politics. He became a founding member of the Transvaal Labour Party in November 1904 (a socialist leaning political organization aimed at representing white artisanal labour union trade interests), and served as its first secretary.[2]

Hossack rose to prominence in the national South African Typographical Union (SATU), acting as its Vice-President between 1911 and 1914, and then as President of the Johannesburg branch in 1920. He would be awarded a Gold Union badge by SATU in 1921 for his services to the South African print trade. Not content with exercises in union management and political leadership, Hossack also threw himself into local activism, negotiating with employers for increases in pay and better working conditions, playing a key role in supporting strategic strikes in 1914 in Pretoria battling the de-unionizing of shop floors, and overseeing and singlehandedly

---

[1] Hossack's father, also named Alexander Hossack, is recorded in Edinburgh post office directories from 1887 until 1913 as owner of a small print shop located first at 71 and then at 68 Bristo Street, near the central campus of the University of Edinburgh. See for example *Post-Office Edinburgh and Leith Directory, 1887–88* (Edinburgh: Morrison and Gibb, 1887), p. 562. Hossack's compositor son James W. Hossack, who with Alex junior, worked for several years with his father, created marketing material for the firm: a business card sample composed and printed by James, for example, appears in *The Printers' International Specimen Exchange*, vol. 10 (London: The British Printer, 1889). Hossack died in Edinburgh on 17 March 1914, following which the firm was taken over by Thomas Paris, who had previously worked at Murray and Gibb for several years (union records indicate he had started there in 1888 and was there until at least 1903). See 'Statutory Registers, Deaths', ed. Crown Office (Edinburgh: National Records of Scotland, 1914) and 'Edinburgh Typographical Society Contributor Records, 1861–1900', in *Edinburgh Typographical Society Records* (National Library of Scotland). The firm subsequently traded under the name Hossack and Paris through to Paris's death in 1938: 'Bailie Paris. Edinburgh Magistrate's Death', *The Scotsman*, 29 December 1938.

[2] British Labour Party records hold correspondence with Hossack between 1906 and 1914 related to the early period of the Transvaal Labour Party: see, for example 'Hossack, Correspondence', in *Labour Party Archives* (Labour History Archive and Study Centre, People's History Museum/University of Central Lancashire, 1906).

writing and typesetting propaganda material and strike proclamations during union confrontations. Sandy was not the only one in his family to have taken his trade skills overseas: his father, also named Alexander Hossack, having trained in Edinburgh and worked for the small jobbing printers Muir and Paterson in Clyde Street, 'lifted' his union card in 1873 to work for a period in Boston, before returning to Scotland to start his own business.[3]

The Hossacks were just some of the thousands of English-speaking journeyman printers and compositors who moved across transnational borders to bring their skills elsewhere. Hossack (junior) was also an archetype of the mobile, active, and engaged printer and compositor that featured in the Victorian print economy. He, like many others chronicled in this book, was highly literate, engaged, outwardly facing, creative, and committed to expanding labour infrastructures and opportunities. Yet the roles individuals such as Hossack played in developing transnational print economies during the Victorian and Edwardian periods have not been well served in past studies. In part this has been due to the compartmentalization of labour studies within a sociological or economic framework, with investigations focused on the trade infrastructure of a nation, on a single union, or on case study exemplars.[4] Such is also the case with several labour histories documenting the rise of Scottish and English unions and of the skilled compositor, whose focus is on explaining how print unions were organized and what part they played in labour movements of the nineteenth and twentieth centuries.[5] What's missing, as one recent study has acknowledged, are insights into the social and economic conditions of compositors, especially as they relate to conditions at work.[6] A survey of PhD dissertations between 1970 and 1984 related to US printing history found 120 projects issued during that period, of which only three dealt with the trade experiences of print workers.[7] There are some exceptions to this national and subject specific focus, as for example Gary Marks's comparative work on nineteenth-century union politics in Germany, Britain and the USA.[8]

---

[3] Details recorded in 'Edinburgh Typographical Society Contributor Records, 1861–1900'.

[4] Useful exemplars include A. J. Downes, *Printers' Saga, Being a History of the South African Typographical Union* (Johannesburg: South African Typographical Union, 1952); Elaine N. Katz, *A Trade Union Aristocracy: A History of the White Workers in the Transvaal and the General Strike of 1913* (Johannesburg: University of Witswatersrand, 1976); Gregory S. Kealey, ' "The Honest Workingman" and Workers' Control: The Experience of Toronto Skilled Workers, 1860–1892', *Labour/Le Travail* 1 (1976); *Toronto Workers Respond to Industrial Capitalism, 1867–1892* (Toronto; Buffalo; London: University of Toronto Press, 1991); Seymour Martin Lipset, Martin A. Trow, and James S. Coleman, *Union Democracy: The Internal Politics of the International Typographical Union* (New York and London: Free Press; Collier-Macmillan, 1956); Mark D. Steinberg, *Moral Communities: The Culture of Class Relations in the Russian Printing Industry, 1867–1907* (Berkeley: University of California Press, 1992).

[5] Examples include union histories such as Sarah C. Gillespie, *A Hundred Years of Progress: The Record of the Scottish Typographical Association, 1853 to 1952* (Glasgow, 1953); A. E. Musson, *The Typographical Association: Origins and History up to 1949* (London: Oxford University Press, 1954); John and Peter Bain Gennard, *A History of the Society of Graphical and Allied Trades* (London: Routledge, 1995); John Gennard, *Mechanical to Digital Printing in Scotland: The Print Employers' Organisation* (Edinburgh: Scottish Printing Archival Trust, 2010).

[6] Patrick Duffy, *The Skilled Compositor, 1850–1914* (Aldershot: Ashgate, 2000), p. 12.

[7] Ibid., p. 12.

[8] Gary Marks, 'Variations in Union Political Activity in the United States, Britain, and Germany from the Nineteenth Century', *Comparative Politics* 22:1 (1989), pp. 83–104. See in particular Chapter 4, 'Printing Unions and Business Unionism', pp. 120–54, in *Union in Politics: Britain,*

Equally, recent anglophone print culture studies have tended to view print worker lives and activity through the lens of book culture, marginalizing the role of community-based printers as cultural connectors, and favouring studies of book printing over coverage of a wider range of printing work that extended beyond books and newspapers to cover jobbing work as diverse as journals, labels, leaflets, newsletters, pamphlets, posters, printed packaging, receipt books, tags, and other commercial material.[9] Again, some exceptions exist, as for example Isabel Hofmeyr's study of Gandhi's experiment in South African-based printing, and Siân Reynolds' study of Edinburgh women compositors.[10]

It should be acknowledged that anglophone initiatives in the histories of the book in America, Australia, Britain, Canada, Ireland, and Scotland have heroically dug away and presented us with details of the infiltration and development of national print infrastructures across the centuries, imported and developed from Western European print technology and traditions.[11] Many of these have focused on textual transmission and the spread of books, newspapers and journals as expressions of cultural expansion, as opposed to thinking through the simultaneous spread via skilled workers of jobbing print knowledge and print trade enterprise. This has been less true of studies of earlier periods of print trade activity. Spurred on by the pioneering work of Lucien Febvre and Henri-Jean Martin in their 1957

Germany, and the United States in the Nineteenth and Early Twentieth Centuries (Princeton, NJ: Princeton University Press, 1989).

[9] Such sidelining can be seen in the following examples, outstandingly comprehensive though many of them have been in other ways: Michael F. Suarez and H. R. Woudhuysen Suarez, *The Oxford Companion to the Book*, 2 vols. (Oxford: Oxford University Press, 2010), The *Print Networks* series issued by Oak Knoll Press and the British Library.

[10] Isabel Hofmeyr, *Gandhi's Printing Press: Experiments in Slow Reading* (Cambridge, MA: Harvard University Press, 2013); Siân Reynolds, *Britannica's Typesetters*, ed. Colin Bell, Edinburgh Education & Society Series (Edinburgh: Edinburgh University Press, 1989).

[11] See among others Hugh Amory and David D. Hall, eds., *A History of the Book in America*, vol. 1: *The Colonial Book in the Atlantic World* (Chapel Hill: University of North Carolina Press, 2007); John Barnard and D. F. McKenzie, eds., *The Cambridge History of the Book in Britain*, vol. 4: *1557–1695* (Cambridge: Cambridge University Press, 2002); Bill Bell, ed., *The Edinburgh History of the Book in Scotland*, vol. 3: *Ambition and Industry 1800–1880* (Edinburgh: Edinburgh University Press, 2007); Stephen Brown and Warren McDougall, eds., *The Edinburgh History of the Book in Scotland*, vol. 2: *Enlightenment and Expansion, 1707–1800* (Edinburgh: Edinburgh University Press, 2011); Scott E. Casper et al., eds., *A History of the Book in America*, vol. 3: *The Industrial Book, 1840–1880* (Chapel Hill: University of North Carolina Press, 2007); David Finkelstein and Alistair McCleery, *The Edinburgh History of the Book in Scotland*, vol. 4: *Professionalism and Diversity, 1880–2000* (Edinburgh: Edinburgh University Press, 2007); Yvan Lamonde, Patricia Lockhart Fleming, and Fiona A. Black, eds., *History of the Book in Canada*, vol. 2: *1840–1918* (Toronto: University of Toronto Press, 2005); Robert A. Gross and Mary Keller, eds., *A History of the Book in America*, vol. 2: *An Extensive Republic, Print, Culture, and Society in the New Nation, 1790–1840* (Chapel Hill: University of North Carolina Press, 2010); Carl F. Kaestle and Janice Radway, eds., *A History of the Book in America*, vol. 4: *Print in Motion: The Expansion of Publishing and Reading in the United States, 1880–1940* (Chapel Hill: University of North Carolina Press, 2009); Patricia Lockhart Fleming, Gilles Gallichan, and Yvan Lamonde, eds., *History of the Book in Canada*, vol. 1: *Beginnings to 1840* (Toronto: University of Toronto Press, 2004); David McKitterick, ed., *The Cambridge History of the Book in Britain*, vol. 6: *1830–1914* (Cambridge: Cambridge University Press, 2009); David Paul Nord, Joan Shelley Rubin, and Michael Schudson, eds., *A History of the Book in America*, vol. 5: *The Enduring Book: Print Culture in Postwar America* (Chapel Hill: University of North Carolina Press, 2009); Michael F. Suarez and Michael L. Turner, eds., *The Cambridge History of the Book in Britain*, vol. 5: *1695–1830* (Cambridge: Cambridge University Press, 2009).

translated text *The Coming of the Book*, book historians of the early print period have mapped the flow of skills and expertise from Germany across Europe in the late fifteenth century, and then outwards through the sixteenth to eighteenth centuries.[12] By the time we reach the nineteenth century, the continuation of one-way transmission of print knowledge through colonial expansion and missionary and state needs and interests is taken for granted. A strange lacuna exists in our knowledge of the industrialized Victorian period and beyond. As Aileen Fyfe has commented recently, 'Historians of the Book have long recognized that there were significant changes in the production and distribution of printed matter in the nineteenth century. In contrast to the voluminous scholarship on the "printing revolution" of the fifteenth century, the nature of these changes remains little studied.'[13] To expand somewhat on that, we have no map of the global nature of industrialized, nineteenth-century printing activity in English speaking worlds (or others for that matter), nor is there a clear map of the flow of skills, tools, people, knowledge, and information circulating around global print networks and geographical nodes. The chapters that follow attempt to redress this in modest form, demonstrating how print networks were developed across the anglophone world, and through what means such networks enabled transnational trade communication and information flows across space and time.

NATIONAL IDENTITY FORMATIONS

Benedict Anderson's now overused pronouncement on national identity established the idea of the collective 'imagined community', partly shaped by a common, shared language inculcated through shared print media sources such as newspapers and books.[14] The idea of a national identity based on culture, language, and print is naturally a contested point in areas that experienced colonization and conquest by others during the eighteenth and nineteenth centuries: the cultural stories and identities that dominate can be based equally on power structures and hierarchies as on a shared alphabet. But if the 'imagined community' is a troubled concept for many, implicit in its acceptance is the assumption that print culture infrastructures supporting its development were uni-directional and effortlessly created: printing presses somehow appeared, technology and colonial manpower to run them were invariably imported into foreign lands, texts were subsequently produced, and in time indigenous workers were allowed induction into the mysteries and the art of the printing press, subsequently ushering in an era of self-expression and creative endeavour.

---

[12] Febvre and Martin, *The Coming of the Book*, pp. 167–97; see also Adrian Johns, *The Nature of the Book: Print and Knowledge in the Making* (Chicago: University of Chicago Press, 1998); Miles Ogborn and Charles W. J. Withers, eds., *Geographies of the Book* (Farnham: Ashgate Press, 2010).

[13] Aileen Fyfe, 'Steam and the Landscape of Knowledge: W & R Chambers in the 1830s–1850s', in *Geographies of the Book*, ed. M. Ogborn and C. Withers (Farnham: Ashgate Press, 2010).

[14] Benedict Anderson, *Imagined Communities: Reflections on the Origins and Spread of Nationalism* (London: Verso, 1991).

Unpack this, particularly in relation to Britain and its dependencies in the nineteenth century, when new technology enabled print production to expand exponentially at cheaper cost and more quickly, and you face some interesting questions. What infrastructures and mechanisms underpinned such print culture developments? What cultural values and trade skills were transmitted and embedded in indigenous settings by workers who flowed into and through established and developing territories? And what was transmitted back through 'imperial' circuits and networks? Who manned the machines, what skills and talents did they bring to such tasks, and who created the copy and bankrolled the distribution of print in all its forms (from ephemeral to pamphlet, journal, newspaper, and printed book). What prompted print workers to move about? How did locals and incomers alike deal with each other in such work-spaces?

Studying these questions at a general level offers insights into the shaping of local print economies. Local printers produced newspapers and formed part of self-sufficient market town print economies, offering personal printing services to local merchants and farmers that small print shops were well qualified to do. A question arising from this point, which this volume seeks to address, is how did local print economy traditions and forms translate across transnational settings? The period chosen for studying this issue, 1830–1914, covers the rise of print unions across the anglophone world from the 1830s onwards, the expansion of letterpress printing technology and consequent employment opportunities during the period 1840–1880, and the transnational extension of print networks that concludes with the outbreak of the First World War.

This book is an interdisciplinary study of, to draw on Tony Ballantine's phrase, the 'webs of empire' that underpinned and enabled skilled print labour networks over the Victorian and Edwardian periods.[15] It is a cultural history, with substantial chapters incorporating original material linked to labour history, literary culture, migration studies, social history, and print culture studies. Drawing on a range of unique primary and secondary sources covering Australia, Canada, England, Ireland, New Zealand, Scotland, South Africa, the United States, and Wales, it focuses on the 'typographical web' that encompassed print economies across these regions. It offers insights into how print culture structures translated across national boundaries, how print workers were mobilized and organized as the century progressed, and how shared craft identities, creative endeavours, and trade press publications created a sense of moral community that linked the printing fraternity across space and time.

The first chapter of the book addresses the phenomenon of the 'tramping typographer', the roving printer who travelled across cities and nations seeking work, establishing trade and labour networks, and participating in a skills exchange process that expanded trade knowledge across national borders. It examines how international labour networks developed between 1830 and 1914 to support such interchanges locally and transnationally, including union backed 'tramping

---

[15] Tony Ballantine, 'Empire, Knowledge and Culture: From Proto-Globalization to Modern Globalization', in *Globalization in Modern History*, ed. A.G. Hopkins (London: Pimlico, 2002).

schemes' and emigration grants. It offers a typology of the migrant worker extant during this period of great mobility, and explores how migrating print workers played key roles in settler communities and union initiatives.

Chapter 2 addresses the methods by which workers were mobilized and trade unions communicated during a series of strikes sparked by the 'nine-hour' movement in the 1870s. The nine-hour movement, to lower working weeks from sixty to fifty-four hours, had gained impetus in Great Britain following a successful strike in 1871 by Newcastle-based engineers. Print trade strikes allied to the movement took place across Canada, England, Ireland, and Scotland over the following decade. Some ushered in a general shift to improved working hours and conditions across major labour sectors (not just in printing). Another led to the opening of the composing room to women workers. A late 1870s Irish strike provoked parliamentary inquiries and debates about protectionism and the tensions between supporting national labour interests while enabling government-sponsored transnational print activity. Other strikes demonstrated the difficulties of maintaining a balance between central oversight and localized union actions. Implicit within the debates generated by these events were attempts to define the role of print trade societies within trade guild parameters, and ultimately the forms of social identity and communication networks forged and supported during such labour struggles and encounters.

Chapter 3 concentrates on trade journals started by typographical workers between 1840 and 1900. The typographical trade press featured a great number of works by creative compositors. Topics reflected upon in poems, short stories, and memoirs included reading experiences, literacy, working class culture, the art of printing, and union solidarity. A survey of the extant material, of the background of creative compositors and printers, of the format of the journals in which such material appeared, and of the themes and topics they addressed, offers valuable insights into the way creativity was harnessed by printers to address trade specific social, cultural, and work-based themes and concerns.

The three chapters of this book are meant to illustrate how individuals, shaped by local print economies, interacted within larger global frameworks, whether through extended travel networks, through coordinated strike actions, or through creative processes and trade press outputs. Printers were joined via a complex web of personal interchanges linked to changes in technology, businesses practices, labour organization, and communication. British and anglophone trained compositors and journeyman printers, moving between local and international settings, played important and unacknowledged roles as key transmitters of knowledge within a global 'typographical web'. They were connected by a craft identity that encouraged notions of printers as part of a larger moral community.

The formation of a moral community of compositors and journeyman printers derived from the use of a trade specialism to shape behaviour and conceptions of inclusion and exclusion. The skill of composing movable type was one that underpinned printing as a profession from the trade's inception in 1450, when Gutenberg launched the printing press revolution. Until the early 1800s, composing type, working it off a press, and reading and correcting the resulting proofs had often been performed by an individual printer, aided by apprentices or a small number of co-workers, who were multi-skilled and trained to manage the full range of printing work. By far the most skilled and demanding part of this process was typesetting, the casting of metal type into lines that would be locked into a form of flat boxed structure, over which ink would be rolled, paper placed, and pressure applied to transfer the results. As one account notes, typesetting or composing was a process 'which demanded not only a high degree of dexterity, but for good work an aesthetically discriminating eye'.[16] In the nineteenth century, as new techniques and technology (such as lithography) added complexities to the printing process, and print firms expanded to accommodate rising demands for print in all forms, these tasks began to be compartmentalized, with men offered the opportunity to specialize as compositors, pressmen, and/or correctors of press work. Often some would move from one specialization to another during their working lives, with compositors taking on editorial or general management roles, or becoming proof correctors and press contributors. Regardless, the long, seven-year apprenticeships which most individuals underwent, ensured printers were inducted into the full range of tasks associated with the craft of printing with movable type. As print unions began to be established from the 1830s onwards, dominated by the composing wing of the trade, the term printer would become synonymous with the typographically skilled and trained practitioner. They would prove organized and active participants of transnational networks that would materially shape the Victorian anglophone print trade world.

The space these printers inhabited was a gendered, male space. Until the 1860s and 1870s, women compositors were few and actively discouraged by British and Irish trade societies and unions. This would change following the industry strikes of the 1870s, documented in Chapter 2 of this book. In the USA, women compositors were accommodated more readily, particularly with the rise of the 'swifts', compositors, both male and female, renowned for their accuracy and speed in typesetting, whose reputations would be made through numerous composing races instituted from the late 1860s onwards.[17] One such exemplar, Augusta Lewis, would found the Women's Typographical Union no. 1 in 1869, the first all-woman labour union in the USA.[18]

Despite these incursions, the print floor remained primarily a male space for most of the century. Within this male space, the printing fraternity imposed codes of conduct on individuals joining the ranks: strict oversight of behaviour and activity was engrained into the workplace, as well as being part of the training of an apprentice printer, monitored and overseen in firms by the chapel system.

---

[16] J. Hagan, *Printers and Politics: A History of the Australian Printing Unions, 1850–1950* (Canberra: Australian National University Press, 1966), p. 2.

[17] Walker Rumble, *The Swifts: Printers in the Age of Typesetting Races* (Charlottesville and London: University of Virginia Press, 2003). See also Walker Rumble, 'A Showdown of "Swifts": Women Compositors, Dime Museums, and the Boston Typesetting Races of 1886', *The New England Quarterly* 71, no. 4 (1998).

[18] *The Swifts: Printers in the Age of Typesetting Races*. See in particular the chapter on August Lewis, 'Augusta Lewis and Women's Typographical Union No. 1', pp. 62–83.

The chapel system was a workplace structure stretching back to pre-industrial print beginnings, which combined economic, social, and political concerns into a recognizable pattern of interaction. Compositors enmeshed themselves within a workplace community with well-established boundaries and codes of conduct. Chapel membership dues were a required part of the structure, meant to cover expenses of work rituals and social occasions. Frequent meetings were held to discuss communal concerns, as well as manage through collective democratic means the apportioning of work and the managing of time and space between colleagues. Rituals covering apprenticeship, the joining and leaving of the work community, and the general conduct within the work space were also part of chapel rules and processes. As Gary Marks points out, the principle behind such management was twofold: 'maintaining the autonomy of the printers' craft from employer supervision, while opposing any possible threat to the printers' occupational solidarity'.[19] The meshing of these two themes, autonomy and solidarity, into a work scenario where regulations on ratios of apprentices to qualified printers were strictly patrolled by the workers, rates of pay were minutely calculated and watched, and division of work was managed internally, were means by which print workers 'sought to restrict the freedom of employers to compartmentalize and divide the work force'.[20]

UNIONS

Nineteenth-century print unions grafted themselves onto pre-established chapel systems. Unions created similar rites, codes, and methods of overseeing membership. They required union dues as means of creating collective responsibility, issued membership and travelling cards to facilitate belonging to and movement between print networks, used communication sources such as monthly journals, bulletins, and union meetings to inform wider print trade communities of individual achievements and warn of transgressors, and sponsored public events to celebrate and commemorate key moments of print trade history and activity.

During the nineteenth century, four major print trade unions developed in the British Isles to service key regional areas and printing centres, and represent journeyman printers and compositors. These included the Dublin Typographical Provident Society (DTPS), founded in 1809, later to be more fully organized and reinstituted in 1825, and on which scholars such as Charles Benson, Mary Pollard, and Vincent Kinane have written.[21] A short-lived regional union, the Irish Typographical Union, was also extant between 1836 and 1841. In the 1850s and

---

[19] Marks, 'Variations in Union Political Activity in the United States, Britain, and Germany from the Nineteenth Century', 90.

[20] Ibid.

[21] See Charles Benson, 'The Dublin Book Trade 1801–1850, 4 Volumes' (PhD, Trinity College, Dublin, 2000); Vincent Kinane, *A History of the Dublin University Press, 1734–1976* (Dublin: Gill and Macmillan, 1994); Vincent Kinane, 'Irish Booklore: A Galley of Pie: Women in the Irish Book Trades', *The Linen Hall Review* 8, no. 4 (1991); Vincent Kinane, 'Printers' Apprentices in 18th- and 19th-Century Dublin', *The Linen Hall Review* 10, no. 1 (1993); Mary Pollard, *A Dictionary of the Members of the Dublin Book Trade, 1550–1800* (London: Bibliographical Society, 2000).

1860s, Irish union activity began gathering momentum and strength, with the revitalization of the DTPS, the absorption of Irish regional printing union clusters into the English-based Typographical Association, and the parallel development of its Scottish counterpart, the Scottish Typographical Association (STA). The DTPS was representative of most Dublin members of the trade at the time, though exact numbers of print workers in Dublin during the latter half of the nineteenth century are hard to come by. One source quotes a total of 899 letter press printers employed in the 1860s, while union records for 1870 show membership standing at just over 690, or roughly 77 per cent of Dublin's estimated total workforce.[22]

London print workers were supported by the London Society of Compositors, formed in 1848 from previous mergers of competing unions and because of London compositors seceding from the National Typographical Society to form a separate entity focused on London's print industry. Reporting a membership in April 1848 of 1,100 members, by 1902 numbers had risen to 11,244, and by 1914 it was reporting membership figures of 12,384.[23]

Scottish printers were at the forefront of union activity in the early nineteenth century, and one of the first trade union groups for printers and typographers to seek general organization, with a start in Glasgow in 1817. A more enduring Scottish-based organization rose from such beginnings in 1853 with the founding of the Scottish Typographical Association, which grew into a regional bastion of union activity, expanding from a general annual membership in 1857 of around 600 in five key centres to around 4,700 members in 1910 based in twenty-five Scottish towns and cities.[24]

By far the largest in terms of membership was the Provincial Typographical Association, which emerged in 1849 from previous short-lived associations (the Northern Typographical Union, 1830–44, and the National Typographical Association, 1844–1848). In 1877, it merged with another organization, the Relief Association, to form the Typographical Association, under which it remained titled until mergers with other regional associations in the second half of the twentieth century. Starting with nineteen branches and 481 members mainly concentrated in Lancashire, Cheshire, and the West Riding, by 1914 the Association had expanded to 157 branches and 23,310 members based in England, Wales, and Ireland, though excluding Dublin and London.[25]

In other anglophone countries, unions were founded later in the century. In the USA, the National Typographical Union, first mooted in 1850, would fully emerge after initial meetings between eleven print trade societies in 1852; it would change its name in 1869 to the International Typographical Union to acknowledge

[22] Nicholas McGrath, 'Meandering through the Past', in *Dublin Typographical Provident Society Records* (Trinity College Dublin), p. 1870.

[23] Ellic Howe and Harold Waite, *The London Society of Compositors (Re-Established 1848): A Centenary History* (London: Cassell and Company, 1948), pp. 86, 340.

[24] Gillespie, *A Hundred Years of Progress*, pp. 54–5, 233; Arthur Marsh and John B. Smethurst, *Historical Directory of Trade Unions*, vol. 5: *Including Unions in Printing and Published Local Government, Retail and Distribution, Domestic Services, General Employment, Financial Services, Agriculture* (Aldershot: Ashgate, 2006), pp. 93–4.

[25] Musson, *The Typographical Association*, pp. 91–3.

the incorporation of Canadian print trade branches, and grow from just over 2,000 members in 1853 to 51,100 by 1914.[26] Australia witnessed early union organization in the 1850s, with one of the first compositors' union being founded in Melbourne in 1851 as the Victoria Typographical Association. It was followed by small typographical associations founded in the mid- to late 1850s in Ballarat, Hobart Town, Sydney, and Adelaide, among others.[27] Economic depression, failed strike actions, and determined opposition of print establishment owners, saw several of these association branches disappear by the early 1860s, except for Ballarat, which quietly soldiered on intact through to the end of the century and beyond. It was not until the 1870s and 1880s that print unions would regain a foothold in Australia and neighbouring New Zealand, as economic expansion and improved trade conditions drew new recruits and able trade organizers to Australasian shores. The New Zealand Typographical Association would take shape following a meeting of delegates in Dunedin in July 1881, following which union branches were established in Auckland, Dunedin, Napier, and Wellington.[28] A national South African Typographical Union emerged in 1898. Print trade organization came much later in India, with the founding of the Indian Printers' Union in Calcutta in 1905. Like its anglophone antecedents, it established social benefit schemes for its members, including mutual insurance, night schools, educational stipends, and funeral allowances.[29] As discussed more fully in Chapter 1 of this volume, many of these print union branches were built upon the organizational work of anglophone roving printers.

Unions became powerful arbiters in the print work place, actively lobbying for better working conditions and pay, and offering members access to a variety of benefits such as sick pay and unemployment relief. As the trade union movement in general began gathering force from the mid-nineteenth century onwards, print union representatives became involved in significant initiatives to improve workers' rights and wages across the printing sector, going on strike in response to local or regional circumstances, circulating news items and information on working conditions and, through annual congresses, leaflets, monthly journals, and annual reports, seeking to ensure and strengthen communication and practical links with print trade members and other trade unions. From there they progressed into wider lobbying efforts, participating in wider trade union organized movements and initiatives, such as the nine-hour working week movement documented in Chapter 2 of this study.

Another feature of the printing fraternity was the emphasis on and support for trade mobility and the development of a transnational 'printing diaspora' of linked

---

[26] George E. Barnett, 'The Printers: A Study in American Trade Unionism', *American Economic Association Quarterly* 10, no. 3 (1909). Appendix 7; and Leo Wolman, *The Growth of American Trade Unions, 1880–1923* (New York: National Bureau of Economic Research, 1924), pp. 110–19.

[27] Hagan, *Printers and Politics*, p. 32.

[28] Peter Franks, *Print & Politics: A History of Trade Unions in the New Zealand Printing Industry, 1865–1995* (Wellington: Victoria University Press, 2001), p. 32.

[29] Rajendra Kumar Sharma, *Social Disorganisation* (New Delhi: Atlantic Publishers and Distributors, 1998).

unions and print networks. Victorian print trade unions and benevolent print trade societies, as noted in Chapter 1 of this study, were keen promoters of free movement of people, ideas, and skills across the English-speaking world. English speaking printers were key players in printing diaspora networks developed via the unions at local and international levels: individual members circulated between regional and overseas union branches, acted as transmitters of union values and trade skills, and became central to the expansion of labour interests in new territories. They wrote letters to colleagues letting them know of their experiences, produced memoirs of their working lives, contributed to trade journals, founded and edited newspapers, and served as cultural connectors locally and transnationally. Chapter 3 of this volume explores how these connections manifested themselves in the creative and cultural material produced by compositors and journeyman printers in the monthly print trade journals that were founded from the 1840s onwards in Great Britain and Ireland, Australasia, North America, and South Africa. Previously unheralded and unknown 'labour laureates' made their mark in the pages of these journals, publishing poetry and prose on labour themes in dialect form, and frequently infusing contributions with print trade specific language and terminology. Such contributions were then circulated and shared internationally by the print trade press, creating a 'typographical web' of knowledge exchange transcending national boundaries.

THEORIZING TRANSNATIONAL FLOWS

The flow of skills, tools, people, and print knowledge around global networks and geographical nodes, and the place of trained printers in this circulation of print knowledge, has great implications for understanding how trade knowledge was spread, print communities formed, and nation building projects and identity enabled by globally informed but locally developed print infrastructures. Printers in the Victorian world participated in a rapidly industrialized global setting, drawing on union supported emigration grants to shift continents when the need arose, or making use of tramping networks codified by unions to support regional migration when jobs were scarce or union actions required it.

Migration internally and overseas enabled insertion of trade skills into local and general spaces and the transfer of knowledge and skills between incomer and indigenous workers. Much has been written about general nineteenth-century migration flows, but not in relation to transnational print worker concerns. If we are to understand fully the construction and dissemination of cultural knowledge during the industrialized period, what is needed is 'a fuller appreciation of what we might term the "architecture of empire", its fundamental structures, the levels at which knowledge was created, consumed and transmitted'.[30]

Extant union membership lists, minute books, and other records offer insight into the way print trade union branches used their organizational structures to

---

[30] Ballantine, 'Empire, Knowledge and Culture', p. 127.

sustain a cohesive sense of social identity and elite trade status amongst their members across space and time. The various forms in which such identities were effectively supported and monitored shaped regional, national, and transnational flows of skills, knowledge, and labour traditions throughout the English-speaking world in the nineteenth and early twentieth centuries. Ultimately, what I hope this work provides are new insights into how print culture structures translated across national boundaries, how print workers were mobilized and organized as the century progressed, and how shared craft identities and creative endeavours created a sense of moral community that linked the printing fraternity across space and time.

1

Roving Printers

International Printer Migration, Skills Exchange, and Information Flow, 1830–1914

INTRODUCTION

Migration was a key tool for building the social, cultural, and economic infrastructures of the Victorian and Edwardian world throughout the nineteenth and early twentieth centuries. Between 1815 and 1930, an estimated 12 million Britons left the British Isles for North America, Australasia, and South Africa.[1] During the same period, 7 million Irish emigrated to the USA and the British Dominions.[2] A similar deluge of migrating families came out of Europe: one estimate suggests that between the end of the Napoleonic Wars in 1815 and the depression of the 1930s, over 50 million people left Europe for overseas destinations.[3] Such displacement of people contributed to imperial and labour diasporas driven by economic necessity during this period of extensive movement and change. Print culture (and its practitioners) was crucial to the communication structures supporting such diasporas. And members of a highly skilled, mobile 'printing diaspora' who could help construct and promote political and cultural identities through the agency of print were, from the outset, high on the preferred occupation lists.

English-speaking printers and printing unions were key players in such printing diaspora networks, at local and international levels: individual members circulated between regional and overseas union branches, acting as transmitters of union values and trade skills, and becoming central to the expansion of labour interests in new territories. By what means this was accomplished is the subject of this chapter. Among areas to be explored will be: the phenomenon of the 'tramping typographer', peripatetic roving printers who travelled along established print networks in search of work; emigration networks that facilitated transnational migration of skilled print workers; types of skilled trade movement evident from union records and archives; and the role of transnational print migrants as community anchors and labour organizers.

---

[1] Dudley Baines, *Emigration from Europe, 1815–1930* (Basingstoke: Palgrave Macmillan, 1991), pp. 7–9.

[2] Ibid.

[3] Dudley Baines, 'European Emigration, 1815–1930: Looking at the Emigration Decision Again', *Economic History Review* New Series 47, no. 3 (August 1994), 525.

PRINT TRADE MOVEMENT

The local, regional, and transnational circulation of highly skilled workers played its part in the development of nineteenth-century anglophone print economies. Between 1830 and 1914, supported by travel subsidies and emigration and removal grant schemes, British and Irish printers and print union members circulated overseas in great numbers, part of a larger, global movement of people and skills. New York City's Castle Garden emigration processing centre alone saw 4,830 international compositors, printers, type cutters, type founders, type makers, typesetters, and typographers flow through its gates between 1840 and 1890, of whom 2,273 were British and Irish, as Table 1.1 makes clear.[4] The latter group arrived via ships from Glasgow, Liverpool, Newcastle, Southampton, and Queenstown in Ireland.

During the same period, English-speaking printers from Britain, North America, and elsewhere moved into British colonial spaces to participate in what has generally been termed 'settler capitalism', setting up businesses, engaging in labour and union politics, and creating the print culture infrastructures that sustained social, communal, and national communication and identity in such territories.[5] Equally there was movement by workers across and between North America, the British Isles, Australasia, India, and South Africa that attested to the globalized nature of print work.

But in print culture terms, few have considered the cultural and social impact of such fluid transactions across nineteenth- and early twentieth-century borders. As

Table 1.1 Print Trade Worker Registrations, Castle Garden Immigration Centre, New York, USA, 1840–1890

Country or Region of Origin	Primary Occupation Listed				Total numbers
	Compositor, Typographer	Printer	Type cutter Typefounder Type maker Typesetter	Pressman	
England	97	1017	11	6	1131
Ireland	66	638	10	6	720
Scotland	72	321	11	3	407
Wales	0	15	0	0	15
Grand Totals	**235**	**1991**	**32**	**15**	**2273**

---

[4] In 1890 Ellis Island replaced Castle Garden as the emigration processing centre for emigrants arriving via New York, thus the cutoff date used for data gathering purpose. Data was retrieved from www.castlegarden.org, accessed 13 March 2017. A global search of the records using the 'fuzzy terms' print*, type*, typo* and composit* yielded a total of 4,800 non-native print trade emigrants to New York, of whom 2,258 were English, Irish, Scottish, and Welsh workers listing their profession as printer, compositor, type cutter, type founder, type maker, typesetter, or typographer.

[5] Donald Denoon, *Settler Capitalism: The Dynamics of Dependent Development in the Southern Hemisphere* (Oxford: Clarendon Press, 1983).

William Pretzer summarizes in an astute study of nineteenth-century US print tramping customs, we have still a great deal to learn regarding the nature of geographical mobility amongst print workers, the role of travel in sustaining social and cultural traditions, and the impact of technology and unions in supporting or terminating itinerant work systems.[6] The impact of mobility and skills flow on nation building and social structures is an important one worth considering in wider contexts.

It is also worth reflecting that such mobility meshed with an intensive period of expansion in print infrastructures across the English-speaking world. In Britain, improvements in print technology, allied to slow but steady repeals from the 1820s to the 1860s of the so-called 'taxes on knowledge', steep tariffs on ads, paper, ink, and newspapers imposed because of political fears of public access to news and information following the French Revolution of 1789, saw a corresponding expansion of local print shops and print trade worker numbers. Between 1831 and 1851, the UK Census records the numbers of print trade workers over the age of twenty in England and Wales rising from 9,000 to 23,600.[7] Some 8,000 of the latter number were located in London, working across 423 offices.[8] Of these London offices, only four were large enough to employ more than 100 compositors (Clowes, Spottiswoodes, Hansards, and Savill and Edwards), while as many as 288 were small, 'backroom' operations employing fewer than three compositors.[9] Scottish census records only began recording occupations in 1841: returns suggest print and allied trade numbers rose from 7,195 to 13,235 between 1841 and 1851.[10] In Ireland, letterpress printing numbers rose more slowly in the same period, from 1,717 workers recorded in the 1841 census to 2,178 workers in 1851.[11]

From 1851 to 1891, UK print trade worker numbers rose further as opportunities expanded in the wake of the repeal in 1861 of the paper tax, the last of the 'taxes on knowledge'. The number of print workers listed in the UK Census for England and Wales more than tripled between 1851 and 1891, rising from 23,600 in 1851 to 44,100 in 1871, then to 82,000 in 1891.[12] Of these census totals, Welsh and Monmouthshire printers accounted for 343 in 1851, 700 in 1871, and

---

[6] William S. Pretzer, 'Tramp Printers: Craft Culture, Trade Unions, and Technology', *Printing History: The Journal of the American Printing History Association* 6:2 (1984), 3.

[7] A. E. Musson, *The Typographical Association: Origins and History up to 1949* (London: Oxford University Press, 1954), p. 18; John Child, *Industrial Relations in the British Printing Industry: The Quest for Security* (London: Allen and Unwin, 1967), p. 107.

[8] Musson, *The Typographical Association*, p. 18. Ellic Howe and Harold Waite, *The London Society of Compositors (Re-Established 1848): A Centenary History* (London: Cassell and Company, 1948), pp. 147–8.

[9] Howe and Waite, *The London Society of Compositors*, pp. 148–50.

[10] Ross Alloway, 'Appendix A: Personnel in the Print and Allied Trades', in *Edinburgh History of the Book in Scotland*, vol. 3: *Ambition and Industry, 1800–1880*, ed. Bill Bell (Edinburgh: Edinburgh University Press, 2007).

[11] Kinane, 'Irish Booklore: A Galley of Pie: Women in the Irish Book Trades', p. 11.

[12] Child, *Industrial Relations in the British Printing Industry*, p. 107.

2,000 in 1891.[13] In Scotland, it was a similar story, with census figures on workers in print and allied trades rising from 13,235 in 1851 to 22,248 in 1871, and then to 33,752 in 1891.[14] Ireland saw equally steady expansion, with letterpress printer numbers rising from 2,177 in 1851 to 3,421 in 1871 (of which twenty-five of the latter were women compositors).[15] Irish census returns from 1881 through to the end of the century did not include analysis by occupation for the whole country, but Dublin censuses did. Dublin returns indicate a continuation of a slow but steadily upward trend across the sector of previous decades, with compositor numbers rising from 1,477 male and nineteen female workers in 1881 to 1,817 male and forty-seven female workers in 1891, and concluding with 1,901 male and eighty-seven female workers in 1901.[16]

The rapid, nineteenth-century settlement westwards across both Canada and the USA witnessed similar dynamic expansions in print activity. In Canada, printing trades grew quickly in the second half of the century, with worker numbers rising from 752 in 1851 to over 4,200 in 1871, and then more than doubling as migrants flooded in to encompass 9,006 workers in 1891 and 11,576 workers in 1901.[17] In the USA, the 1840 US national census recorded 1,573 printing offices employing 11,622 workers, responsible for producing 1,403 newspapers alongside other print material.[18] Two-thirds of those printing offices were in rural villages.[19] A wider picture of the print trade emerges in later census data. In 1850, there were 1,605 firms involved in printing, book, and stationery trades, employing 15,420 men over the age of sixteen and 6,631 women over the age of fifteen. As Table 1.2 shows, numbers rose exponentially over the next thirty years, so that by 1880 the census returns listed 5,863 firms employing 80,198 men over the age of sixteen, 23,234 women over the age of fifteen, and 8,643 youth.[20]

Jack Larkin tellingly concludes that such expansion aligned with a wider cultural phenomenon, whereby 'printing offices became a characteristic feature of the commercial villages emerging in the American countryside, and printers moved westward alongside farmers, merchants, and other artisans'.[21] These social shifts

---

[13] Aled Jones, *Press, Politics and Society: A History of Journalism in Wales* (Cardiff: University of Wales Press, 1993), p. 77.

[14] Alloway, 'Appendix A'.

[15] Kinane, 'Irish Booklore: A Galley of Pie: Women in the Irish Book Trades', p. 11.

[16] Ibid., p. 12.

[17] Eric Leroux, 'Trades, Labour, and Design', in *History of the Book in Canada*, vol. 1: *1840–1918*, ed. Yvan Lamonde, Patricia Lockhart Fleming, and Fiona A. Black (Toronto: University of Toronto Press, 2005), p. 77.

[18] Robert A. Gross, 'Introduction', in *A History of the Book in America*, vol. 2: *An Extensive Republic, Print, Culture, and Society in the New Nation, 1790–1840*, ed. Robert A. Gross and Mary Kelley (Chapel Hill: University of North Carolina Press, 2010), p. 37.

[19] Jack Larkin, '"Printing Is Something Every Village Has in It": Rural Printing and Publishing', in *A History of the Book in America*, vol. 2: *An Extensive Republic, Print, Culture, and Society in the New Nation, 1790–1840*, ed. Robert A. Gross and Mary Kelley (Chapel Hill: University of North Carolina Press, 2010), p. 146.

[20] Scott E. Casper, 'Introduction', in *A History of the Book in America*, vol. 3: *The Industrial Book, 1840–1880*, ed. Scott E. Casper, Jeffrey D. Groves, Stephen W. Nissenbaum, and Michael Winship (Chapel Hill: The University of North Carolina Press, 2007), pp. 10–17.

[21] Larkin, '"Printing Is Something Every Village Has in It"', p. 146.

Table 1.2 US Census Data, Printing, Book, and Stationery Trades Workers

Census Year	# of Firms	Men over 16 years	Women over 15 Years	Youths	Total # Workers
1840	1,573	11,622	—	—	11,622
1850	1,605	15,420	6,631	—	22,051
1860	2,941	30,604	10,255	—	40,859
1870	3,553	41,345	12,711	4,273	58,329
1880	5,863	80,198	23,234	8,643	112,075

encouraged geographical mobility amongst American journeymen printers working between urban areas and rural communities. Later print historians would feelingly describe such journeymen as 'birds of passage' who 'journeyed more often and farther than other American artisans'.[22]

Jobbing printers were called upon to manage production of a complexity of print material, from local newspapers and pamphlets to business cards, labels, greeting cards and other print paraphernalia. New settlements called for skilled workers who could keep the populace informed and help promote the town to the wider world. Equally, the legal requirement in many emerging settlements that land purchases by individual stakeholders be advertised locally in printed form created revenue opportunities for enterprising printers. Local communities also needed avenues to promote settlement opportunities. A contemporary typographer would recall that 'it was not at all uncommon, where no printer appeared to start a newspaper for such a budding community, for the citizens or promoters of the prospective city to assume the financial obligations entailed in order to encourage some member of the craft to set up a press and to give the location publicity'.[23]

Print represented progress, and local newspapers represented community knowledge and a territorial marking. Reflecting on the establishment of the first newspaper in Kansas in 1854 in Leavenworth, which had preceded the establishment of more conventional social infrastructures, the typographer memoirist John Edward Hicks drew attention to the symbolic significance of such an act: 'The spirit of adventure thrust it forward ahead of the calaboose, the post office, the school, the church, and made of it a symbol of conquest.'[24]

In Britain, the shift from concentration of print activity in a small number of urban centres to wider, diffuse networks of locally and regionally based jobbing print businesses was equally tangible to those studying the rise of British unionized labour. The labour historians Sidney and Beatrice Webb neatly summarized the results in their influential 1897 study *Industrial Democracy*, commenting that

The printing trade, on the other hand, once concentrated in half a dozen towns, has to-day crept into every village, the vast majority of printing offices being tiny enterprises of small working masters. The compositor, moreover, has to deal with a

[22] Ibid., p. 151.
[23] John Edward Hicks, *Adventures of a Tramp Printer, 1880–1890* (Kansas City, MO: Midamericana Press, 1950), p. 17.
[24] Ibid.

variety of employers, from the London daily newspaper or the great publishers' printer, down to the stationer's shop in a country town or the fore man of a subsidiary department of a railway company, wholesale grocer or manufacturer of india rubber stamps.[25]

The mobile printer was an example and representative of expanding labour and trade connections. Studying the methods by which their cross-cultural border crossings were supported over the course of the nineteenth and early twentieth century helps us gain insight into their roles as connecting and mediating links between economic structures and craft cultures.[26]

ON THE TRAMP

Printers on the move over the course of the Victorian period often covered great distances and took their time doing so. Such was the case when a compositor stepped out of London on 1 March 1848, to undertake a grand tour that lasted a year, covered 1802 miles, and included stops at Southampton, Bristol, Birmingham, Gloucester, Liverpool, Carlisle, Newcastle, and through into Scotland. His peregrinations subsequently took him to Glasgow, Stirling, Stranraer, and then to Ireland, where he visited the major printing centres of Belfast and Dublin, as well as nineteen other Irish towns. Crossing back to mainland UK, our indefatigable typographer passed through Manchester, Leeds, Nottingham, Leicester, and Cambridge, before completing his tramp back in his old haunts in London.[27]

Sixty-five years later, Timothy J. Ryan, a young printer from St John's, Newfoundland, traversed Canada, and parts of the United States, on a similar peripatetic and unstructured tour. He would take up print work where and when it suited, was not averse to occasional stints of manual and farmhand labour, and over the course of twenty months, between 1913 and 1914, crossed the entirety of Canada, taking in Ottawa, Regina, Calgary, Banff, and Vancouver among others, then moved across the US border to tramp through Seattle, Spokane, and Butte (Montana), before returning to Regina and onwards to Port Arthur, Ottawa, Montreal, and finally home to St John's. His journey would take in twenty-three distinct towns and cities and cover a total of 8,865 miles.[28]

Though some generations apart, such related examples of print migration fluidity and mobility are worth pausing over. Peregrinations of this type were common amongst trained printers and compositors over the long nineteenth century. Indeed, these typographers were participating in a tradition amongst skilled artisanal workers

---

[25] Sidney Webb and Beatrice Webb, *Industrial Democracy*, New Edition (London: Longman, Green and Co., 1897), p. 465.

[26] Pretzer, 'Tramp Printers: Craft Culture, Trade Unions, and Technology', p. 3.

[27] 'If the System of Tramping', *The Typographical Protection Circular*, May 1849.

[28] Robert H. Babcock and T. J. Ryan, 'A Newfoundland Printer on the Tramp', *Labour/Le Travail* 8/9 (1981–1982). Starting and ending in St John's, Newfoundland, the full itinerary included the following towns and cities: Ottawa; Winnipeg; Regina; Moose Jaw; Calgary; Banff; Ravelstoke; Vancouver; Bellingham; Seattle; Auburn; Moses Lake; Spokane; Missoula; Butte, Montana; Great Falls, Montana; Lethbridge; Medicine Hat; Moose Jaw; Regina; Brandon; Hartney; Fort William; Port Arthur; Ottawa; Montreal.

that dated back several centuries. It was part of the so-called 'tramping system', which organized print trade unions in Britain and elsewhere had adapted from guild traditions and used throughout the Victorian era as a means of organizing and controlling labour activity in local and regional areas. Used throughout Britain and its dependencies, it was also common in other European states, in Canada and in the USA, a fundamental aspect of print trade work culture that was 'critical in both sustaining and spreading it'.[29]

The tramping system as it was practised in the Victorian world acted as a method of circulating skilled workers across space and time. In Britain, tramping relief was organized and resourced by national typographical unions that had their roots in benevolent society organizations begun in the late eighteenth and early nineteenth centuries. Such typographical benefit societies emerged with a strong remit of offering support on a reciprocal basis to printers travelling in search of work. The earliest such association in London, for example, grew from a meeting at the Hole-in-the-Wall Inn in Fleet Street on 12 March 1792, where a group of compositors established 'The Phoenix (or Society of Compositors)'.[30] It would become registered under the 1793 Friendly Societies Act, evolve into the London Trade Society of Compositors, formed in 1816, with one of the objects being 'the Relief of its Members when out of Employment', then become the London Union of Compositors in 1834.[31] This would in turn evolve into the London Society of Compositors, established in 1848 with similar benevolent intentions.

Regional variations were to follow. One of the first benevolent societies in Ireland was started in Dublin in 1809, though a slow beginning would lead to a revitalized relaunch in 1825. In Manchester, compositors combined to establish the Manchester Typographical Society in November 1797, tasked with acting 'for the protection of journeymen's rights', and who from the start established sick funds and tramping relief support. By July 1822, the Manchester society was paying 4 shillings to roving printers passing through the city, a sum subsequently raised in January 1825 to 5 shillings for tramp printers with cards from any other print trade society.[32] However, the large increase in printers seeking relief following the trade wide economic crash of 1826 caused them to begin revising their support, at first lowering the rate to 4 shillings, and then defining who was eligible for funds. Within ten years, it became accepted Manchester policy for relief to be paid only to those printers who carried indentures and membership tickets from approved societies, though some exceptions were made.[33] The sums and numbers supported were still sizeable. Between July 1822 and December 1840, the Manchester society expended over £434 in relieving 2,330 tramping printers

---

[29] Pretzer, 'Tramp Printers: Craft Culture, Trade Unions, and Technology', p. 3.

[30] J. H. Richards, 'Social and Economic Aspects of Combination in the Printing Trade before 1875' (MA thesis, University of Liverpool, 1957), p. 22. Though written over sixty years ago, Richards's work is one of the most valuable and comprehensive studies of the Victorian tramping phenomenon yet produced. It is unfortunate it was never published, denying wider access to its wealth of invaluable data.

[31] Ibid., p. 43.   [32] Ibid., p. 63.   [33] Ibid., p. 64.

passing through their city, of which 1827 had relevant tickets, and 503 did not.[34] The latter number included a number of European and North American printers relieved throughout the 1830s, such as Morris Oppel from Berlin (July 1833), John Crocker from America (October 1833), Signor Antonio Borino from Malta (March 1835), and Louis Poltier from Montreal (November 1840).[35] Several Polish refugee printers were also supported throughout the 1840s.[36]

Manchester played a key part in launching the Northern Typographical Union in 1830, which knitted together print trade centres across the northern English regions until its amalgamation into the National Typographical Association in 1844. The Northern Union, as it was termed, like its predecessors provided tramping relief for printers during its fourteen years of existence, though its resources were often tested by the numbers passing through regional branches. In the year covering 1 May 1841 to 30 April 1842, for example, thirty-nine branches of the Northern Union provided £589.12.6 in relief to 6,036 tramping printers, of which Northern Union cards accounted for 2,975 of the total, London cards 1,302, Irish cards 583, Scottish cards 467, and other societies 455.[37] In contrast, during the same period the five societies that made up the Irish Union relieved 289 cards at a cost of £70.6.6, and the London Union of Compositors relieved 235 cards at a cost of £67.16.6.[38]

In Scotland, typographical societies such as the Glasgow branch, established in 1817, included tramping and unemployment relief in their activities. Glasgow's charter noted that its mission was:

> First, to provide for such members as require to leave the City for want of employment, without having pecuniary means; Secondly, to furnish, with facility, money to such strangers as cannot find employment in the City; and, Thirdly, to co-operate with other places in exposing irregular workmen, and maintaining a friendly intercourse throughout the Trade.[39]

Glasgow offered a sliding scale of relief to roving printers: 7 shillings if one was a member of a corresponding Society, or 5 shillings to non-Society members who could prove they were 'free of professional opprobrium', but nothing to fellow Glaswegian printers who were not Society members.[40] Between 1817 and 1830, tramping relief and allowances to support members leaving town accounted for over two thirds of the society's total expenditures.[41] Other union branches were founded across Scotland dedicated to similar objectives, and in August 1836 ten of these joined together in the shape of the General Typographical Association of Scotland (GTAS), with leadership from the Glasgow branch. It would last until

---

[34] Ibid., p. 65.   [35] Ibid., p. 174.   [36] Ibid.   [37] Ibid., p. 157.
[38] Ibid., p. 158.
[39] Sarah C. Gillespie, *A Hundred Years of Progress. The Record of the Scottish Typographical Association, 1853 to 1952* (Glasgow: Robert Maclehose & Co., 1953), pp. 24–5.
[40] Ibid., p. 25.
[41] Richards, 'Social and Economic Aspects of Combination in the Printing Trade before 1875', pp. 90–1. Tabulating data from the Glasgow society accounts, Richards concludes that of the total expended by the Society during that period (£114.5.1), £42 went towards leaving town allowances, £34.13.6 to tramping relief, £6.8.0 to grants of various kinds, and £31.3.7 to other expenses.

1844, when Scottish unions aligned themselves for a period with the Northern Typographical Association. A disastrous strike in Edinburgh in 1847 decimated Scottish union funds and organization, and it would take until 1853 for Scottish print union strength to reassert itself again into forming the Scottish Typographical Association, which proved more enduring in nature.

Until 1844, under the oversight of the GTAS, and in halting form through the next ten lean years of union activity, Scottish print trade branches operated a relief scheme where numbers relieved at times exceeded the total number of union members registered (which in 1843 totalled 700). Between April 1841 and April 1842, it provided relief of £116.17.0 to 819 travelling printers, with the majority presenting membership cards from the Northern Union (339), followed by Scottish branch members (199), London unions (190), the Irish union (eighty-six), and other English societies (five).[42] The following year, 755 roving printers were given tramping relief totalling £121.16.2, by nine of the seventeen member branches (Aberdeen, Dumfries, Edinburgh, Glasgow, Kelso, Kilmarnock, Montrose, Perth, and Stirling).[43]

Such support could challenge union branch finances, but by providing support to those on the move or in search of work, such co-operation ensured in most cases that the position of local members was not undermined by unemployed men coming into town and taking situations in 'unfair' houses where the wages were below the accepted standard, or there was an ongoing dispute. 'Tramping' was used to manage disputes, with striking print workers being paid to leave town when required. This had the dual benefit of discouraging strike-breaking and protecting individuals from victimization.

As English, Welsh, Scottish, and Irish unions grew in strength and number over the second half of the century, the tramping relief system evolved into a sophisticated travel network that subsidized members with a travel mileage sum (usually between one and sixpence a mile), given on completion of fixed routes between union towns in search of work. On arrival in town, they would present their union card to the secretary (whose hours and place of availability were listed in local typographical journals and membership notes), who would register the card, give them the required stipend, offer them a meal, some drink, a chit for lodgings, and where possible some temporary work in a local union shop. If no work was forthcoming, such tramping typographers were required to move on to the next town in the circuit, continuing the process until they found full employment or ceased tramping. British circuits, built up throughout the eighteenth century through trade guild connections, and carried on in the tramping relief support of early nineteenth century benevolent trade societies, were thus fully formalized through active intervention of the typographical trade unions that emerged from the 1840s onwards.

Other countries and international regions adopted various models for dealing with the same phenomena. In Canada, mobility within the printing trade was initially not a priority when twenty-four Toronto-based printers seeking to 'meet

---

[42] Ibid., p. 158. [43] Ibid., p. 170.

industrial problems, not social and benevolent needs', met in 1833 to found the York Typographical Society.[44] However, labour historian Sally Zerker notes that they did make exceptions, as for example when the society gave financial assistance to a Scotsman named Baird from the Cork Typographical Society to enable him to travel to the United States in search of employment.[45]

The York Typographical Society changed its name to the Toronto Typographical Society in 1835, but subsequently folded in 1837. It was reorganized as the Toronto Typographical Union (TTU) in 1844, under revived direction from Toronto printers identifying themselves as 'part of the continental touring force'.[46] The stated aims of the TTU constitution of 1848 were:

> To promote by every lawful means, the interests of the employers as well as the employed and to uphold the respectability of the members of the Printing profession in the City of Toronto; to preserve from encroachment the present established rate of wages; to raise a fund for the support of its members in sickness, or when out of employment; to assist with money those of its members desirous of leaving the city; to contribute to the funeral expense of deceased members; and to afford pecuniary assistance to those of the profession generally who may require it.[47]

As Zerker notes, 'Printers who came to Toronto were definitely accustomed to the migratory tradition and practice...[and] they willingly adopted the old travel allowance scheme.'[48]

The economic conditions and changes in Canadian printing technology, however, forced the TTU to further adapt its system of mutual aid to meet an increasing demand for casual work and to protect the jobs of its members.[49] The Canadian tramping system 'had to be revised into a travelling scheme with expenditures which accounted for both longer distances and locomotive transport'.[50] In 1844 the flat sum of £1 was given to those unemployed members who required travel assistance, but by 1848, the revised TTU constitution allowed awards of not less than 10s and not more than £1.[51] In line with such focus on unemployment and travel relief, when the TTU decided to join the National Typographical Union in 1866, 'the primary concern at that juncture was the benefit to Toronto's travelling members'.[52]

The US-based National Typographical Union, haltingly founded in 1850 but restarted in 1852 with around 2,000 journeymen printer members across twelve union branches, was later renamed the International Typographical Union when Canadian branches were added to its roster. It would expand to encompass 7,500 members in seventy-nine US and Canadian branches by 1869, and as noted in the introduction, would list more than 50,000 members by 1914. In 1852, it adopted a national policy of having local branches issue travelling cards for departing members, in return accepting card holding incomers from other branches. While allowing leeway on how local branches managed transient printers on the move, the

---

[44] Sally F. Zerker, *The Rise and Fall of the Toronto Typographical Union, 1832–1972: A Case Study of Foreign Domination* (Toronto and Buffalo, NY: University of Toronto Press, 1982), p. 20.
[45] Ibid., pp. 21–2; 54.   [46] Ibid., p. 6.   [47] Ibid., p. 40.   [48] Ibid., p. 56.
[49] Ibid., p. 58.   [50] Ibid., p. 56.   [51] Ibid., p. 40.   [52] Ibid., p. 76.

national union sought to establish general, overarching principles and standards to sit in parallel with local traditions. Thus holders of travelling cards were entitled to admission to local branches without payment of initiation fees; travellers staying less than a month were exempt from paying union dues; 'rats', miscreants or black-listed members reported in the pages of union backed trade journals and official documents were to be rejected even if presenting what purported to be bona fide documentation.[53] Travelling subsidies did not exist at a national level, though local branches and print shops were encouraged to set up support funds or informal work schemes to provide for the more indigent of the tramping print fraternity passing through. The editor of the *Globe-Democrat* in St Louis, Missouri, for example, was known throughout the 1870s and 1880s for his friendliness to tramp printers. He devised a relief scheme whereby printers down on their luck and without work could come in, set several lines from reprint copy put aside in what was called the 'grasshopper cases', 'cash in at the regular scale – and eat'.[54]

The goal of national oversight of travel sitting alongside local custom, as William Pretzer has noted, was to facilitate the movement of union men across North American print centres while simultaneously trying to control the effect of such mobility on local rates and establishment wages. 'While local unions focused on wage scales, apprentice regulations, and work rules', Pretzer concludes, 'the national organization concentrated on controlling the movement of men and preventing employers from using travelling printers to depress wages or break strikes.'[55]

Unions and trade groups established later in the century in Australia, Canada, South Africa, and New Zealand imported and adapted versions of the British tramping system. As opportunities arose for international print worker migration traversing continents and cultures, such systems required mechanisms to manage complex movements across colonial routes. Trade movements also cut across colonial communication circuits, and complicated the standard narrative of colonial and national development. Print workers did not merely move from centre to periphery (often characterized by British observers as moving from the UK to overseas colonial spaces, or from urban print centres to rural locations), but equally moved between regional circuits and across national borders. The Toronto Typographical Society minute books of 1859–1864, for example, offer evidence of printers arriving from other Ontario locales such as Hamilton and Peterborough, and traversing to and from American border cities such as Detroit and Buffalo. They also shuttled between Toronto and American printing centres such as Chicago, New Orleans, New York, and Memphis, as for example Patrick Boyle, who deposited a New Orleans union card on 3 July 1860, withdrew it on 5 March 1861 to return to New Orleans, then reappeared in the Toronto union lists on 1 October 1861.[56]

---

[53] Pretzer, 'Tramp Printers: Craft Culture, Trade Unions, and Technology', p. 7.
[54] Hicks, *Adventures of a Tramp Printer, 1880–1890*, p. 45.
[55] Pretzer, 'Tramp Printers: Craft Culture, Trade Unions, and Technology', p. 7.
[56] Toronto Typographical Union, 'Minute Books, 1859–1871, Toronto Typographical Union (Local 91)', ed. Archives of Ontario (Toronto: Archives of Ontario, 1978). I am grateful to Greta Golick for researching the Toronto Typographical Union records on my behalf for such examples.

Scots émigrés feature in Toronto membership lists throughout the second half of the century, with over one hundred names potentially linking back to Scottish union membership records. It is difficult, however, to establish exact correlations and intersections between Scottish and Torontonian member listings due to issues such as multiple entries for similarly named individuals, and insufficient supporting evidence to establish exact matches. There are a few corresponding matches, such as John Laird, who deposited a Glasgow Scottish Typographical Union card and signed the membership roll of the TTS on 6 September 1859. Listed in the 1861 Census of Canada as resident in St Patrick's Ward, York, Canada West, Laird would remain in the Toronto area for over thirty years, changing occupation at some point after 1861 to join his brother in becoming a picture framer and gilder.[57] Several decades later, the TTU Account Book for 1908–9 records recent Scots émigré William Reid depositing his Scottish Typographical Association card (No. R 456) in March 1909, then being invited to sign the membership roll as a full member on 1 May 1909.[58] The same Account Book records James McIlroy, recently arrived from the 'Belfast Branch' Typographical Association, similarly joining the TTU on 13 April 1909.[59]

It was not uncommon for skilled workers to include multiple moves across the British Isles, the USA, Canada, Australasia, and South Africa within their working lives. Such was the case of Jack Farrell, 'Australian Jack' or 'Transvaal Jack' as his South African colleagues knew him. Born in Ireland but a young émigré to Australia, he learned his trade in Victoria, then throughout the 1880s and early 1890s took up itinerant print work, tramping through New Zealand, fetching up in San Francisco, sojourning in Denver, Chicago, New York, Philadelphia, Cincinnati, and Arizona, then returning via San Francisco to Sydney, Australia. In 1896 he shifted to Johannesburg, South Africa, where he would play a key role in founding the South African Typographical Union in 1898, serve as its first president, help launch the *South African Typographical Journal* and form part of the advance guard that established the Government Printing Office in Pretoria in 1900.[60]

As noted already, the typographical unions that developed from the 1830s onwards encouraged such mobility amongst union members as a means of monitoring and controlling supply and demand for labour. Tramping circuits

---

[57] See ibid. John Laird is noted in the 1861 census of Canada as living in a household with his brother, twenty-six-year-old Robert Laird, employed as a gilder, Margaret, a 71 year-old widow [possibly his mother], and possibly a widowed sister. In 1871, John Laird is listed as part of a household that includes his brother, sister-in-law, and his nephew, with his occupation listed as picture framer. In 1877, John Laird [listed as gilder] married Jane Best. The 1881 and 1891 census returns list Laird as a gilder (1881) and then a picture framer (1891). Data from http://www.bac-lac.gc.ca/eng/census/Pages/census.aspx, accessed 22 March 2017.

[58] 'Account Books, 1908–1909, Toronto Typographical Union (Local 91)', ed. Archives of Ontario (Toronto: Archives of Ontario, 1978).

[59] Ibid.

[60] 'J. P. Farrell', *South African Typographical Journal* 1, no. 20 (1900). See also 'J. Farrell, First President S.A.T.U.', *South African Typographical Journal* 4, no. 39 (1902). A brief contextual reference to Farrell also features in Sydney J. Shep, 'The Printer's Web: New Tools to Crack Old Chestnuts', in *Advancing Digital Humanities: Research, Methods, Theories*, ed. Paul Longley and Katherine Bode Arthur (Basingstoke: Palgrave Macmillan, 2014), p. 70.

strategically removed excess labour from key sites of strike action, and cemented union organization and membership cohesion. They also fitted within an artisanal trade vision of kinship joined to individualism, a moral community supporting individual labour within unified trade structures. Union membership allowed members to be simultaneously autonomous and part of a larger trade community. One could enjoy the benefits accrued from membership, such as health and social welfare support, while at the same time being supported to shift locations when the need or desire struck. To be a printer on the move required little extra baggage, as one memoirist recalled of his tramping days in the 1850s: 'Printers need to carry few tools. A composing stick and an apron were all I required to begin work anywhere, and even these were not indispensable.'[61] Knowing where to find work was also essential. As one old-timer remarked, anyone who couldn't 'smell a print shop a mile away' wasn't a good union man.[62] Those without a good sense of smell had to rely on trade bulletins listing 'fair' printshops, as well as printed lists of union officials with the time and places when they were available to direct arrivals to likely accommodation and work.

The most important item for a tramping typographer was an up-to-date typographical union card, certifying that one was a member in good standing. Some cards merely certified that an individual was a bona-fide member of a union branch, as in the case of the cards issued by the London Society of Compositors (LSC) from 1858 onwards, such as the example of Figure 1.1.

In late 1907, the LSC initiated an annual design competition to produce a yearly membership card, the impetus having been an outcry over that year's card design (see Figure 1.2), which several members had deemed a 'monstrosity'.[63] The aim was to stimulate union members to design cards that were both aesthetically pleasing and typographically innovative. In the first year of competition, seventy entries were submitted anonymously under entry numbers, and were judged by Harry Whetton, editor for over fifty years of the *British Printer*, whom a contemporary described as invaluable in his role as 'stimulator of good craftsmanship and a whole hearted propagandist for British printing'.[64] Whetton announced the results in the October–November 1907 issue of the *British Printer*, accompanying the statement with a page reproducing eighteen of the shortlisted entries. In his summation, Whetton paid tribute to the design skills of those who had entered the competition, noting 'I do not remember a Job Competition in which the average was so high, largely because there is scarcely a single example devoid of some good points, and this to me is very interesting as significant of the standard of workmanship represented by the membership of the London Society of Compositors.'[65] He offered more restrained praise for the winning entry, listed

---

[61] W. E. Addams, *Memoirs of a Social Atom*, 2 vols. (London: Hutchinson & Co., 1903), p. 292.

[62] Hicks, *Adventures of a Tramp Printer, 1880–1890*, p. 13.

[63] George E. Rowles, *The 'Line' Is On: A Centenary Souvenir of the London Society of Compositors 1848–1948* (London: Co-Operative Printing Society, Ltd, 1948), p. 51.

[64] Ibid.   [65] 'LSC Membership Card Competition', *The British Printer* 20, no. 119 (1907).

Figure 1.1. London Society of Compositors card, 1859

Figure 1.2. London Society of Compositors card, 1907

Figure 1.3. London Society of Compositors card, 1908

as number 1,020, calling it 'an all round, neat, useful, effective and workmanlike design'.[66] It would feature as the 1908 membership card (see Figure 1.3).

The design competition ran under the auspices of the LSC until 1955, when the LSC amalgamated with another union to become the London Typographical Society (LTS). The competition continued for another eight years under LTS patronage until 1963, when the practice was stopped after a further amalgamation with the Typographical Society to form the National Graphical Association.[67]

Other union cards were less aesthetically focused but more practically orientated. Some, such as Figures 1.4 and 1.5, consisted of 'withdrawal' or 'travelling' certificates, cards, or booklets, which declared holders had left branches in good standing, and which, when presented at another branch, entitled them to membership without penalty, fines or entry fees. After 1877, The Provincial Typographical Association issued English, Welsh, and Irish trade members on the move with either a first or second-class travelling 'card', which entitled holders to different mileage rates depending on the class of card held. It was essentially a pocket-sized booklet with tabulated pages on which union branch secretaries recorded arrivals, departures and allowances given to the holder, as per example Figure 1.6. Still others consisted of small, four-sided membership 'working' cards that included details of the relevant branch on the front cover, space for dues paid stamps or notes inside, and branch rules on the back cover. (See Figures 1.7 and 1.8.)

The printer J. W. Rounsfell's well-known account of tramping around England in the 1880s makes clear how important the difference was between a British first

---

[66] Ibid.   [67] John Gorman, *Images of Labour* (London: Scorpion Publishing, Ltd, 1985).

NATIONAL TYPOGRAPHICAL ASSOCIATION.

No. ....

Certificate granted ....

Arrears ....

Entitled to Relief ....

To ....

NATIONAL TYPOGRAPHICAL ASSOCIATION.

Established January 1, 1845.

No. ....

.... District. .... Branch.

This is to Certify, That[1] .... quits this Branch of the Association ....

Having been a Member[2] .... than Six Months, he is[4] .... entitled to receive the Unemployed Benefit of the Association.

Entered, ... 184 Issued, ... 184

.... Treasurer.

.... President.

.... Secretary.

To ....

Should the bearer not obtain Work in the town where he applies for Relief, this Certificate is to be endorsed, upon payment; and unless it bear the signature of the Secretary for the previous week's relief, the Member be charged the full rate of subscription, supposing him to have been employed.

ANY ERASURE OR ALTERATION MADE IN THIS CERTIFICATE WILL RENDER IT INVALID.

[1] Name. [2] Either clear, or so much in arrears. [3] More or less. [4] Is, or is not.

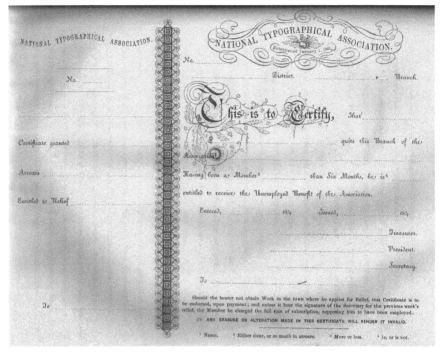

Figure 1.4. National Typographical Association leaving certificate, 1840s

HONORABLE WITHDRAWAL CARD

International Typographical Union

INSTITUTED MAY 1852

THIS CERTIFIES Denver, March 9, 1908.

That Chas. A. Ellis *the holder hereof, is at this day and date a member in good standing of* Denver Typographical *Union No.* 49, *of the* State *of* Colorado, *and is granted this Honorable Withdrawal Card, which exempts him from all dues or taxes whatsoever, and acquits him of all rights to benefits of any kind whatsoever in said organization; and he is required to deposit same with the proper officer before seeking work under the jurisdiction of any subordinate union; and he promises not to violate any trade requirement of the said International Typographical Union, or its subordinate bodies, while holding this Card.*

WITNESS Our hands and the seal of the union, the day and year first above written.

J. W. Bramwood
Secretary-Treasurer International Typographical Union

W. E. Shields *President*

F. C. Birdsall *Secretary*

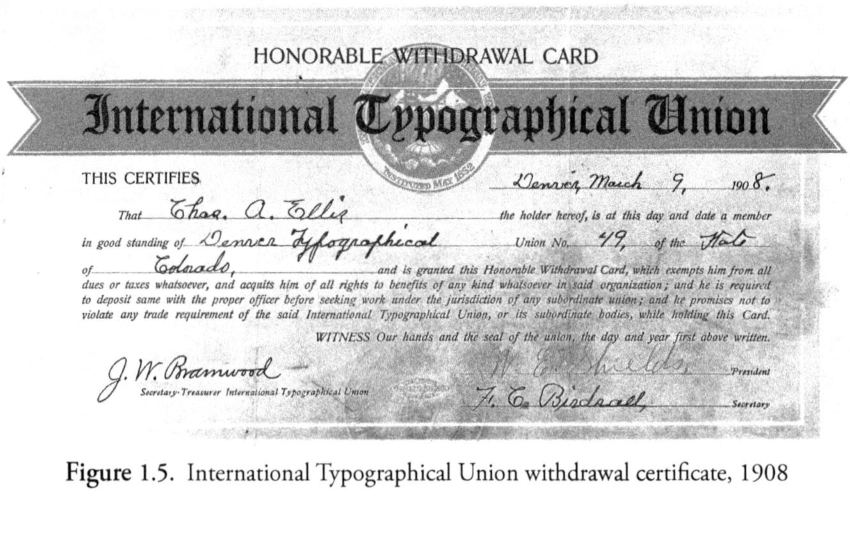

Figure 1.5. International Typographical Union withdrawal certificate, 1908

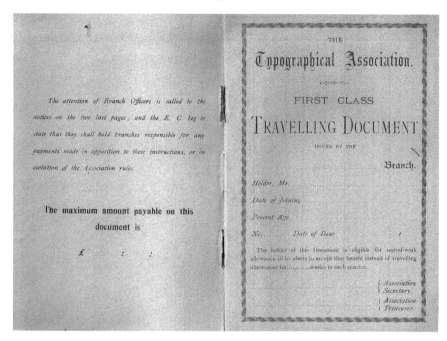

Figure 1.6. Provincial Typographical Association First-class travelling card, 1871

and second class 'ticket', the first of which entitled a printer on the move to compensation of a penny a mile, against the second-class rate of a half-penny for each mile travelled. The half-penny extra per mile could mean the difference between eating well or starving at the end of the day. Tramping printers would use maps such as Figure 1.9 outlining tramping routes and distance to make fine-gauged calculations of mileage required to keep on the right side of hunger.

Thus, Rounsfell's first encounter with a veteran roving printer starts with the tramp snatching up Rounsfell's tramping map and engaging in just such travelling calculations, much to Rounsfell's mystification:

'Chesterfield 24 – mileage shilling – chapel ninepence', muttered the man with the map. This would have been sufficient evidence to one used to the road that the individual beside me was travelling with a Second-class or ha'penny a mile document. But at that time I was too green and inexperienced to know the difference between the First and Second-class, although of course I knew that my First-class Doc entitled me to a penny a mile, but had not the slightest notion then how the chapels worked out.[68]

Union cards were not confined to English-speaking trade organizations. There is evidence that typographical unions in other countries adopted union membership

---

[68] J. W. Rounsfell, *On the Road: Journeys of a Tramping Printer* (Horsham: Caliban Books, 1982), p. 4.

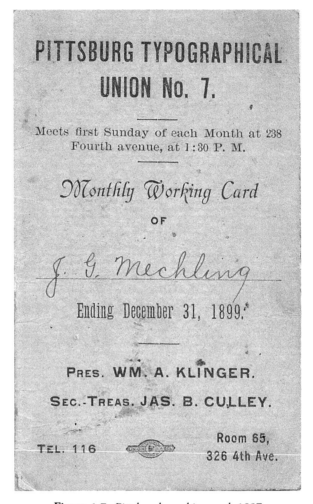

Figure 1.7. Pittsburgh working card, 1897

and travelling cards to identify workers in good standing, as for example Figure 1.10, a card issued by the Spanish union branch of Orense in 1907.

A compositor could think of offering examples of work when seeking a job, but the union card was the ultimate key to entry into unionized and non-unionized print shops along tramping routes. As a young printer was advised in 1913 by a fellow travelling compositor on producing a sample of his work early into a tramping stint across the USA, 'Listen, kid, we printers who call ourselves, never carry samples around with us to show what we can do, or have done. Our card is the only credential we need to prove to prospective employers that we *are* printers.'[69]

[69] Linafont Brevier, *Trampography: Reminiscences of a Rovin' Printer, 1913–1917* (Glendale, CA: n.p., 1954), p. 3

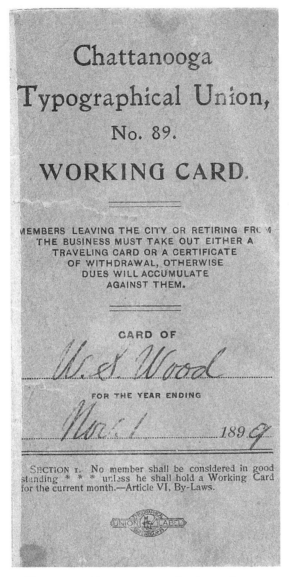

Figure 1.8. Chattanooga membership card, 1899

The union travelling card was, in the words of a mid-twentieth century chronicler of the typographical traveller, 'a certificate to a doubting world that the bearer was a qualified journeyman printer no matter what he outwardly appeared to be'.[70] It was a travelling typographer's most valuable piece of documentation, 'his passport to strange lands, his only bank account, the secure rock on which he rested'.[71]

---

[70] Paul Fisher, *An Uncommon Gentry* (Columbia: University of Missouri, 1952), p. 11.
[71] Ibid., p. 12.

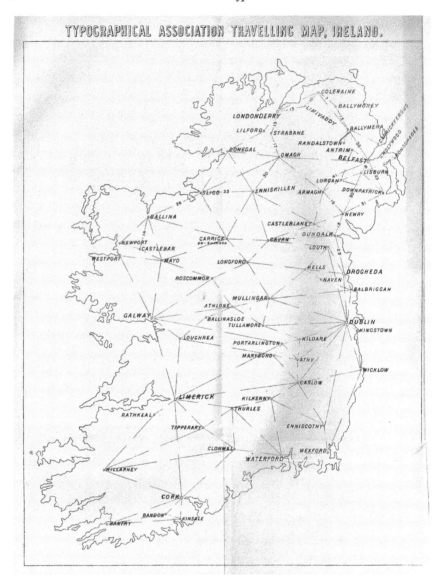

Figure 1.9. Irish travelling route map, 1870s

The totemic power of a union card in US print circuits persisted through to the 1950s, as one female compositor who began her career as a fifteen-year old apprentice in 1917 recollected in 1988: 'I always put a lot of faith in that card. If you saw that card, you knew that you were going to get justice.'[72]

---

[72] Amelie Purves, quoted in Maggie Holtzberg-Call, *The Lost World of the Craft Printer* (Urbana and Chicago: University of Illinois Press, 1992), p. 65.

Figure 1.10. Orense typographical union card, 1907

Packing up a union card in an old kit bag was easy, and moving on when work was short or demand was low led to a high degree of trade mobility in the printing trade across many regions throughout the century.[73] In the USA, data on roving printers was gathered at a national level between 1857 and 1892 under the instigation of the International Typographical Union.[74] Analysis of the resulting local admissions by travelling card suggested tramping was extensive, particularly after the conclusion of the US Civil War and through to the 1890s. Between 1857 and 1865, union membership fluctuated between 1,300 and 3,500, but local admissions by travelling card were less than 20 per cent of total national membership reports. Ratios of travelling card admissions rose in subsequent years, along with union membership. In the post-Civil War period, travelling card membership accounted for between 30 and 40 per cent of total admissions, hitting higher ranges during periods of national and worldwide depression (1872–1873, 1875).

---

[73] See for example I. C. Cannon, *The Compositor in London: The Rise and Fall of a Labour Aristocracy* (London: St Bride Library, 2011), pp. 50–1; E. J. Hobsbawn, 'The Tramping Artisan', *The Economic History Review* 3, no. 3 (1951); Pretzer, 'Tramp Printers: Craft Culture, Trade Unions, and Technology'; Lloyd Ulman, *The Rise of the National Trade Union* (Cambridge, MA: Harvard University Press, 1955), and in particular pp. 62–7; Zerker, *The Rise and Fall of the Toronto Typographical Union, 1832–1972*, pp. 58–65.

[74] The subsequent US data and summary analysis is drawn from Pretzer, 'Tramp Printers: Craft Culture, Trade Unions, and Technology', p. 9, and Ulman, *The Rise of the National Trade Union*, pp. 64–5.

Between 1883 and 1892, travelling card admissions remained above 40 per cent, and in the early 1890s rose to nearly two-thirds of total membership reports.

In Canada, similar membership mobility rates were recorded in union registers, such as those kept by the Toronto Typographical Union (TTU) branch on amalgamation with the ITU. Overall the migration ratios noted in the TTU records were less dramatic in range, though at key historical points they rose to reflect economic challenges such as the worldwide depression that affected global trade between 1873 and 1879. From 1867 to 1871, membership in the TTU rose from 72 to 190, with travelling card admissions making up between 12.5 per cent and 16.5 per cent of the total. Between 1873 and 1877, reflecting economic downturns across the print sector, the percentage of travelling card admissions rose from 25.1 per cent to 36.3 per cent, before dropping to fluctuate between 10 and 20 per cent from 1879 to 1892.[75]

Often, patterns of movement were conditioned by seasonal work rhythms. In Britain, some tramping typographers timed their movements to coincide with an upsurge in work occasioned by the printing of Parliamentary papers, court session rulings and other government documents at key points in the year. In New Zealand, tramp printers worked a circuit based on locations of events such as seasonal horse races and agricultural shows. Increased demand at each venue for printed flyers, promotional leaflets, and other related print jobs would tax local printers' resources, and incoming piece rate workers would be hired to manage the overflow. One long-time union member later recalled, describing the seasonal print workers who had passed through his father's Blenheim printshop in the late nineteenth century, 'Those itinerant comps would follow the A & P [Agricultural and Pastoral] shows and race meetings, for there were few country offices that could cope with the extra hand setting required for special publications. These men would work diligently till the job was finished…Then they would walk to the next place already decided upon.'[76]

Tramping circuits supported by print trade societies also existed in continental Europe, a by-product of long-standing guild traditions dating back centuries, though differences would emerge between continental Europe and Britain in terms of expectations. European counterparts were expected to incorporate an element of mobility into their early training. As the Webbs pointed out in 1897, continental apprenticeships featured a 'wanderjahre' period, or 'customary years of travel from town to town at its close', which was not required of British apprentices (though many did so as part of a general wanderlust and a response to trade conditions when work was tight).[77] Eighteenth- and nineteenth-century Franco-Swiss networks saw transient print workers shuttle between France and Switzerland, such as those who flowed through the premises of the Société Typographique de Neuchatel, a key supplier of French language texts in the eighteenth

[75] Zerker, *The Rise and Fall of the Toronto Typographical Union, 1832–1972*, p. 62.

[76] Eric Wakelin, quoted in Peter Franks, *Print & Politics: A History of Trade Unions in the New Zealand Printing Industry, 1865–1995* (Wellington: Victoria University Press, 2001), p. 30.

[77] Webb and Webb, *Industrial Democracy*, p. 455, footnote 1.

and nineteenth centuries.[78] Similarly, Germano-Scandic-Russian tramping networks extant throughout the nineteenth and early twentieth centuries supported compositors traversing across Germany, Sweden, Denmark, Finland, and Russia.[79] Emigrant printers, many from Germany or German trained, dominated Russian print economies: in St Petersburg, for example, 44 per cent of private print shops were owned either by German nationals (23 per cent), immigrants from the Baltic provinces (9 per cent), or Jews from the Pale of Settlement (12 per cent).[80] In Moscow in 1885, 20 per cent of print firms were run by ethnic non- Russians, with 14 per cent owned by mostly German foreign nationals, 4 per cent owned by individuals born in the Baltic provinces, and 2 per cent owned by Jewish printers, contrasting with the low number overall of ethnic non-Russians living in Moscow at the time (5 per cent).[81]

US networks witnessed influxes of young trainee compositors making excursions as early as seventeen or eighteen years of age. This was due in part to the compressed apprenticeship practices that increasingly featured in non-unionized rural centres. Instead of the seven-year apprenticeship system favoured by British and European counterparts, new entrants in the USA found themselves pushed through three–four-year stints, due in part to the desire to cut costs and lower wage bills in small town print shops. From the 1820s and into the 1850s, the number of relatively inexperienced young compositors and pressmen let loose in the US marketplace was particularly high. Their travels took in work at both unionized and non-unionized print shops. The result was that during the period leading up the 1860 US Civil War, the typographical tramping circuit was often treated as a concluding part of an apprenticeship, a 'recognized study in the curriculum of the trade'.[82] Journeymen printers disparagingly labelled such entrants 'two-thirders', and resented the resulting downward pressures on wages and quality caused by such influx of less skilled personnel across the industry.[83]

US-based printers on the move were not just youngsters wet behind the ears. More experienced migrant compositors could be found acting as union missionaries,

---

[78] Robert Darnton, *The Literary Underground of the Old Regime* (Cambridge, MA: Harvard University Press, 1985), pp. 148–67. See also *The Great Cat Massacre and Other Episodes in French Cultural History* (New York: Viking, 1984), pp. 80–2.

[79] Lars Olsson, 'Tramping Typographers–National and Trans-National Labour Migration at the Break Though of Industrial Capitalism in Northern Europe', in *Eighth European Social Science History Conference* (Ghent, Belgium, 2010). My thanks go to Dr Simon Frost for referring me to this interesting piece on Germano-Scandic printer migration circuits. For Russian connections, see Mark D. Steinberg, 'Culture and Class in a Russian Industry: The Printers of St. Petersburg, 1860–1905', *Journal of Social History* 23, no. 3 (1990), pp. 513–33; Mark D. Steinberg, *Moral Communities: The Culture of Class Relations in the Russian Printing Industry, 1867–1907* (Berkeley: University of California Press, 1992).

[80] Ibid., p. 13. The Pale of Settlement was the term applied to the western region of Imperial Russia that permitted Jewish settlement and included Latvia, Lithuania, Ukraine, and Moldova and extended to the borders of Prussia and Austria-Hungary.

[81] Ibid.   [82] J. Lumley, 'The Printer', *The Printer* 6 (1866).

[83] William S. Pretzer, ' "Of the Paper Cap and Inky Apron": Journeymen Printers', in *A History of the Book in America*, vol. 2: *An Extensive Republic, Print, Culture and Society in the New Nation, 1790–1840*, ed. Robert A. Gross and Mary Kelley (Chapel Hill: University of North Carolina Press, 2010), p. 166.

starting up unions in towns along regional networks, and playing key roles as informants, cultural transmitters, and social networkers. 'No printer ever loved his union with the singular devotion of the old, handset tramp', recalled one contemporary chronicler, 'no printer was ever so sure of the union's capability to overcome any obstacle'.[84] There were multiple cases of migrant printers instigating labour organization activities where they found it was needed. When the union in Columbus, Ohio collapsed in 1858, incoming tramp printers stepped in quickly to successfully reorganize what survived, while similar efforts to unionize the Pacific Northwest later in the century were led by tramp printers who had passed through Midwest regions and been schooled in union tactics.[85] A contemporary recalled many of the latter being '*thorough* unionists who fought to create decent pay scales and ethical craft codes'.[86]

Such defences would also extend to acting as spies in 'closed' print shops, or joining vigilance committees to guard against strikebreakers (a point discussed elsewhere in this book). One memoirist recalls patrolling the streets of Kansas City in 1880 during strikes at two city newspapers, on the lookout for rat labour recruits. News of one arrival from Independence, Missouri prompted the formation of a 'reception committee' to meet him at the train station. 'We hustled him down toward the river front and made him believe we were going to drown him; then we walked him up and down the levee until the night train for Independence was due. We put him on the train and never saw him again.'[87]

Robust union actions like these could backfire, leading to accusations of union condoned assault and threatening behaviour. Defending the tramping artisan against general charges of bringing the trade into disrepute, the head of the Chicago Typographical Union wrote in *The Inland Printer* of 1889 that such actions were not the norm. More often, artisan tramp printers were to be seen in the vanguard of defending union rights through their organizing efforts: 'More typographical unions', he concluded, 'owe their inception to the proselytizing efforts of the tramp, than to the organizing agencies of the international body.'[88]

Even Allan Pinkerton, Glasgow-born founder of the eponymous detective agency that by the turn of the twentieth century had become a byword for brutal strike breaking and union busting tactics on behalf of US industrialist owners, grudgingly praised tramp printers for their general acumen and skill. 'There are often among these confirmed tramp printers, many of the most brilliant minds and winning manners', he commented in an otherwise shrill memoir of unions and strikes his firm had battled in the summer of 1877.[89] He also recognized the general principles and tolerance of the typographical tramping urge, for 'tramping

---

[84] Fisher, *An Uncommon Gentry*, p. 11.
[85] Pretzer, 'Tramp Printers: Craft Culture, Trade Unions, and Technology', p. 7.
[86] A. C. Shoemaker, quoted in ibid., p. 7.
[87] Hicks, *Adventures of a Tramp Printer, 1880–1890*, p. 29.
[88] M. J. Carroll, 'The Tramp Printer', *The Inland Printer* 6 (1889). Quoted in Pretzer, 'Tramp Printers: Craft Culture, Trade Unions, and Technology', p. 7.
[89] Allan Pinkerton, *Strikers, Communists, Tramps, and Detectives* (New York: G.W. Carleton, 1878), p. 53.

is a recognized pleasure and necessity among printers'.[90] For Pinkerton, the difference between a tramp printer and other migrant artisans was 'greater versatility, and possibly readier wits', and a knowledge of current events that enabled the tramp printer, when in the company of other transient workers, to hold 'something of the position of an oracle'.[91] As a result of this, and of having experienced the tramping life as a roving cooper when he was younger, he was disposed to see typographical tramps in a kind light, for 'as a class they are not criminals, and we have no right to take such measures against them as will make them such'.[92]

Timothy J. Ryan, the young Canadian tramping typographer mentioned earlier, emerged from his pre-war peregrinations with a keen sense of union needs. His travels opened his eyes to the lack of unionization across Newfoundland in 1914. 'They don't seem to realize the situation and take the initiative and try to help themselves', he remarked in his short account of the trip.[93] Jobbing printer numbers had risen exponentially in Nova Scotia over the decades previous, as firms expanded workforces to deal with new opportunities. Census returns between 1891 and 1911, for example, record a jump in Nova Scotian workers from 478 to 635, employed in 39 firms, though little seems to have been done to effectively organize these print trade workers.[94] Such expansion was part of a national trend: as Éric Leroux points out, between 1891 and 1911 the number of employees in the Canadian printing sector more than doubled, from 9,006 to 19,263.[95] Ryan became part of a labour leadership determined to unionize this emergent workforce, joining the printers' local union in May 1915, then taking on leadership roles as vice-president and secretary-treasurer with a view to extending union representation across the region.[96]

Printers were not the only ones to develop tramping circuits. E. J. Hobsbawm noted in his 1951 groundbreaking piece on migrant artisans that by the midnineteenth century the artisanal tramping system was widespread throughout Great Britain and elsewhere. In 1860, for example, it was known to be in use among lithographers, tailors, coachmakers, bookbinders, smiths, engineers, steam-engine makers, stonemasons, carpenters, iron-founders, coopers, shoemakers, boilermakers, plumbers, bricklayers, and various other crafts.[97] Union tramps were celebrated in trade lore for representing craft independence, integrity, and ingenuity. By the 1860s, however, the overuse of the system and the move to regulate trade conditions and industrialize trade work patterns saw middle class observers stigmatizing the tramp as part of an immoral system.[98] As one chronicler astutely observed, 'To the middle-class observer it seemed immoral that a worker should tramp the roads, living on the charity of his mates, in preference to working at the rate the employer

---

[90] Ibid., p. 55.   [91] Ibid.   [92] Ibid., p. 66.
[93] Babcock and Ryan, 'A Newfoundland Printer on the Tramp', p. 267.
[94] Leroux, 'Trades, Labour, and Design', p. 77.   [95] Ibid., p. 79.
[96] Babcock and Ryan, 'A Newfoundland Printer on the Tramp', p. 262.
[97] E. Hobsbawn, 'The Tramping Artisan', *The Economic History Review* 3, no. 3 (1951), p. 305.
[98] See for example 'The Trade Tramp', *Leisure Hours*, 1 June 1868.

saw fit to offer. To the organized worker this *was* the moral thing to do. To work, however "honest" the work, under rate was the depth of immorality.'[99]

Part of the problem, frequently acknowledged by typographical union officials, was that as the system evolved to cope with increasing numbers, there was a persistent level of misuse by unscrupulous print trade members. The tramping relief offered in Scotland was often railed against in the pages of the *Scottish Typographical Circular*, the monthly union journal started in 1857. Typical was the following view expressed in the leading article for the 5 July 1862 issue: 'The indolent, dissipated, and incompetent naturally, as surely as if they were impelled by a physical law, seek that calling where their qualifications find some reward: and so long as the tramping system is maintained as at present, there will always exist a class who will make tramping their vocation.'[100] Branch minutes recorded similar complaints about compositors seeking handouts with little intention of working when opportunities became available. 'It is to be feared that many of these who take to the road do so', reported the Banff branch in 1856, 'not because they have no work to do, but because they have no will to do it.'[101]

In Ireland, the mobility of journeymen printers could leave unions shouldering unanticipated wage bills. Vincent Kinane notes that the Dublin union faced frequent cases of union members leaving 'horse' behind them, that is, skipping town for a short period after 'filling out bills on Saturday for more than they had actually done, with the intention of compensating for it in the following week's bill'.[102] The Dublin Typographical Provident Society (DTPS) was frequently called on to pursue errant journeymen for retroactive payments, and in some cases ended up compensating employers directly from their own funds. In one such case, the Dublin University Press applied to the DTPS in December 1846 to force payment of £1.3.0 'horse' left by J. Armstrong. Armstrong had a reputation for serial offences of this type, apparently, having joined the DUP earlier that year after ducking similar 'horse' commitments at his previous employer, McDonnells.[103] Twenty-odd years later, the DTPS were still covering dunning notices for missing 'horse' payments. For example, tucked away in the official quarterly returns of receipts and expenditures for 1870–1 are several notes of payments made on behalf of absconding union members. These included: 2s 3d for '"Horse" left by Mr. Edward Scall', (30 June 1870 accounts); 5s 6d for '"Horse" paid for Mr R. Fitzgerald' (31 December 1870 accounts); and 5s 10d for '"Horse" paid for Mr. J. Power' (31 March 1871 accounts).[104]

Such 'flying brethren', as unscrupulous journeymen trampers were disparagingly termed, were not above faking union cards to gain access to union benefits. To guard against such frauds, union officials would report infractions to central committees and 'name and shame' through publishing the names of 'worthless

---

[99] R. A. Leeson, *Travelling Brothers* (St Albans: Granada Publishing Ltd, 1979), pp. 152–3.
[100] 'Tramping', *Scottish Typographical Circular* Third Series, Volume 1, no. 11 (1862), p. 171.
[101] Quoted in Gillespie, *A Hundred Years of Progress*, p. 78.
[102] Kinane, *A History of the Dublin University Press, 1734–1976*, p. 136.   [103] Ibid.
[104] 'Dublin Typographical Provident Society Committee Minute Books', in *Dublin Typographical Provident Society Records* (Trinity College, Dublin).

members of the profession in search of employment' in the monthly typographical trade press, in annual reports, and in union circulars.[105] The typographical trade press and union congresses across various countries spent a great deal of time debating the issue, highlighting egregious examples of misconduct, as well as noting the financial strain upon individual branches of 'relieving tramps' during economic downturns. In such ways, by the 1870s the professional tramp (as opposed to the occasional printer on the move), 'acquired an almost proverbial reputation for being idle, dissolute, and inferior workmen'.[106] But as one British union chronicler has noted,

> The system certainly tended to foster 'professional roadsters'. On the other hand, there were 'many instances of men who have tramped long and hard, and yet have never... brought the least disgrace upon their own characters, or upon the profession'. The misconduct of a few, no doubt, resulted in exaggerated statement about all tramps.[107]

To be fair, trade debates acknowledged that tramping as a long-term activity was hard on the body and the soul. It might suit the younger, fitter compositor just starting out in the business, but a constant pace of travel in intemperate weather and across rough terrain took its toll. For each anecdotal tale of educated and philosophical tramp printers inspiring and entertaining trade members on their arrival in town, there were equal numbers of accounts of travellers broken by their travails. An editorial account of the 'monstrous evils and injustices of the tramping system' in the February 1844 issue of *The Printer*, began by quoting an elderly typographical tramp who had spent the winter travelling over six hundred miles in search of work. The shattering results were seen to be even worse than the degrading prospect of entering a workhouse: 'Should I live until next year, and be out of employment', the roving printer concluded, 'I will go into the workhouse sooner than draw my card and tramp.'[108]

J.W. Rounsfell's memoir of tramping across England in the 1880s describes similar views from and affecting encounters with professional tramping typographers. One compositor encountered on the road to Sheffield confessed he continued to travel though he knew he was 'already past it', reduced to scrounging from friendly trade members who were keenly aware he was no longer able to work a composing stick. 'The word "already" had a painful significance', Rounsfell commented, 'for he couldn't be over forty years old at that time, yet he was socially and industrially done for, and had to beg his way continuously through the country.... Once he had glided inside either a union or non-union shop, all the staff would not be strong enough to get him out again till he had been relieved.'[109] As noted elsewhere in this volume, the typographical trades press on occasion featured obituaries and valedictory poems commemorating fallen tramping typographers. When William Craven, a Leeds based compositor, died in November 1844 after a period of ill health brought on by the travails of the road, an obituary and a short

---

[105] Musson, *The Typographical Association*, p. 51.   [106] Ibid.   [107] Ibid.
[108] Anon., *The Printer* 2 (1844). Quoted in Helen Williams, 'Regional Print Economies in 19th-Century Scotland' (PhD thesis, Edinburgh Napier University, 2018).
[109] Rounsfell, *On the Road*, p. 101.

poem contributed by a compatriot featured in the pages of *The Printer*. Explicit in these contributions was an acknowledgement that the tramping life had led to his early demise, his health compromised and 'materially hastened by repeated journeys in search of employment'.[110] Such examples provided impetus for the establishment by many union branches of benevolent and sick funds to support trade union members in times of illness, with members contributing to the general pot to access free medical attention when needed.

Despite the duress of life on the road, and the effect it had on the health and morale of many who were forced to take up such travelling cycles, a mythology grew up centred round the image of the charismatic, colourful, and philosophical tramp printer, particularly in the USA, where many a young apprentice was enticed onto the road by tales of trade lore and adventure told them by transient typographers. One memoirist recalled vividly his fourteen-year-old apprentice self being entranced by a journeyman printer who had paused at his workplace for a short stint. A talkative, charismatic character, the journeyman 'had been sub-editor, proofreader, engineer, press feeder, ad solicitor, and had plugged type in hundreds of jim crow towns and large cities. He quoted Shakespeare, Lincoln, Mark Twain and the Bible. His tales of travel carried me away to many unfamiliar spots, everything made vivid and real to me as I sat spellbound.'[111] The boy went to bed dreaming of strange adventures, setting out on a journey with the journeyman compositor 'in which we met and talked with Shakespeare, and Adam and Eve (to whom we passed our cards), made a speech at a Sunday school picnic, set type on the Bible, were thrown off coal cars, rode with engineers, sharing the contents of their lunch boxes, and saw all of the West and most of the East'.[112] The apprentice worked his way through his apprenticeship and at the first opportunity, aged nineteen, set off on his own peregrinations, which would last ten years and take in much of the U.S. mid-West.

Colourful if roguish characters may have enlivened conversation as they briefly entered the print workplace, but the evanescent nature of their links to such establishments was a cause for concern for many union offices and indeed for some itinerant compositors themselves. J. W. Rounsfell, English printer on the move in the late 1880s, spoke for many on recollecting the feeling of dismay and loneliness he felt on being forced to move on when work dried up. 'The truth must be told', he confided, 'with the exception of the necessary linen change and socks, the penny-a-mile traveller "moves out" unhampered by luggage, unnoticed by acquaintances, unwept by friends, and often un-"soled and heeled" through the sudden and unexpected collapse of a "permanency".'[113]

Small regional centres such as Kansas City in the USA, the Scottish border town of Dumfries, and other nodal points in the international tramping circuit, were subjected at seasonal times to a large transient population of men as they moved between major print cities. Kansas City saw a great number of roving printers

---

[110] 'Death of Mr Craven, Compositor', *The Printer*, no. 2 (1844).
[111] Hicks, *Adventures of a Tramp Printer, 1880–1890*, p. 13.   [112] Ibid.
[113] Rounsfell, *On the Road*, pp. 93–4.

passing through, given it was, as one commentator noted, 'the gateway to the West, being the place where the trails branched out, taking settles and traders to California and the Oregon country; to Pike's Peak, and to Santa Fe'.[114] The Scottish town of Dumfries was a similar, convenient border point between Scottish and English print centres, serving in particular the heavily trafficked routes between Manchester and Edinburgh.[115] The accounts of the Dumfries Typographical Association between July and September 1840, for example, record a multi-regional mixture of men passing through the town, sixteen in total from places such as Belfast, Birmingham, Dublin, Glasgow, Kilmarnock, London, Manchester, Nottingham, Preston, Stafford, Sunderland, and Wigan. For the whole year, benefits were paid to twenty-six individuals, only five of whom were from Dumfries itself.[116] Passersby appear in the records of benefits paid at such meeting points, but played no other part in the print economy of the town visited.

Likewise, key British port cities such as Liverpool, Newcastle, and Southampton saw influxes of printers touching down at crucial periods before embarking on overseas adventures. Gold rushes in Australia, New Zealand, the USA, and South Africa in the 1860s, 1880s and 1890s enticed many to pass through on their way to such overseas destinations. On reaching such exotic destinations, they would either move on quickly or fall back on their composing skills, once gold fever had subsided and they had failed to make their fortune panning for elusive ingots.

COMMUNICATION CIRCUITS

Records exist for several key union centres in England, Scotland, and Ireland, offering fine-grained details of the levels of mobility and skills transfer amongst union registered compositors, pressmen, and journeyman printers during the Victorian era. Tramping was only a part of the picture of worker mobility in the nineteenth-century printing trade. Sample data drawn from extant union records demonstrates clearly the variety of ways in which union members participated in communication and trade networks that encouraged and supported skills transfer and mobility between printing centres locally, regionally, and internationally. It enables an interesting picture to be built up of the communication and mobility circuits through which print workers engaged with each other in the Victorian era.

Many viewed the links forged as members in the union as valuable and sustaining to their professional endeavours. DTPS records note cases such as Henry Sweetman, émigré to New York in 1892, who having been awarded £3 from the union's Foreign Emigration fund, wrote to the union committee soon after arrival to state he had found work. He enclosed £4 to be put towards union membership dues during his period abroad. The committee returned his donation, explaining he could not hold membership with them while overseas, but rather needed to join

---

[114] Hicks, *Adventures of a Tramp Printer, 1880–1890*, p. 28.
[115] Williams, 'Regional Print Economies'.   [116] Ibid.

a local branch in New York.[117] Sweetman returned to Dublin shortly after, but emigrated again in August 1895, and remained in New York for over forty-five years, popping up occasionally in newspaper reports and the International Typographical Union journal.[118]

If communication from members to unions was frequent, equally, communication between unions was vital for such matters as confirming the legitimacy of individual membership applications or keeping abreast of local pay rates and work practices. Edinburgh union minutes offer striking examples of information requests and responses from trade counterparts through what was in effect a global union communication network. When John McMannus junior sought Edinburgh union entry in August 1853, his application was supported by various documents confirming his apprenticeship record and good character, along with a letter from the Halifax union branch 'showing the honourable position he held while working there'.[119] The character testimonial helped sway the committee, and he was duly admitted on paying an entry fee of £2. William Pagan's application to join the Dumfries union branch in July 1857, after a stint in Glasgow, prompted the executive committee to instruct its secretary to 'write to the Glasgow Secretary to ascertain how Mr Pagan left the Glasgow Society, before admitting him as a member of the Dumfries Branch'.[120] Positive responses prompted the committee to admit him to the Dumfries ranks the following month.[121]

Similarly, Dublin records note multiple examples of the admissions committee contacting relevant overseas branches to request further information on new applicants, and then rejecting, accepting, or accepting with fines based on the responses forthcoming. For example, DTPS minute books record a Michael McGowran, who having been a member of the Dublin union from June to September 1872, left in 1872 and then returned from London in April 1875, applying for membership on 24 April 1875 based on a London Society of Compositors membership card. A response received by 18 May 1875 confirmed his standing, though it revealed he owed the London union a fine for working in a 'closed' or non-unionized shop. He was subsequently enrolled with a fine on 22 May 1875.[122]

---

[117] 'Dublin Typographical Provident Society Committee Minute Books', 5 July 1892, OL Microfilm 703.

[118] *The Typographical Journal*, for example, noted his application in 1935 for a pension from the Typographical Union, no. 6, the New York branch of the ITU. It was turned down for 'insufficient membership.' 'Pension Application Disapproved', *The Typographical Journal*, July 1935. However, by 1941 he was being listed in the I.T.U. honour roll for having achieved fifty years of membership. '"Big Six" Honor Roll, 50 Year Membership I.T.U.', *American Labor World* 1941.

[119] 'Edinburgh Typographical Society Minute Books', in *Edinburgh Typographical Society Records* (National Library of Scotland).

[120] Ibid.

[121] Pagan must have returned to Glasgow at some point over the coming year, as he is recorded in the Glasgow membership records as leaving 15 April 1861, then re-entering the rolls in March 1862 as an employee of the *Daily Herald*. He would feature on and off over the coming decades in the Glasgow records until October 1880, when the membership lists note him as 'dead'. See 'Glasgow Typographical Association Membership Lists', in *Glasgow Typographical Association Records* (Strathclyde University Archives).

[122] 'Dublin Typographical Provident Society Committee Minute Books', August-1872–July 1875, OL Microfilm 703, roll 90/40.

Robert McKay was proposed for membership on 13 September, having just arrived from Edinburgh. Edinburgh union branch correspondence confirmed him as a long-time member, though in membership arrears of £2.7.0. He was admitted to the Dublin union on 10 January 1873, 'with a 10/- fine before reading Declaration'.[123]

Such status verifications between union branches were important for authenticating individual access to membership rights and privileges. But it also highlighted how unions dealt with errant members if they had left owing money for dues or fines. In February 1865, several requests for authentication and character testimonials of former Edinburgh members from London, Manchester and Liverpool branch Secretaries caused the Edinburgh union committee to discuss how best to manage errant union debtors located elsewhere. Until then, debts accumulated by members who had left town had been written off. However, the way such debtors subsequently used their membership cards to gain access to other union branches without penalty suggested this policy needed to change. As the union secretary noted, the recent rise in communications from sister branches had highlighted that 'persons were ready enough to refer to their connection with the Society when they found it be their interest in London, Manchester etc, who would have repudiated all obligations thereto had they remained in Edinburgh'.[124] It was suggested that some claim ought to be made against such persons when reference requests were received. Edinburgh members concurred, and after brief discussion the committee adopted the motion that when a member who had left in debt to the Society was found applying for admission into another union, a note of his liabilities was to be sent to the branch Secretary and payment reclaimed. Other unions in turn adopted similar policies, and letters of clearance became standard tools in the process of assimilating new members into local unions.

Authentication via written form also applied to confirming a compositor's trade expertise. Interesting examples of transnational transfer requests by former apprentices, acceptance of which depended upon the production of appropriate documentation, appear in several union records. In December 1874, for example, Joshua Matthews applied for Dublin union membership, having recently arrived from Barbados. He was placed on the non-members list while confirmation of his status as journeyman printer was sought from the *Barbados Agricultural Reporter*, where he had done his apprenticeship. The *Barbados Agricultural Reporter*, founded in 1862, was a key training ground for Caribbean based printing trade personnel, in continual publication until 1930. Matthews' apprenticeship papers took a year to be returned to Ireland, and at an executive committee meeting on 14 December 1875, Matthews was finally accepted for admission as full member of the union.[125] In another instance, the Edinburgh union received an application for membership in November 1855 from Samuel Bishop, a machine press operator apprentice recently arrived from the USA, who was unable to provide satisfactory union documents covering his US apprenticeship work. Given the length of time it took

---

[123] Ibid. August-1872–July 1875, OL Microfilm 703, roll 90/40.
[124] 'Edinburgh Typographical Society Minute Books'. Vol 1, 1848–1856, 1 February, 1865.
[125] 'Dublin Typographical Provident Society Committee Minute Books'.

to communicate with overseas union partners, the committee agreed to allow him to work as an apprentice in Edinburgh until matters were settled. Reconsidering Bishop's case in January 1856, the union committee then permitted him entry on payment of £1, but in effect treated him as a journeyman apprentice for a further two years, given further proof from the USA was unforthcoming.[126] Union lists suggest Bishop continued to work in Edinburgh until at least April 1863, when he was struck off the union roll for membership arrears.[127]

Testimonials and confirmation of good standing were not the only items to be transmitted through such contacts. Also included were frequent requests for work rates, updates on union actions, warnings of strike break recruitment, and calls for support of other trade actions. A good example involved letters to Edinburgh from the Liverpool union in July 1853 requesting information on piece rates. The details were to be factored into Liverpudlian demands for fair rate increases at a local newspaper press. Shortly after, a recruiter arrived in Edinburgh scouring for scab workers to break the resulting strike at a Liverpool daily paper. News of the recruitment effort was sent back to Liverpool, and a circular was issued across Scotland 'cautioning the whole Profession'.[128] As the strike dragged into September, the Edinburgh branch helped Liverpool insert advertisements in the *North British Advertiser* warning workers against taking up positions in the affected print shop.[129]

CYCLES OF CIRCULATION

Throughout the nineteenth and early twentieth centuries, union sponsored emigration and removal grants enabled union members in England, Ireland, Scotland, and Wales to circulate along transnational routes as key players in social and trade union networks, setting up businesses, engaging in union politics, and creating the print culture infrastructures that enabled social, communal, and national communication and identification.

Emigration grant schemes sponsored by typographical unions were part of a more general trend of industrial emigration that had started in the 1830s and developed more fully throughout the 1840s and 1850s. The Dublin Typographical Provident Society was founded in 1825 in response to high unemployment resulting from the depression of the period, with the express purpose of funding unemployment and migration relief for fellow print workers.[130] Others followed suit in establishing support structures for print trade emigrants in the 1840s and 1850s, including the National Typographical Emigration Society (NTES), formed in

---

[126] 'Edinburgh Typographical Society Minute Books'. Vol. 1, 1848–1856, 1 November, 3 November 1855; 5 January 1856.
[127] 'Edinburgh Typographical Society Contributor Records, 1861–1900'.
[128] 'Edinburgh Typographical Society Minute Books', Vol. 1, 1848–1856, 21 July, 3 August 1853.
[129] Ibid. Vol. 1, 1848–1856, 4 September 1853.
[130] Kinane, *A History of the Dublin University Press, 1734–1976*, p. 83. Though it is traditionally believed that the DTPS was founded in 1809, Kinane offers convincing evidence that such early foundations were not long lasting, and that archival material supports 1825 as a more likely founding date.

February 1852 through a combined effort of eleven English print union branches.[131] During its twenty-two-month existence, however, it made little impact on migration numbers: in its first five months, only five applicants, all from Liverpool, were sent out, including three to the USA and one to Australia. By the time the scheme closed on 19 November 1853, it had expended £165.5.0 supporting twenty-one emigrants in total.[132] The emigration committee of the London Society of Compositors ran a parallel scheme overlapping the NTES, establishing an emigration committee that operated between 1853 and 1857. It seemed to have been even more profligate and ineffective in its migration efforts. Labelled a farce towards the end of its life by the LSC's secretary, it spent over £800 in emigration grants, loans, and travel subsidies to support a mere forty-one printer emigrants.[133]

A more effective scheme was the one operated by the Dublin Typographical Provident Society, which had supported emigration requests since its founding in 1825. Between 1856 and 1859, for example, it provided emigration allowances to 120 printer emigrants shifting to mainland Britain or other overseas destinations.[134] It would continue to offer grants through to the turn of the century, over the years steadily increasing its sliding scale of payments to reflect seniority and length of service. In May 1875, for example, reflecting increased travel costs, it raised its emigrations grants to £5 for three years' service, £7 for five years' service, £9 for eight years' service, and £12 for eleven plus years of service. It also adjusted its 'British emigration allowance' upwards to £3.[135]

In 1870, the London Society of Compositors revived its emigration scheme, offering similar grants pegged to length of service: members of two years' standing were offered £5; three years, £6; four years, £7; five years, £8; six years, £9; ten years and over, £10.[136] Strict rules were enforced regarding returning emigrants to prevent the abuses of previous years: anyone who received a grant and returned had to rejoin the union as a completely new member, losing built up entitlements and benefits. This was a powerful disincentive, and the scheme lasted into the twentieth century with little difficulty in implementation.

From 1890 through to the 1950s, the Scottish Typographical Association operated a similar emigration scheme for its members. In its first four years of existence (1890–1893), the scheme paid out £105.16.0 in grants to outgoing members. Funding requests rose significantly after this, peaking between 1903 and 1912, when the union paid out a staggering total of £1626.10.0 in emigration grants.[137]

---

[131] Richards, 'Social and Economic Aspects of Combination in the Printing Trade before 1875', p. 330. Richards reproduces the accounts for the Society covering 1 February 1852 to 31 March 1853, noting that £108.16.4 was subscribed to the scheme by the following union branches: Bedford, Cardiff, Durham, Halifax, Huddersfield, Liverpool, Newport, Preston, Sheffield, Sunderland, Wigan. By far the largest contributors to the scheme were Liverpool, who contributed £67.5.4, and Sheffield, who donated £14.17.0.

[132] Ibid., p. 329–33.

[133] Wilbur S. Shepperson, 'Industrial Emigration in Early Victorian Britain', *The Journal of Economic History* 13, no. 2 (1953), p. 183; Richards, p. 342.

[134] Richards, 'Social and Economic Aspects of Combination in the Printing Trade before 1875', p. 344.

[135] Ibid.   [136] Ibid, p. 345.   [137] Gillespie, *A Hundred Years of Progress*, pp. 248–55.

Through such means skilled print artisans were encouraged to circulate widely, though not all did. As I have written about before, information from British and Irish print union records and other print sources suggest at least four categories of print worker circulation existed across Victorian print networks.[138] These included:

- the local anchor;
- the regionally mobile artisan;
- the nationally mobile typographer;
- and the outward facing, international migrant print worker.

Within these categories, as Helen Williams has noted, there were significant variations based on time and space.[139] Some workers remained settled in one job with one employer for a significant period of time; others went 'on the road' for a single journey to a neighbouring town before returning to assume an anchoring role; still others took extended journeys between single points in print shop networks, while others undertook circular routes (returning to the original branch) with few or many calling points; Others went on frequent and repeated periods of travel, interspersing these with short periods of settled work (though not necessarily in the original branch); and finally, there was the peripatetic traveller, whose appearance across several print network sites suggested a constantly moving approach to work in the trade. With such caveats, however, trade documentation suggests that a common typology of network actors could be found amongst those who worked globally in the English-speaking printing trade during the Victorian and Edwardian periods.

LOCAL ANCHOR

There was the solid, long lasting anchor, the 'home guards', as one memoirist termed such 'stay at home' workers, whose presence in the union was constant over decades and whose place as motivator and conserver of traditions was often extolled in obituaries and retirement notices.[140] A good example was John Carbery, whose death in 1868 at the age of fifty-six occasioned a fulsome tribute in the *Scottish Typographical Circular*. Carbery, a staunch union member who had spent his working life in Edinburgh since his apprenticeship at Mr Shortrede's, 'the printing birthplace of many sterling men', had been a key player in union activities, initiating many of the union's welfare initiatives. He was hailed as 'a real hero of industry', boisterous, earnest, upright, honest and 'the possessor of a generous heart'.[141] His many accomplishments included being 'the principal founder of our Funeral Scheme, an active promoter of the Sick Scheme, a great admirer and patron of our Library till the day of his death, and an intelligent maintainer of the principles of

---

[138] David Finkelstein, 'Nineteenth-Century Print on the Move: A Perilous Study of Translocal Migration and Print Skills Transfer', in *Theory and Practice in Book, Print and Publishing History*, ed. Jason and Eve Patten McElligott (Basingstoke: Palgrave Macmillan, 2014).

[139] Williams, 'Regional Print Economies'.

[140] Hicks, *Adventures of a Tramp Printer, 1880–1890*, p. 20.

[141] 'Obituary: John Carbery', *Scottish Typographical Circular* (1868).

trade unionism, fearless of all consequences, and that, too, at a time when to do so was not the order of the day'.[142]

Another compositor celebrated for his anchoring role was David Lockhart, a union member in the Blackwood publishing firm. The *Scottish Typographical Circular* marked his death in July 1888 with the following encomium: 'a first-class compositor – indeed, in the opinion of many, he stood unrivalled in every kind of work which was put into his hands. At his death, he was one of the oldest hands in the office, having been about thirty-four years there. Mr Lockhart was a staunch unionist, and was one of the oldest members of the Edinburgh Branch of the Scottish Typographical Association. Eminently straightforward, upright, and conscientious in all his actions, he was emphatically a "man" in the highest sense of the word.'[143] Equally, the *Typographical Circular* of March 1918 recorded in commendatory prose the retiral of R. G. Fobister, Scottish trained compositor who, after stints in Scotland, crossed regional borders to become a stalwart member for almost forty years of the Liverpool Typographical Association. His long association with the Liverpool union included acting as secretary and member of the Executive Council, and involving himself in the society's superannuation and benevolent funds. He would be praised as a union member who 'persistently identified himself with everything that made for the progress of the craft of which he was a proud member'.[144]

REGIONAL CIRCULATION

A second category was that of the local and regionally mobile artisan, whose movements within regional printing networks were frequent and wide-ranging, and involved multiple shifts across local and regional printing establishments, such as Robert Andrews, who between 1870 and 1878 shifts employment in Glasgow four times and across three establishments;[145] Charles Arroll, who between 1872 and 1876 changes employment in and around Glasgow five times;[146] and John Farquarhson, who between 1887 and 1903 shuttled around Edinburgh, Aberdeen and Glasgow, sometimes working for a few months, at other times undertaking multi-year labour stints.[147] Some more extreme examples are recorded in Dublin

---

[142] Ibid.   [143] 'Obituary', *Scottish Typographical Circular* (1888), p. 676.

[144] 'A Veteran Treasurer', *Typographical Circular* (March 1918), p. 5.

[145] 'Glasgow Typographical Association Membership Lists'. Membership list notes offer following gloss on his movements: 'left *Daily Herald* for *Express*, Feb 1870; at *Star* from Jan 1871; at *News* from Jan 1874; back at *Herald* from Jan 1877; Left town [Feb 1878]'.

[146] 'Glasgow Typographical Association Membership Lists'. The full notes in the membership lists record his many shifts as follows:

'left Macrone for *Christian News*, Jan 1872; Left town [April 1872];
at Aird & Coghill from Jan 1874; Left town clear [Nov 1874];
at Mackay & Kirkwood from March 1875;
at Barbow from Jan 1876.'

[147] Edinburgh records note Farquharson moving to work in Aberdeen in 1890, Newcastle in 1894, and Glasgow in May 1902; In Edinburgh he is registered working at various firms, including Neill & Co.,

union lists of multiple entries and exits, such as William Morgan (senior) who between 1870 and 1898 is registered twenty-five different times and for varying periods, and John McLoughlin, who between 1877 and 1898 also shifts in and out of the Dublin union twenty-five times. In Morgan's case, patterns of arrival and departure suggest peripatetic moves matching seasonal work opportunities in the Irish provinces and mainland Britain. In some cases, Morgan is expelled for arrears and returns within a few months. In other circumstances, it is clear he has been 'tramping' for key months of the year, particularly where membership notes refer to Morgan having shifted to Irish towns such as Portlaoise, usually for short periods of between one to four months between August and December.[148] John McLoughlin's record is equally complex, but suggests more lengthy tours of Irish locations in tandem with long spells of work in mainland Britain. Membership records also show him interspersing short periods of absence (between two weeks and four months), with longer periods of up to a year working in other locations.[149]

Colston & Co., and the Edinburgh Cooperative Printing Company. 'Edinburgh Typographical Society Contributor Records, 1861–1900'. Accession 4068, no. 88.

[148] His record reads as follows:

'Expelled for arrears, rejoined 6 August 1870'.
'Drew card and £1-10-0' 30 September 1871. 'Returned' 2 December 1871.
'Drew card & £1-10-0' 7 September [1872]; 'Returned' 12 October 1872.
'Drew card & 15/-' 5 July 1873; 'Returned due 10/-' 16 August 1873.
'Drew card & £1-10'—15 August [1874]; 'Returned' 3 October 1874.
'Drew card & £3-0-0'—3 September 1875; 'Returned' 11 December 1875.
'Drew card & £3'—12 August [1876]; 'Returned' 2 December 1876.
'Drew card and £3'—9 June 1877; 'Returned' 11 August 1877;
'Drew card and £3-0-0'—23 March [1878]; 'Returned' 22 June 1878; 'Gone to England' July [1878]; 'Returned' 14 September 1878;
'Drew Card and £1-10-0'—1 February [1879]; in rolls from 22 March [1879]; 'Gone to England'—2 August 1879;
'In rolls' from 24 April 1880;
'In Maryboro' [Portlaoise]'—16 December 1882;
In rolls from January 1883; 'Drew Card and £1-10'—15 September [1883]; in rolls from 1 December 1883;
'Drew Card and £3'—12 December 1885; 'Returned' 9 January 1886; 'Drew card and 15/-'—27 November 1886;
In rolls January [1887]; 'Drew Card and £3'—28 May 1887; 'Returned'—26 November 1887;
'Drew Card and £1'—30 May [1891]; 'Returned' 4 July 1891;
'Drew Card & £3'—17 September [1892]; 'Returned' 26 November 1892;
'Card and £1'—29 July [1893]; in rolls from 11 November 1893.
'Card and £1-0-0'—9 June [1894]; 'Relodged' 23 June 1894; 'Card and 10/-'—10 November 1894;
'Card relodged' 22 February [1896]; 'Card and 5/- loan granted' 18 April 1896;
'Card Lodged'—5 March 1897; 'Card 5/- loan'—17 July 1897;
'Proposed' 10 December 1898.

[149] McLoughlin first appears registered on the rolls on 19 March 1877, though he is not proposed for full membership until 19 May 1877. His record of comings and goings subsequently is documented as follows:

'Card and grant of £1-11'—16 March 1878; 'Returned' 30 March 1878;
'In Provinces'—15 March 1879;
In rolls from 18 September 1880;

Another Irish contemporary, Hugh Logue, presented himself in January 1878 for admittance to the Dublin union with a *curriculum vitae* that encompassed fourteen years of work across an extensive Irish regional network. Logue began his typographical life as an apprentice at the *Coleraine Chronicle*, staying on for a further year as a journeyman printer in 1864–5. He subsequently embarked on a nine-month tour of Glasgow print shops, returned to work in the *Chronicle* for two years, shifted to Belfast to work for the *Belfast Newsletter* (three years), started his own print shop in Antrim (18 months), returned for a short stint in Belfast (nine months), then hopscotched across Omagh, Lurgan, Drumpatrick, and Sligo for three and a half years. In 1877, he took up residence in Dublin, working for the *Irish Times* and then Browne and Nolan.[150] He was eventually admitted to the union in May 1878 after paying a £3 fine for having worked as a non-union employee in Dublin beforehand. He continued as a union member until his death in June 1892.[151]

Wales had its share of mobile printers, though union networks were less extensive in this region than in Northern England, Scotland, and Ireland. Ifano Jones and Aled Gruffydd Jones draw attention to the roving Welsh printer George Jenkin Jacobs, whose fifty-year career encompassed multiple moves between towns and print establishments, composing work on multiple newspapers, the founding and running of his own newspapers, and then a rise in rank to become a master-printer and owner of significant printing works in Rhymney.[152] Born in 1837 on a farm

'In the Provinces'—15 July–12 August 1882;
'Away'—4–24 April 1885;
'Drew Card and £3'—3 April 1886; 'In England' July 1886;
In rolls from 19 March 1887; 'Drew Card and 10/-'—1 October 1887;
In rolls 10 March [1888]; 'Drew Card and £3'—9 June 1888; 'Returned'—25 August 1888;
'Drew card and 10/- to be charged to acct. on return (overclaiming)'—16 February [1889]; 'Returned' 1 June 1889; 'In the Provinces'—July [1889]; 'Returned' 16 November 1889;
'Drew Card and £3 (Did not leave Town)'—14 June 1890;
'Expelled by vote of Trade'—2 May 1891; 'Rescinded' 6 June [1891]; 'Lifted Card' 12 September 1891;
'Returned' 23 January 1892; 'Re-lifted card' 10 September [1892]; in rolls from 8 October 1892; 'Drew Card'—15 April 1893; In rolls from 2 September 1893;
'Card and £3'—20 January [1894]; in rolls again on 10 March and from 22 December 1894;
'By Order of Com. Card and 10/-'—2 February [1895]; in rolls from 1 June 1895;
'Advanced 7/6 Rail Fare'—18 January [1896]; in rolls 25 January [1896]; 'Advanced 2/6'—1 February 1896; 'Loan 10/-'; 'Away (in hospital)'—4 July [1896]; 'Card and 10/- (loan)'—8 August [1896]; in rolls from 29 September; [1896] 'Rail fare 2/-'—17 October 1896;
In rolls from 23 January [1897]; 'card and £3'—27 March [1897]; in rolls from 24 April 1897; 'Card relodged'—21 August [1897]; 'Card' 18 September 1897;
In rolls from 22 January [1898]; 'Loan 5/-'—14 May 1898; 'Expelled for Arrears'—2 July 1898.
In 'New' rolls only on 17 December 1898.

[150] Browne and Nolan was based at 24 Nassau Street and advertised itself as an account book manufacturer, printer, lithographer, and stationer. See *Kelly's Directory of Stationers, Printers, Booksellers and Publishers of England, Scotland, Wales and Ireland* (London: Kelly and Co., 1880), pp. 958–63.

[151] See 'Dublin Typographical Provident Society Committee Minute Books'. Tuesday 15 January 1878, and 'Classified Ad 94', *The Scotsman*, 27 March.

[152] Ifano Jones, *A History of Printing and Printers in Wales to 1810, and of Successive and Related Printers to 1923. Also, a History of Printing and Printers in Monmouthshire to 1923* (Cardiff: William Lewis (Printers), Ltd, 1925), p. 282; Jones, *Press, Politics and Society*, pp. 79–80.

in Whitland, Pembrokeshire, Jacobs served a seven-year apprenticeship in Llanelli until 1856, when he turned nineteen. In 1857, he took up work in Cardiff at the *Cardiff and Methyr Guardian*, shifted a year later to Aberdare to work on the Welsh language newspapers *Gwron Cymreig* and *Y Gweithiwr*, then in 1859 returned to Llanelli to help launch the quarterly magazine *Y Beirniad*. In 1865, he is listed as a compositor in Merthyr working on the *Merthyr Telegraph*, though he leaves town in 1866 in consequence of a printer's strike. Further short-term stints follow in Newport and Merthyr. In 1870 Jacob relocates permanently to Rhymney, where he sets up as a newspaper proprietor, publishing the short lived weekly newspaper *Tredegar Telegraph*. His business expands, he launches more publications, such as the *Tredegar Guardian*, the *Monmouth Guardian* and the *Bargoed and Caerphilly Observer*, and by the time of his death in 1908, he has become an affluent master-printer, managing with his two sons a large firm with strong Welsh roots. Jenkins' also played an important anchoring role in his local area. He would prove an able and active promoter of Welsh language and culture, not just through his work in printing Welsh language material but also through his keen support of the Eisteddfod movement. He would found the Gwent Semi-National Eisteddfod at Rhymney, serve on committees dedicated to bringing the National Eisteddfod to Rhymney, write extensively on Welsh subjects, serve on local cultural and trade committees, and act as local correspondent for the *South Wales Daily News*.[153]

NATIONAL CIRCULATION

A third category of circulating compositors was the skilled journeyman printer who ranged across national printing networks, such as George Mackay, whose obituary notice in the November 1869 issue of the *Scottish Typographical Circular* was accompanied by a long encomium extolling his skills and abilities, and commenting on his particularly mobile career in rural and suburban locations, which ranged across Edinburgh, Glasgow, London, and Crieff. 'Reckoned a swift and good compositor', Mackay moved positions several times within towns and across regional borders. The list was extensive, as the following demonstrates:

> He had held the situation of overseer in Mr Hugh Paton's, in the late *Edinburgh Advertiser* office, and in the Glasgow *Sentinel* office. He was afterwards sub-editor of the *Weekly News*; of the Glasgow *Daily Mail*; and, subsequently, of *The Press*, London. He left London for Crieff, where he edited and printed the *Strathearn Herald*; returning to Edinburgh from Crieff, to edit and print the *Scottish Press*. But ever-recurring illness laid him up, and he had repeatedly to relinquish good positions. In his later years, Mr Mackay was in close connection with the press of Edinburgh.[154]

Another example was William Bradbury, who secured short- and long-term work in England, Scotland, and Ireland between 1885 and 1899. In April 1885,

---

[153] 'Obituary. Welsh Newspaper Proprietor. Mr G. J. Jacobs, Rhymney', *Cardiff Times and New South Wales Weekly*, 17 October 1908, p. 7.
[154] 'The Late George Mackay', *Scottish Typographical Circular* (1869), p. 241.

William Bradbury, compositor/journeyman, joined the Edinburgh Typographical Association. An employee of Constable's the printers, he paid union dues until September 1886, then left to begin a series of short-term peregrinations between Aberdeen, Edinburgh and London.[155] This was to culminate in a two-year stint between February 1892 and March 1894 for the printer Thom's in Dublin, where he would also become a member of the Dublin Typographical Provident Society.[156] He returned to Edinburgh in March 1894, re-registering with the Edinburgh union branch and taking up work in the printing firm Neill & Co. It seems he took to the post, as he remained embedded there until at least January 1899, when we lose sight of him in union lists, as he was struck off for nonpayment of dues.[157] William Bradbury's Scottish, English and Irish migration and mobility patterns, like many of his contemporaries, built on the networks of national unions that took shape in the nineteenth century. Bradbury's earlier pattern of short-term contracts suggested a peripatetic approach to work, akin to the tramping typographer of earlier years. Unlike the tramping typographer of yore, the migration and mobility patterns of members like Bradbury often saw transfers between recognized centres and secured jobs gained through word of mouth and personal contacts.

Equally peripatetic was Andrew Bothwell, another entrant to the Dublin union, whose petition to be admitted to its rolls on 8 March 1879 included a lengthy resumé of his regional experiences. Having started his apprenticeship in Aberdeen (on the *Aberdeen Free Press*), he concluded his training at the *Northern Whig* paper in Belfast. He would move on to join the union in Bradford, return to Belfast to work as a journeyman printer on the *Northern Whig* and the *Morning News*, sojourn for a period in Aberdeen on the *Aberdeen Journal*, move to Nottingham to take a place on the *Nottingham Daily Guardian*, then shift to Dublin in November 1878 to take up work in the Dublin Steam Printing Company.[158] His application was eventually approved and he was admitted to the Dublin union on 14 June 1879.[159]

INTERNATIONAL CIRCULATION

The fourth category was that of the transnational migrant, the wandering typographer who sought work across international borders. From the 1840s onwards, and particularly in the 1880s to the 1900s, British and Irish print union members proved extraordinarily mobile across international spaces, with many playing key roles in establishing key print establishments or advancing union practices across the English-speaking world.

A good example of the cross-border printer adventurer was John Wilson (1802–1868). An 1868 obituary notice in the *Boston Daily Advertiser,* subsequently

[155] 'Edinburgh Typographical Society Contributor Records, 1861–1900'.
[156] 'Classified Ad 94'.
[157] 'Edinburgh Typographical Society Contributor Records, 1861–1900'.
[158] 'Dublin Typographical Provident Society Committee Minute Books'. Roll 90/114.
[159] 'Classified Ad 94'.

picked up and reprinted in the *Scottish Typographical Circular*, took note of Wilson's multi-regional and international career, which included an apprenticeship in Glasgow, taking charge of a large printing establishment in Belfast, working in Manchester at the *Manchester Guardian* newspaper, then emigrating to Boston in 1846. In Boston, the staunchly Glaswegian Wilson and his son would establish the successful printing firm John Wilson and Sons. The business would carry on after his death under the direction of his son John Wilson junior (1825–1903), also Scottish born and trained. In 1879, through a series of shrewd investments, John Wilson junior would take over Welsh, Bigelow & Co., who had been the main printers for Harvard University. Wilson consolidated businesses to form the University Press–John Wilson and Co., and under that imprint over subsequent decades would go on to publish significant titles by Bostonian authors such as Oliver Wendell Holmes, Longfellow, Hawthorne, Whittier, Emerson, and Lowell.[160]

Emigration to the USA by such British and Irish trained printers throughout the Victorian period was encouraged and supported by unions, and as noted already, several thousand made the journey from British and Irish ports over the second half of the century. In conjunction with this, there were multiple flows back and forth between the USA and the British Isles by members when job opportunities arose. In addition to the already mentioned Henry Sweetman, who moved fluidly between Dublin and New York several times in the 1890s, there were other examples such as James Warnock. Born in Paisley in 1827, after a Scottish-based apprenticeship he spent some time as a printer in Liverpool, emigrated in the 1850s to New York, then returned to Glasgow in 1862 with a young family and an appetite for work. Over the next five years he would take up work in six print shops in Ayr and Glasgow before returning to the USA in late 1868.[161] At a presentation organized by colleagues at the end of July 1868 to mark his departure, reported in the *Scottish Typographical Circular*, he was dined, serenaded and given a 'handsome silver snuff box, to serve as a memento of the many friends left in Glasgow'.[162] William Govan, Secretary to the Glasgow branch of the Scottish Typographical Association, oversaw the proceedings and praised Warnock for his indefatigable efforts on behalf of the print profession, commending him as 'one who was ever ready to place his time and his talents at the disposal of the Society – and as one who, notwithstanding all his labours, modestly considered he had only endeavoured to do his duty'.[163] As was usual at such occasions, 'Song and sentiment now followed freely, and made a pleasant evening glide only too quickly away.'[164] There is evidence to suggest that by 1871 Warnock had taken up a position in the New York printing department of the Erie Railway Company, and over the next twenty

[160] 'John Wilson Dead', *Cambridge Tribune* 26, no. 11 (1903).
[161] 'Glasgow Typographical Association Membership Lists'. Union membership lists record him: re-entering the Glasgow union branch in August 1862; working for Anderson; lifting his card for Ayr in January 1863; returning to work in the *Gazette* in January 1864; shifting to Eadie's in January 1865; then leaving for McCorquodale in October 1865. Between then and early 1868 he takes up employment in Hutchison's, a point noted in the notice of his farewell presentation in the *Scottish Typographical Circular*. See 'Trade News: Glasgow', *Scottish Typographical Circular* (1868), p. 72.
[162] 'Trade News: Glasgow'.   [163] Ibid.   [164] Ibid.

years he would play an anchoring role in Scots-American diaspora societies such as the New York Caledonian Club and the Thistle Benevolent Society.[165]

In January 1906, the *London Typographical Journal* reprinted an obituary of the transnational migrant printer Concannon Richards, lifted from the *Australian Typographical Journal*, which highlighted the extraordinary range of workplaces and jobs British printers found for themselves across the world. (The reprint was yet another example of the transnational circulation of typographical press information noted later in this book.) Bidding farewell to this Brighton-born journeyman printer, who died on 26 July 1906, the notice recalled his social skills as a singer and offered a brief synopsis of his career, which included employment in a London music-printing house, an extended period overseeing a print firm in Valparaiso, Chile, short stints back in London as print owner and then reader for several legal and literary journals, and then emigration to Australia in 1883 to join the staff of the *Illustrated Sydney News*. In Sydney, he instigated a short-lived 'Society for the Correctors of the Press' like one that existed in London, but with less success. Further work in other Sydney print firms was succeeded by a final stint as owner of a print firm in Miller Street, which he ran until shortly before his death.[166] The career of Richards offered an interesting arc of activity that encompassed work on several continents, stints as both employed and employer, a role as trade union activist and involvement in the social community of the Sydney print trade.

PRINTERS AS SETTLER CAPITALISTS

New Zealand had similar print trade pioneers landing on it shores. New Zealand colonial development in the nineteenth century was a direct result of British migration, investment, and expansion, as Donald Denoon has pointed out in his classic study *Settler Capitalism*.[167] Many British roving printers became key community members through their participation in the print economy of expanding towns. Taking on such roles in undeveloped frontier towns required stamina and strong communication skills. A good example of such colonial encounters and printers who played key civic roles in extending colonial settlements can be seen in Andrew Ferguson's career as printer in New Zealand. Ferguson, born in Dunfermline, Scotland on 16 December 1838, had been apprenticed to the Edinburgh printing firm Thomas Constable. On completing his training, he moved to London to join

---

[165] The 12 October 1871 issue of the *New York Herald* notes donations being made by James Warnock and thirty-three other colleagues of the Erie Railway Company Printing Department towards relief funds for victims of the Chicago fire that year. (The department raised $100 in total, with Warnock donating $2.50 to the cause.) See 'Better Than Speeches. The Army of Subscribers to Relieve the Sufferers', *The New York Herald*, October 12 1871. A small obituary in the same newspaper appears on 22 September 1894, recording Warnock's death on 20 September 1894 in New York City at the age of sixty-seven. See 'Deaths', *The New York Herald*, 22 September 1894.

[166] 'The Following Appeared in the October Issue of the *Australian Typographical Journal*', *London Typographical Journal* 1, no. 2 (1906).

[167] Denoon, *Settler Capitalism*.

Smith, Elder and Co., where he claimed to have overseen two 'class journals'.[168] In 1867 he emigrated to Dunedin to join his cousins Joseph Mackay and John Mackay II in running the daily *Bruce Herald*, an example of 'chain migration', in which family and/or trade contacts smoothed the entrance of skilled artisans into overseas workplaces.

On a subscription drive for the *Bruce Herald* across the Otago region in late 1867, Ferguson visited the town of Lawrence. The town was originally established as Tuapeka in 1861, following the discovery by Gabriel Read of gold in a nearby ridge. 'Gabriel's Gully', as the goldfield was christened, sparked a gold rush to the Otago region that swelled Tuapeka's population from a handful in 1861 to over 11,500 by 1862. In 1862, it was renamed Lawrence in honour of Henry Lawrence, the British general who gained fame for his role in defending the Indian city of Lucknow during the Indian revolt of 1857.

Lawrence initially was host to a moribund weekly newspaper, the *Tuapeka Press*, started in 1865 by John R. Robb to inform the mining community. In an 1866 letter published in the *Scottish Typographical Circular*, a thirty-year-old Scottish jobbing printer, who had emigrated to New Zealand and found temporary employment in the *Tuapeka Press*, described its setup and that of Lawrence itself. 'The place from which I now write is about seventy miles above Dunedin, on the once famous Gabriel's Gully Goldfields, in the wilds of New Zealand', he noted. 'It is a small township of about thirty houses, surrounded by diggers' tents, hemmed in by high hills, and within thirty miles of the Blue Mountains.'[169] The general print shop layout was as rudimentary as could be expected in a mining town: 'The office is half tent, half house—a rum case-room, I can assure you, from the windows of which we can see the miners at work.'[170] Though in Lawrence he faced 'a rough part of the country, and a rough life', the roving printer had no regrets in leaving Edinburgh for new experiences in such frontier towns, for 'the life of a printer up here is much different from that at home, and I like it as well again, even although the pay were no better'.[171]

The Scots printer may have enjoyed his time at the *Tuapeka Press*, but the newspaper's sparse fare soon had locals agitating for more substantial information sources. Ferguson's conversations in 1867 with Lawrence residents suggested an opportunity to establish a livelier competitor title, buttressed by a jobbing print shop servicing local mining needs. Ferguson pooled resources with two partners, Andrew Burns and John Ludford, and bought old printing equipment from owners of the defunct *Bruce Independent*, which had operated out of Milton. The machinery was transported to Lawrence, where it was installed in a corrugated iron shed that became the temporary base for the business. Ferguson and his partners commenced publishing the four-page weekly *Tuapeka Times* on 15 February 1868.

Ferguson and his companions issued a bold statement of intent in the first issue. Their goal was to create a paper that would guide public opinion, help to maintain

---

[168] 'Memories of the Tuapeka Times', *Tuapeka Times*, 4 February 1905.
[169] 'New Zealand', *Scottish Typographical Circular* (1866), p. 415.   [170] Ibid.
[171] Ibid, p. 416.

a wholesome moral sentiment, and 'materially contribute to the making of a district great, and keeping it so'.[172] 'Our endeavor shall be', the opening editorial continued, 'calmly and deliberately to weigh every variety of sentiment which pervades the community, and give an honest expression to that aggregate of thought which is what we term Public Opinion, and the ventilation of what we conceive to be the legitimate function of the journalism of a country.'[173]

Such lofty ambitions were nurtured under rudimentary circumstances. To save money, during the early years the partners lived, worked, ate, and slept in the print shop. 'We converted a corner of the office into a kitchen and, with the aid of a stove, the apprentice managed, with a little assistance, to cook all we required', recalled Ferguson many years later.[174] At night the divisions between the printing frames were used as dormitories by Burns, Ludford and an apprentice, with Ferguson bunking down under the counter. Bedding initially consisted of old copies of the *Bruce Independent* that had been used as packing to transport the print equipment to Lawrence.[175] Though the paper was issued weekly, the presses were kept busy with job printing of general items such as handbills, invoices, labels, cards and forms, and space in the paper was reserved for advertising such services. As the first issue announced in bold letters on the front page, 'Ferguson, Burns, & Ludford beg to intimate to the inhabitants of Lawrence and surrounding districts, that, having furnished their Office with NEW AND ELEGANT TYPE, they are prepared to execute every description of ORNAMENTAL, COLORED, AND PLAIN PRINTING, at Moderate Prices, and on the shortest notice.'[176]

Newspaper circulation slowly built up, encouraged by much personal lobbying and delivery by horseback to rural subscribers. New owners of the rival *Tuapeka Press* injected an element of competition into the press environment, but by 1869 Ferguson and his partners' acumen and hard work led to them buying out the *Tuapeka Press*, leaving the *Tuapeka Times* pre-eminent in the field. They would shift premises shortly after. Ludford and Burns's shares in the business were subsequently bought out in June and October 1870 respectively by Ferguson, who brought in a new partner, John C. Brown, to help run the business. Brown lasted a little over a year before he in turn was bought out by Ferguson. Ferguson assumed sole control of the business in December 1871, and in November 1873 he converted the paper into an eight-page, bi-weekly issue.[177]

Ferguson arrived as Lawrence began to develop civic structures and to establish a more permanent town identity, moving beyond stakeholder gold rush circumstances. Over the years he lived there, the township expanded to include a school, a courthouse, a jail and police station, a post office and other government buildings. Discoveries of quartz and coal created new mining opportunities to compensate

---

[172] 'The Tuapeka Times', *The Tuapeka Times*, 15 February 1868.   [173] Ibid.
[174] 'Memories of the Tuapeka Times'.   [175] Ibid.
[176] 'Tuapeka Times General Printing Office', *Tuapeka Times*, 15 February 1868.
[177] See 'Dissolution of Partnership', *Tuapeka Times*, 23 June 1870; 'Dissolution of Partnership', *Tuapeka Times*, 28 December 1871.

for a drop in temporary residents once the initial 'gold rush' had died down.[178] With central government support and funding, dams and aqueducts were built to create water reservoirs and channel water through to the township, and after much lobbying, a railway line was built in 1877 linking it via the South Main Line to Dunedin, Invercargill, Lyttelton, and Christchurch.

Among the reforms and initiatives championed by Ferguson in his newspaper editorials and his civic activities were seeking funds to build roads, bridges, and general infrastructure, establishing a fire brigade, pushing for a regulated mining industry, and lobbying for a railway link to the town. He became a key proponent of the local land settlement movement, seeking to release large sheep farming runs for general farming use. New Zealand at the time was gripped by a shortage of land available to small farmers, as more than half of all privately owned land was locked up in large sections of 5,000 acres under control of a small elite of 584 owners.[179] Ferguson supported steps taken to establish a land league to combat this locally with 'the most prominent men of the town and district taking a leading part in it'.[180] 'Land for the people, and people for the land' was the motivational statement frequently repeated in his editorials.[181] The move was successful, with several Tuapeka runs eventually being released by the Government for sale or lease as workable farmland.

Ferguson took seriously his role in Lawrence as printer, editor and journalist, describing it as one of civic responsibility that at times could be trying and 'far from pleasant'.[182] Public documents and local news items hint also at his close engagement with Lawrence's civic society in other forms: he acted as a witness to wills and an executor of estates; he served as local councillor and ran for mayor in 1874 (losing by four votes); he served as juror on civil court cases, and in 1879 was appointed a Justice of the Peace for the Colony; and he helped set up a cooperative building society to support the savings and loans needs of local farmers, businessmen and townsfolk.[183] He would also maintain the cycle of 'chain migration' of relatives that had initially drawn him to New Zealand, bringing his seventeen-year-old London-born nephew William Epps to Lawrence in 1879, where Epps was to spend the next two years helping to edit and produce the paper.[184]

---

[178] Information about the early history of Lawrence can be found in Margaret Allen Jennings, 'The History of Lawrence, Otago, New Zealand, from Earliest Times to 1921, Including a Review of Its Future Prospects' (MA thesis, Canterbury University College, 1921).

[179] Denoon, *Settler Capitalism*, pp. 73–4.   [180] 'Memories of the Tuapeka Times'.

[181] Ibid.; 'Social Gathering', *Tuapeka Times*, 22 February 1882.   [182] 'Social Gathering'.

[183] 'Telegrams', *Clutha Leader*, 23 July 1874. 'Local Intelligence', *Tuapeka Times*, 4 March 1874; 'Jottings from Lawrence', *Lake Wakatip Mail*, 4 August 1874; 'Building Society Meeting', *Tuapeka Times*, 11 September 1875; 'Supreme Court. -in Banco', *Tuapeka Times*, 13 April 1878; 'The New Zealand Gazette', *Otago Daily Times*, 21 June 1879.

[184] 'Lawrence Revisited, after an Absence of Thirty Five Years', *Tuapeka Times*, 8 December 1917. William Epps (1862–1946) would later work for newspapers in Melbourne and Sydney, act as secretary of the Australasian National League, and serve for thirty years (1902–1932) as Secretary of the Royal Prince Alfred Hospital in Sydney, Australia; 'Mr William Epps. Presentation by Hospital Staff', *The Sydney Morning Herald, 16 June 1932;* 'Presentation to Retiring Hospital Secretary', *The Sydney Morning Herald, 16 June 1932.* 'Deaths', *The Sydney Morning Herald, 17 June 1946;* 'Try to Live to 150 Ends at 83', *Sunday Mail, 14 July 1946.*

In 1882, Ferguson sold his business interests to local partners and returned to Edinburgh, where he established the firm of Scott and Ferguson, Burness and Co., a specialized print firm employing around eighty people that was an amalgamation of a jobbing printshop and a lithographic business.[185] In 1896 the firm was bought out and absorbed into Morrison and Gibb (a well-known local print firm), of which Ferguson remained as Secretary until his retirement in 1915. He returned to New Zealand in 1905 for an extended visit to his old haunts, and was touched by a warm, welcoming civic reception hosted in his honour in Lawrence, attended by over 100 ex-colleagues and friends. He died in Edinburgh in 1917.[186]

AUSTRALIAN SKILLS CIRCULATION AND UNION ORGANIZATION

Skills transfer and civic development were not the only aspects of such migratory experiences. Equally important was the way trade and labour practices and values were exported overseas and integrated into indigenous settings. This was particularly the case when overseas labour forces began organizing more robustly towards the end of the century.

In Australia, the labour movement was materially helped by the expertise of labour leaders who either brought over skills and experience from Britain, or though native born, were highly mobile across transnational networks and borders. As one historian has noted, by the 1900s the Australia labour movement was led by two categories of tough minded, independent, determined, and resourceful leaders: 'the pioneers and veterans of "the movement" who were predominantly British in origin; and younger, mainly native-born, men, often in their twenties and early thirties, highly mobile geographically and full of energy, enterprise and initiative'.[187]

A good example of such robust input into Australian typographical union activity was the expansion of the Melbourne Typographical Society between the 1880s and early 1900s, spearheaded by strong minded English and Scottish-born union organizers such as John Hancock and Robert Elliott, who brought their knowledge of British trade practices to bear upon Australian soil. John Hancock (1846–1900), Clerkenwell-born and London-trained, had emigrated to Melbourne in 1884, where he joined Sands and McDougall as a reader. Within five years, he had taken on significant roles in the trade union movement, including Secretary of the Melbourne Typographical Society, editor of the *Australian Typographical Journal,* and President of the Trades Hall Council, the umbrella organization coordinating union links across the city trades. Described as a dynamic leader, as head of the Trades Hall Council Hancock personally oversaw the organization and

---

[185] 'Through Our Exchanges', *Bruce Herald,* 1 August 1882.

[186] A brief biographical description of Ferguson can be found in William Pike, ed., *A Dictionary of Edwardian Biography: Edinburgh and the Lothians* (Edinburgh: Peter Bell, 1983), p. 259.

[187] Neville Kirk, *Comrades and Cousins: Globalization, Workers and Labour Movements in Britain, the USA and Australia from the 1880s to 1914* (London: The Merlin Press, 2003), p. 112.

linking into the Council of twenty-five different societies, turning it into an effective lobbying force. He would also lead on fund raising for labour causes, for example successfully rallying the trades to contribute to the £35,000 raised in support of the ultimately unsuccessful Melbourne Maritime strike of 1890. Hancock's political career did not end there: he would become a member of the Australian Parliament in 1891, and represent first Collingwood and then the Footscray district until shortly before his death in 1900.[188]

His counterpart Robert Elliott, born in Hawick in 1864, entered the print trade at the age of ten, subsequently serving a seven-year apprenticeship on the *Hawick Express*. On completion of his indentures he shifted to Dingwall and then to Edinburgh, where he worked as a compositor for the print firm Turnbull and Spears and then for Morrison and Gibb.[189] Edinburgh records note his presence as a vocal member of the typographical union between 1883 and 1886, following which he 'lifted card' for Australia in June 1886.[190] Elliott joined Sands and McDougall as a compositor on arrival, overlapping with John Hancock for several years. In 1893 Elliott joined the Government Printing Office, and then moved over to the firm of D. W. Paterson, having been poached by the owner, who had been a foreman at Sands and McDougall.[191] From his arrival in Melbourne he took on significant leadership roles within the union, serving as a member of the Melbourne Typographical Society (MTS) Board of Management, as a member of its Executive, as its vice president, as treasurer for nine years, and then as representative of the branch at the Australasian Typographical Union's tri-annual trade conferences.[192] In 1909 he was elected the Melbourne Typographical Society's first organizer, and by driving forward new initiatives and inclusive policies based on his early experiences of union membership and organization, within four years union membership more than doubled from 875 to 1800.[193] He became general secretary in 1912 after an administrative re-organization of union management, serving in that role until 1921. He would take on other senior roles in the Australian print trade union hierarchy through to his death in December 1931.[194]

In his study of nineteenth-century Australian labour movements, Neville Kirk notes examples of other foreign-born typographical union leaders who worked in parallel with Elliott and Hancock. One such was Thomas Boreland McKnight, who on his death at the age of eighty-six in 1912 was mourned by the *Australian Typographical Journal* as 'one of the oldest printers in Victoria'.[195] McKnight's long career encompassed multiple stints on several continents and countries. Born in

[188] For biographical information on Hancock, see 'Death of Mr John Hancock, M.L.A.', *South African Typographical Circular* 1, no. 17 (1900). See also R. T. Fitzgerald, *The Printers of Melbourne: The History of a Union* (Melbourne: Sir Isaac Pitman and Sons, Ltd, 1967), p. 72–3.
[189] 'The M.T.S. Organiser', *The Australasian Typographical Journal*, 7 October 1909.
[190] 'Edinburgh Typographical Society Contributor Records, 1861–1900'.
[191] 'The M.T.S. Organiser', p. 99.   [192] 'The M.T.S. Organiser'.
[193] J. Hagan, *Printers and Politics: A History of the Australian Printing Unions, 1850–1950* (Canberra: Australian National University Press, 1966), p. 149; R. T. Fitzgerald, *The Printers of Melbourne: The History of a Union* (Melbourne: Sir Isaac Pitman and Sons, Ltd, 1967), pp. 99, 115.
[194] Hagan, *Printers and Politics*, p. 344.
[195] Quoted in Kirk, *Comrades and Cousins*, p. 114.

Scotland in 1826 and apprenticed for seven years at the *Dumfries Herald*, he worked for a period in London on the *Morning Post*, emigrated to the USA in search of work, returned for a stint in Scotland, and in 1853, at the age of twenty-seven, took passage to Victoria to seek his fortune in the gold fields. This venture proving unsuccessful, he made his way to Melbourne where he served time on the *Argus*, worked in various offices as a journeyman printer, served in the union and later ran his own enterprise, proving a model employer in the latter position. The obituary concluded in true labour union style that McKnight had been 'a congenial companion, and good unionist, ever ready to assist a fellow-workman'.[196]

Similarly, the Scots-born, Edinburgh-trained compositor Sam Mackie received encomiums in trade press obituaries on his death in August 1912, where his work at the *Ballarat Star* was highlighted, alongside his role as a founding member of the Ballarat Typographical Society in 1857.[197] Due to the organizing efforts of Mackie and others, the Ballarat Typographical Society would be one of the few print unions founded in the 1850s to survive the challenges faced during the late 1850s and 1860s by the print trade labour movement. As one chronicler has noted, while other contemporary Australian print unions crashed and disappeared during that period, 'The Ballarat Society lived on quietly, keeping itself alive, the only link in time between the societies of the fifties and their first new stirrings in the seventies.'[198]

JOURNEYMEN IN SOUTH AFRICA

A prime site where importation of ideas and people was also key to the organization of print unions was South Africa. A trickle of wandering compositors came over in the 1870s and 1880s, attracted by the lure of the diamond mines then being uncovered, inspired by a general wanderlust, or drawn by other factors such as family 'chain migration'. The trickle turned into a flood following the discovery of gold in Witwatersrand, Johannesburg and other parts of the Transvaal region from 1886 onwards. Once wandering printers had exhausted their patience digging in the gold fields, they turned their attention to seeking print work where available.

Transnational emigrants from both northern and southern hemispheres worked in tandem to establish South African print union infrastructures in the 1880s and 1890s. Newspapers and print outlets grew exponentially as the colony expanded. Exact statistics of growth are hard to come by, but by 1905, the Master Printers' Association of the Transvaal was claiming that next to mining, printing 'afforded employment to the largest number of white men' in the area.[199] The print trade union was equally acknowledged to be the most 'powerful organization in South Africa', due to its organizing strengths, cohesion, and ability to incorporate members arriving to work in the trade.[200]

---

[196] Ibid.   [197] Ibid.   [198] Hagan, *Printers and Politics*, p. 35.
[199] E. Katz, *A Trade Union Aristocracy: A History of the White Workers in the Transvaal and the General Strike of 1913* (Johannesburg: University of Witwatersrand, 1976), p. 3.
[200] Ibid., pp. 251–2.

Print trade organization in South Africa began in the 1880s and 1890s. It was during this period that South African-based print union organizers established union offices and began agitating for standardized work practices, improved wages and enhanced labour conditions. Most were printers on the move with international experience, as for example 'Transvaal' Jack Farrell, peripatetic Irish-born compositor mentioned earlier, whose working life prior to arrival at the Cape in 1896 encompassed stints in Australia, New Zealand and across the western states of the USA. The earliest South African typographical association was started in Cape Town sometime in 1881–2, though it was fairly dormant until more robust leadership revived it in 1889.[201] Other typographical society branches followed, among them Durban and Maritzburg (1889), the Transvaal Typographical Society in Johannesburg (1893), Pretoria (1894), and Kimberley (1895).[202] In January 1898, at an inaugural conference in Johannesburg involving delegates from across the South African region, a national South African Typographical Union was established, with Jack Farrell elected as its first President. Farrell would go on to edit the union's monthly journal, launched in March 1898, as well as lead on general organizational efforts and national strike actions over the coming years.

For such journeymen printers, early setups in South Africa were rudimentary. Typical was the Kimberley printshop from which was issued the *Daily News*, and in which one itinerant compositor worked for six months in the early 1890s. The office, 'shanty would be a better name', was staffed by a foreman more often to be found in the local saloon than at the print works.[203] Putting together the news-paper involved standing at a composing frame with guttering candles perched perilously close to the type case, into which candle wax would fall and coagulate around the letters. 'When I made a dig for a lowercase "d", I would lift about half a pound of them in a solid lump', recollected the amused compositor.[204] It took some disentangling to move forward with reading and typesetting relevant copy, which was kept in a cigar box nearby. When the typesetter ran out of 'lowercase d' letters, he was casually told to use whatever came to hand: 'Oh, use italic, or any type that will justify. Everything goes here.'[205]

Other challenges awaited the enterprising compositor, such as contending with foreign type setups. In June 1900, at the height of the Anglo-Boer war (1899–1902), Boer held Pretoria fell into the hands of the British army. In August 1900, the British government moved to re-establish a Government Printing Works in Pretoria (for this purpose taking over the premises of the Staats Drukkerij, which had been the Boer office equivalent). The government requested that the South African Typographical Union (SATU) supply skilled men to reopen the previously Dutch held space. A multinational team of twelve men (seven Scotsmen, three Englishmen and two South Africans), dubbed the 'Twelve Apostles' or 'Pilgrim Fathers', was

[201] A. J. Downes, *Printers' Saga, Being a History of the South African Typographical Union* (Johannesburg: South African Typographical Union, 1952).

[202] Ibid., pp. 1–40.

[203] J. P. Ingram, 'At the Cape', *Pacific Union Printer* (1893), reproduced in Alastair M. Johnston, ed., *Typographical Tourists: Tales of Tramping Printers* (Berkeley, CA: Poltroon Press, 2012), pp. 80–3.

[204] Ingram, 'At the Cape'.   [205] Ibid.

selected by the South Africa Typographical Union for the task.[206] The already mentioned 'Transvaal' Jack Farrell was among those selected for this posting, classified as one of the South African-based compositors. The challenges they faced included martial law and strict curfews, and a composing room and type geared to service Dutch language needs. 'The cases are a bit comical at first, but we are becoming experts at Dutch and Dutch cases now', noted a correspondent in the October 1900 issue of the *South African Typographical Journal*.[207] The letters were different, the case set up entirely unfamiliar, and type available either too copious or too spare. 'There are no thick spaces, only middle, thin, and hair, and the lack of thick space seems an awful drawback to the British comp', continued the bemused commentator, though there were no complaints about the working space, which was 'a splendid, roomy place, with all convenience of type, furniture, stones, frames, cabinets, racks, etc. etc., and it is sincerely to be hoped that in the near future it will be the scene of the employment of a large staff of printers.'[208]

In the early 1900s, South African print trade recruiters took to advertising for large batches of printers to support the expanding print economy of the country. Some were legitimate recruitment drives to serve expanding business or community needs. Others, however, were operations designed to break local strikes and trade disputes. Such was the case in 1902, when the Durban and Maritzburg-based printer Pete Davis and Sons attempted to import British journeymen printers to work on the *Natal Advertiser*. The impetus for this move had been a long-fought battle by the Durban and Maritzburg unions to raise minimum wages for established hands from 66 shillings to £3 12s per week (72 shillings). After a mediation session held in Durban in March 1902 between proprietors and unions, the Master Printers acceded to the demands, though 'under protest', and in July wages were raised accordingly in most participating firms.[209] Pete Davis, however, sought to circumvent the process by importing non-union workers willing to work for less. Stanley Whitehead, a printer agent, was commissioned to travel to England in search of forty printers interested in working a year's contract on the *Natal Advertiser,* paying less than the union rates agreed. Newspaper notices were issued in London, Manchester and elsewhere in May 1902 advertising 'job hands in Natal', and promising up to 70 shillings pay per week to applicants. £15 was to be advanced as passage money, which would then be deducted from future pay at 5 shillings per week.

Whitehead soon achieved his quota of sign ups, but the matter subsequently came to public attention through a Durban court case raised by a union man against Pete Davis and Sons. George Wilkes, compositor, had been recruited from a position at Hall and Sons in Manchester. He had signed a pre-immigration contract in Oldham, initially for a year's work at a weekly salary of 'no less than

---

[206] The advance party consisted of: Alfred Archer (foreman), Sandy Aitken, Bennie Bees, Jack Day, J. Davidson, Jack Farrell, Sandy Fraser, Jack Humphrey, Tom Kirby, David Milne, J. Todd, and Allan Weir. See Downes, *Printers' Saga*, p. 147.

[207] Quoted in ibid., p. 147.   [208] Ibid., pp. 147–8.

[209] A brief synopsis of the events features in ibid. p. 105. Further coverage of the subsequent court case appears in 'A Typographical Dispute', *South African Typographical Journal* 5, no. 49 (1902), p. 4.

66s[hillings]', with the understanding it would be ratified via a second contract at a higher rate of 70 shillings on arrival in South Africa. In Durban, on discovering he and others had been brought over to undercut the agreed union rate of 72 shillings, Wilkes refused to sign the ratifying contract, gave a week's notice, and then sued for breach of contract. The subsequent court case offered interesting details of the recruitment system and the methods used by Master Printers such as Davis to draw on overseas workers to undercut union-led wage campaigns.

Wilkes argued he had been misled into agreeing a contract going against the interests of South African union agreed standards. The case, though, became narrowly centred on whether the contract signed in Oldham was binding in Natal, so superseding any nuanced variations expected by the recruited worker on arrival in South Africa. Labour issues and wage disputes were ignored in the end, though in passing judgement the court acknowledged that Davis had sought through such recruitment tactics to loosen trade union influence in his workplace. 'Whatever the wages were in Natal', news accounts reported of the judge's summary, 'it seemed to him extremely probable that Whitehead was sent Home in consequence of the attitude of the men in Natal, to get men at lower wages than those of the Society in Natal'.[210] Nevertheless, Davis was entitled to recruit in this manner if so desired, for 'his agent could enter into contracts to get people to work for whatever they agreed upon'.[211] As a consequence, the judgement went against Wilkes, based on the argument that it was he who had been in breach of contract by breaking an agreement signed in good faith in Oldham. The print firm was awarded forty shillings plus costs.

CANADIAN PRINT TRADE CASE

A more egregious example of misleading recruitment, which was to have a significant effect on future Canadian and British labour laws, emerged from 1905 print strikes in favour of an eight-hour working day, coordinated across Canada and parts of the USA by the International Typographical Union. The most controversial of these strike actions took place in early September 1905 in Winnipeg, Canada, when union members presented the Winnipeg Master Printers with a memorial calling for lowering the working week from nine hours to eight hours a day, to take effect 1 January 1906. Fifteen firms refused the demand, while an indeterminate number of other firms employing a total of 155 union members agreed. The International Typographical Union subsequently called a strike in the city, and on 18 September 1905, seventy affected members walked out of their workplaces. Determined to break union representation in the workplace, the Winnipeg Typothetae, who represented fourteen of the affected firms, hired a Liverpool-based agent (Charles Brunning) to hire and ship over up to 80 replacement British and Irish workers. Ads were placed in key newspapers across the country, including the *London Daily News*, the *Yorkshire Post*, the *Manchester Guardian*, the *Glasgow Herald*,

---

[210] 'A Typographical Dispute'.   [211] Ibid.

the *Liverpool Echo,* and the Devonshire *Western Morning News.* 'Job compositors, first class and competent linotype operators', seeking guaranteed positions in Canada, were invited to apply to the Liverpool agent. Successful applicants had to pay for their own travel, but were promised that on arrival in Winnipeg they would be offered a two-year, full-time position paying job printers and linotype operators 18 dollars (£3.15.0) and 20 dollars (£4.3.0) per week respectively.[212] Fifty-one responded, travelling to Canada in late October by second class boat and train, unaware that they were being brought in to break the Winnipeg strike.

Matters became clearer when their train arrived on 5 November 1905 at Kenora, just outside Winnipeg. The printshop owners inserted a note in the *Manitoba Free Press* that the British printers had been smuggled into the city that day by vehicle, escorted by the Thiel Detective Agency.[213] Instead, the new recruits were escorted off the train and brought into the city to start work the following day, before the striking printers could become aware of the subterfuge. At this stage, several of the new hires questioned the propriety of the Master Printers misleading them into doing strikebreaking work, but had little option but to take up positions, given their inability to return to Britain without funding. A week later, a further batch of recruits arrived in town, and over the next six weeks several would be sent to allied print shops facing strike action in nearby towns such as Brandon, or coerced into travelling to US border town printshops when needed. In January 1906, around forty of the strikebreakers resigned en masse from seven of the affected printshops, joining the local union in support of the strike. They justified their actions in letters to the press, where they denounced the Winnipeg Typothetae for bringing them to Winnipeg under false representation, 'having been informed that no trouble existed there between the employing printers and their work-people'.[214] Labour trade newspapers responded with expressions of solidarity for these skilled male workers in language framed by race, gender, and class identity. As a leading labour newspaper the *Voice* commented, '[They find] themselves enticed across the ocean to work as "rat" printers for the purpose of defeating the efforts of Canadian and American printers to establish a uniform eight-hour day in the trade. It is not an enviable position for a decent white man to be in under any circumstances.'[215] With support from the local union, thirty-seven of the affected printers issued a petition to King Edward VII complaining of their treatment. The resulting document was forwarded to the Privy Council of Canada, who sent it to the Canadian Department of Labour for investigation. Deputy Minister Hugh Mackenzie King (who would later become Canadian Prime Minister), spent several days interviewing printers and owners alike. His report, issued in March 1906, upheld the complaints of the printers, demonstrating that they had been victimized and misled into signing contracts to replace striking workers rather than take on new

---

[212] 'Canada. Correspondence Relating to the Complaint of Certain Printers Who Were Induced to Emigrate to Canada by False Representations', ed. House of Parliament (London: His Majesty's Stationery Office, 1906), p. 477.

[213] Ibid., p. 467.   [214] 'Strike of Printers at Winnipeg', *The Labour Gazette* (1906).

[215] Quoted in David Goutor, *Guarding the Gates: The Canadian Labour Movement and Immigration, 1872–1934* (Vancouver: UBC Press, 2007), p. 118.

opportunities. The report also offered a clear-eyed indictment of Canadian labour recruitment processes, whereby immigration agents were paid commission to recruit British workers with scant oversight of working methods and processes. As he concluded, in this case the agent in question, Charles Brunning, had

> deliberately and intentionally misrepresented the facts to men whom he had induced to Canada, or to most of them, by representing that they were being brought to Canada to fill positions which the growth of the printing trade in the West had created, and which they could fill in an honourable way, also by carefully concealing as well as denying the existence of any strike in Winnipeg or any intention on his part to have them act as strike breakers, whereas he knew all the time of the existence of the Winnipeg strike, and had as the chief object of his mission the securing of men to fill the places of Canadian workmen on strike.[216]

He argued that action needed to be taken to protect future workers from being recruited under false pretences. Between July 1906 and April 1907, acts and amendments were enacted in Canada and Britain prohibiting the subordination of working conditions in such ways, and outlawing false representation by immigration agents and promoters in Britain.[217] These developments went some way to curbing irresponsible and morally debatable print migrant worker recruitment over the coming decades, though it did not stamp it out altogether.

CONCLUSION

The interlinked, global migration network that supported the movement of English-speaking skilled printers throughout the nineteenth and early twentieth centuries would be shredded by the onset of worldwide economic depression in the 1930s, and the impact of two world wars bookending this economic crisis. At the same time, British government social welfare schemes to replace trade-based unemployment relief and sick payment schemes from 1909 onwards slowly began tackling the burden and rationale for tramping initiatives previously taken on by trade unions. British print unions finally abolished tramping support in 1913 with a great sigh of relief, acknowledging that such a system was no long fit for purpose in a world where 'an unemployed member preferred to stay in his own town, with his family and friends, eking out existence on out-of-work benefits and what casual employment he could get, waiting for trade to improve'.[218]

During much of the nineteenth and early twentieth centuries, structured and unstructured migration and skilled print worker movement played their part in shaping global exportation and insertion of print trade skills and knowledge into new arenas. Roving printers acted as labour and union missionaries. They started

---

[216] 'Canada. Correspondence Relating to the Complaint of Certain Printers Who Were Induced to Emigrate to Canada by False Representations', p. 482.

[217] D. Goutor, *Guarding the Gates: The Canadian Labour Movement and Immigration, 1872–1934* (Vancouver: UBC Press, 2007), p. 129.

[218] Musson, *The Typographical Association*, p. 279.

businesses that were central to shaping and directing the print economies of new and emerging communities and towns. They parlayed and passed on their knowledge and expertise to others they encountered in their travels. Unions that emerged in the nineteenth century developed complex information and support networks to respond to the need for trade worker movement. They were used to control worker numbers in saturated print centres, to extract workers during strike actions, to support those who could not find long term work, and to create a union-led, global typographical knowledge and skills exchange system. It was also part of a trade craft identity, a thread that runs throughout this book and this chapter. The tramping and migration narratives noted here provide strong insight into how print trade workers saw themselves within a wider world: they understood themselves to be participants in a moral community of artisans, bound together by shared skills and a duty to support others like them when required.

2

Striking Printers
Print Trade Disputes and the Nine-Hour Movement, 1870–1880

The 1870s marked a period of increased UK and transnational trade union and benevolent society mobilization to instigate changes in working conditions, aligned to the 'nine-hour' or 'short-time' movement. It was also marked by key legislative changes that for the first time enabled labour groups to organize themselves and later in the decade supported the right to strike without fear of criminalization. In the UK, the 1871 Trade Union and Criminal Law Amendment Act, put forward by Disraeli's government and then enacted under Gladstone's premiership, allowed trade unions to partially move from being benevolent societies geared solely to the social welfare of its members to more active participants in improving working conditions and pay structures. The act legalized trade societies, enabling them to register as legal entities and gain legal protection for their funds against fraudulent officials. On the other hand, the tacked-on Criminal Law Amendment Act potentially criminalized all peaceful union activity that could be construed as interference in the workplace. This included activities such as union workplace recruitment, or anything that could be classified as 'molestation', 'intimidation', or 'coercion'.[1] It took four years of agitation before the Criminal Law Amendment Act was repealed in 1875 and replaced by a set of laws that gave full legal recognition to trade union collective bargaining, and established principles of civil contracts between employers and employees on equal terms. Similar legal changes occurred in Canada, which followed Britain's lead in offering legal protection to organized trade unions.

Along with such changes came a concerted effort across British and associated English-speaking print trade sectors to shift working hours from sixty+ to an average fifty-four hours a week. The 'nine-hour' movement had gained impetus in Great Britain following a successful strike in 1871 by Newcastle-based engineers, who had sought a shorter working week of fifty-four hours, increased pay and improved working conditions. Other unions followed suit in Britain and internationally, and several key print trade strikes that followed in the wake of this movement are of note and interest for what they reveal about international print politics, identity, and cultural positioning during this period.

This section will focus on important strikes in London, Edinburgh, Toronto, and Dublin that took place between 1872 and 1878. Though some were deemed

---

[1] A. E. Musson, *The Typographical Association: Origins and History up to 1949* (London: Oxford University Press, 1954), p. 300.

failures at the time (and in several cases cataclysmic in terms of trade organization effectiveness), several resulted in key social and organizational changes in relevant regions (some intended, others not). Some strike outcomes ushered in a general shift in improved working hours and conditions across major labour sectors (not just in printing). Others led to the opening of the composing room to women workers, albeit with much resistance. An Irish print strike provoked Parliamentary inquiries and debates about protectionism and the tensions between supporting national labour interests while enabling government sponsored print activity. Still other strikes demonstrated the difficulties of maintaining a balance between central union oversight and localized chapel actions.

Notable about several of these confrontations was the powerful role of key print trade owners in resisting union demands. Strikes in Toronto, Dublin, and Edinburgh faced strong-minded, conservative kingpin figures who used media outlets for propaganda purposes and bankrolled extensive recruitment of outside workers to strike-break and spike opposition. In turn, also revealing is the unknown role of 'vigilance committees' and trade union spies in informing on and combating the strikebreaking actions of employers. Implicit within the debates generated by these events were struggles to define the role of print trade societies within trade guild parameters, and ultimately to highlight what forms of social identity were forged and supported during such labour struggles and encounters.

LONDON STRUGGLES

In the late 1860s the London Society of Compositors faced an organized Master Printers Association (MPA), comprised of key London printing firms, who sought through consolidation to resist worker demands for pay raises and hour reductions. Three separate statements from letterpress societies of compositors, pressmen and machine managers issued to the MPA in 1866 drew attention to the urgent need to negotiate more widely on trade demands. The MPA and compositors met in November 1866 as a joint committee to examine what compromises could be established. Agreement was made to implement a minimum stab wage rise from 33s to 36s, a reduction in hours from 63 to 60, a raise of ½d per 1,000 ens (or letters), and various overtime and Sunday work extra payments.[2] Soon after, similar agreements were signed with pressmen and machine manager representatives. By 1870, however, print trade groups were agitating for further concessions, particularly considering the nine-hour movement sweeping across skilled trade sectors. The London-based MPA collapsed in October 1870, leaving in its wake fractured negotiating parties to face increasingly strident trade demands over coming years.

In April 1871, Sunderland-based engineers came out on strike seeking to negotiate a nine-hour working day and a fifty-four-hour working week. Four weeks later, employers acceded to their demands, and what became known as the nine-hour movement gained momentum in this key trade. Within six months, because of

---

[2] J. Child, *Industrial Relations in the British Printing Industry* (London: Allen and Unwin, 1967), pp. 112–13.

strategic strike action in key cities, the fifty-four-hour week 'became the locally recognized weeks' time in all the engineering trades'.[3] This widely documented struggle became the impetus for similar demands in other skilled trades for wage rises and working hour reductions, with printers at the forefront of such unified expressions. In August 1871, Edinburgh compositors, journeymen, and pressmen secured a fifty-four-hour working week in both newspaper and book offices which was implemented in January 1872, though stab wages at 27s 6d per week remained below comparable Glasgow and London rates (30s and 36s respectively). In January 1872, the London Society of Compositors followed suit, issuing a memorial to individual employers setting out their demands for an increase of ½d per 1,000 ens, the maintenance of the weekly stab rate at 36s, and a reduction in working hours from sixty to fifty-four. As they noted, the demands were in keeping with general practices elsewhere, for 'in all directions and in all sorts of trades, the limitations of the week's work to fifty-four hours, or nine per day, has become an accepted creed with the great mass of skilled workmen'.[4] In addition, they cited health and safety reasons for the requested reduction in hours, lingering on the long travel times and high ratios of lung disease endured by their members:

> The influence of close and unhealthy offices operates fearfully upon our death rate, as is shown in the amount disbursed by our Society in funeral payments, over fifty per cent of our Members dying from diseases of the air passages, which is almost entirely referable to the vitiated atmosphere we are compelled, in too many instances, to breathe, and which, we need hardly say, is intensified by having to work late at night.[5]

As discussions and negotiations dragged on, the union met on 2 March and set 16 March 1872 as a final date for concluding negotiations, at which point its 3700 members were prepared to send in their mandatory two weeks' notice. In a general meeting of key London printers on 7 March 1872, the demands were conceded, and London joined other successful cohorts in celebrating the move to better working conditions.

EDINBURGH BATTLES

With London's print union having secured higher wages for a fifty-four-hour working week, Edinburgh Typographical Association branch members debated in April 1872 pressing for further, more radical workplace concessions. There was a split of views, with press and machinemen urging action, but compositor members holding back. As the union secretary John S. Common noted to his London counterpart Henry Self, 'It will send in smoke in the meantime, as the comps are

---

[3] Sidney Webb and Beatrice Webb, *The History of Trade Unionism, 1666–1920* (London: Self published for the Trade Unionists of the United Kingdom, 1919), p. 314.

[4] Ellic Howe and Bibliographical Society (Great Britain), *The London Compositor: Documents Relating to Wages, Working Conditions and Customs of the London Printing Trade, 1785–1900*, Small Quarto Series/Bibliographical Society (London: Bibliographical Society, 1947), p. 283.

[5] Ibid., p. 284.

opposed to moving at this unseasonable time of the year.'[6] Common added, 'We are, however, committed by a resolution to take action in the beginning of September.'[7] One unfortunate by-product of such internal discussions was a rise in tensions between Edinburgh compositors and machinemen. 'Already there has been a little bad blood spilt', noted Common, 'and there is sure to be more before all is done, which is deeply to be regretted.' Furthermore, he worried that leaks to employers of their discussions would damage union negotiations, with the result that 'the employers know now for certain what we mean to do, and we have kindly given them four clear months to think the matter over, and to make their arrangements for meeting us'.[8]

By October 1872, most Edinburgh branch members had changed their minds, moving for raises of the weekly stab wage to 30s while simultaneously lowering working weeks to fifty-one hours. It was a strategically challenging move, given the union had been financially weakened through a failed three-month strike at the *Scotsman* newspaper unilaterally called in July by fifty-three *Scotsman* press employees. It is worth pausing for a moment to review the circumstances of the *Scotsman* strike, which was to have a major effect on the union's abilities to stave off subsequent moves against it by print trade employers. The event demonstrated the difficulties of restraining individual branch members from rushing into action without wider consultation with union representatives, and the consequent result of unilateral action on union negotiating power. It also highlighted tensions that could exist between localized chapel concerns (often centred on workplace battles over piece rate pay, work place hierarchies and working conditions), and general strategic union concerns (where general focus was on battles for better general pay, better sector wide working hours, safer employment conditions and more harmonious labour relations).

THE *SCOTSMAN* STRIKE

On 18 July 1872, a meeting was called by members of the *Scotsman* chapel to air long-held grievances over the press overseer's allocation of piecework. A complex scale of payment for newspaper piecework (as opposed to weekly wage rates) had been laboriously worked out and implemented by Edinburgh press employers and workers in 1867. Rates were usually calculated by measuring the area of type composed, expressed as 'ems' or 'ens'. Press compositors would be paid a certain number of shillings per 1,000 ems or ens for general work, but there were also special rates set for more difficult work, such as tables and foreign languages. Most lucrative of all were printed advertisements, which though produced at the same piece rate as general material, were easier and quicker to do, given they contained more blank spaces than regular typeset work. These items were known as 'fat' or 'phat' matter, and in most Scottish offices were traditionally distributed by placing

---

[6] 'Edinburgh Typographical Society Outgoing Letter Books', in *Edinbugh Typographical Society Records* (National Library of Scotland), No. 121, p. 383, 10 April 1872.
[7] Ibid. No. 121, p. 386, 12 April 1872.　　　[8] Ibid. No. 121, p. 386, 12 April 1872.

them in a 'box' along with other items to be typeset; compositors would pick up items in order of arrival and in rotational fashion, thus ensuring a fair, balanced distribution of easy and complex copy amongst shop floor journeymen compositors and apprentices. Following a management change in the *Scotsman* in 1869, and the appointment in February 1870 of a new overseer (John Mackenzie Garner), this method of distributing copy ceased.[9] Instead, after complex negotiations with the Chapel hands, the overseer took back the right to select copy for apprentices, and began reserving for them the easiest and 'best copy', leaving complex and less lucrative typesetting work for the established hands. Other infringements of agreed piece rate scales were logged and complained about in the years intervening, until Chapel members decided they had had enough.

Members spent most of the July 1872 meeting venting grievances over key slights: there were too many apprentices taking an unfair share of lucrative piece work; the weather report, laid out in tabular form and requiring minor tweaking each day, had been taken out of the 'box' and kept aside solely for apprentices; 'fat' copy no longer made its way into the 'box'; apprentices were reportedly given up to twenty-four ads at a time to set, when journeymen seldom saw more than four in the box at any given moment; and so on.

Action was needed apparently, and on 20 July 1872 a letter of complaint was sent to the *Scotsman* overseer, signed by fifty-three of the fifty-four members of the Chapel. Castigating the overseer for offering but not delivering on promises made in the past, the Chapel members politely but firmly announced their dissatisfaction with the current state of work distribution. 'One of the principal infringements under which we suffer', they wrote, 'is the system of keeping the Apprentices as fully employed as is possible to do upon the best "copy" that appears in the Paper – a system as unfair to the Apprentices themselves as to the Journeymen.'[10] The system of apprentice piecework allocation, which the Chapel had ceded to the overseer on the basis that fair and equal distribution of material would be maintained, was to their minds not functioning. Procedures needed to return to what they had been. If not, then no copy would be accepted 'over the counter', and 'we shall insist on every line of copy being "boxed" – apprentice and journeyman alike'.[11]

On the night of 23 July, five Chapel members absented themselves from work for varying lengths of time (the chapel clerk came in an hour late; others arrived much later or not at all). Reasons given for such tardiness were hazy: in years to come, the *Scotsman* defended its actions during this period by claiming the men had been drunk, and had threatened through their absence the safe and timely production of the evening edition of the newspaper.[12] Chapel members maintained they had valid reasons for their tardiness, and that their absence had not

---

[9] John Mackenzie Gardner was recorded in a *Scotsman*-reported court hearing as having served as Foreman at the *Scotsman* from February 1870 to 7 August 1872. See 'Desertion of Service by Compositors', *The Scotsman*, 23 August 1872.

[10] 'Minutes of Scotsman Chapel', in *Edinbugh Typographical Society Records* (National Library of Scotland), No. 34, 18 July 1872; 20 July 1872.

[11] Ibid., No. 34, 20 July 1872.

[12] 'The "Scotsman" Strike of 1872: Reason for Non-Union Basis', *The Scotsman*, 13 May 1926, p. 6.

threatened production work. Nevertheless, all five were given two weeks' notice and dismissed. At a Chapel meeting on Wednesday 24th July, members read the overseer's reply to their demands in light of their fellow workers' dismissal, and disapproving of the actions and the overseer's 'evasive and unsatisfactory tone', rushed to tender their resignations.[13]

The unilateral action provoked panic amongst trade union ranks. On immediate receipt of the news, the Edinburgh branch secretary sent an urgent cable to his counterpart at Scottish Typographical Union headquarters in Glasgow. 'Sudden crisis in Scotsman', it read, 'Whole Chapel, on own responsibility, have tendered notice to leave.'[14] He urged his Glasgow contact to call a board meeting for the weekend, where representatives would outline the circumstances leading to this rupture, and asked him to broadcast widely the closure of the *Scotsman* office to union workers. *Scotsman* union representatives met with Edinburgh colleagues on Friday 26 July to explain their actions, running through their list of grievances, noting the dismissal of five men for absence and lateness (including the secretary of the Chapel), and defending the unanimous decision to tender their notice to leave, 'stating as their reason the fact of this clerk having been dismissed for what was no fault at all'.[15] They now asked, after the fact, for approval of these actions, and for support in redressing the wrongs they felt had been inflicted upon them.

The events highlighted the tensions that could develop between Chapels, with a focus on localized grievances and company specific circumstances, and parent trade unions, focused on mediating across larger industry led concerns. The *Scotsman* Chapel's unilateral actions threatened the union's mediating role. The minutes of the relevant meeting record a sense of unease at this threat, which in effect dragged the union into a confrontation not of its own choosing. Possibly addressed but not explicit in the summary were serious questions about whether Chapel grievances were major or minor in context of general trade union concerns, the extent to which the absences could be classed as minor infringements, how fit for work the individuals had been on their return, and to what extent had their absence impeded time sensitive work being completed. Were they, as *Scotsman* reports later made out, drunk, unfit for duty and endangering timely production of that evening's newspaper? The union minutes are silent on these points, but in the end in slightly disappointed tone the Secretary recorded a unanimous decision to back the men and seek support from the union's central office. 'While regretting that the chapel had taken so important a step without first consulting with the Executive Committee', the secretary concluded, 'yet in consideration of the peculiar circumstances of the case, and the imperative necessity for prompt and decided action, approve of the conduct of the Chapel, and resolve to sustain the men in their present endeavour to redress the numerous grievances which have sprung up in the Scotsman office.'[16]

---

[13] 'Minutes of Scotsman Chapel', p. 193, 24 July 1872; *Scottish Typographical Association: A Fifty Years' Record, 1853–1903* (Glasgow: Scottish Typographical Association, 1903), p. 62.

[14] 'Edinburgh Typographical Society Outgoing Letter Books', p. 452, 24 July 1872.

[15] 'Edinburgh Typographical Society Minute Books', vol. 3, Minute Book 7, April 1869–23 October 1875, p. 160, 26 July 1872.

[16] Ibid., pp. 160–1, 26 July 1872.

The strike was scheduled to begin the twelfth of August, on expiry of the official two weeks' notice period given by Chapel members. As the onset of the strike loomed, the *Scotsman* management took active steps to recruit non-union workers to replace union members. Their goal was to establish the *Scotsman* as a fully non-unionized workplace, and this event provided the opportunity for doing so. The philosophy underlying this aggressive countermove by the *Scotsman* was reflective of a general view amongst key Edinburgh print trade employers about ownership and control over the workspace, and the incursion of organized labour into those spaces. For key conservative minded Edinburgh print capitalists, their control of the shop floor was in danger of being superseded by union led worker control. As an editorial in the *Scotsman* made clear, management saw this as an attempt whereby 'the employed shall have the management, and the employers only the risk and responsibilities', with a further erosion of principles to a point where 'employers are to hand over the control of their business and property, not merely to their own employees, but to more or less secret associations of strangers'.[17]

Quick and steadfast action was to mark employer reactions to this strike, and to the more general Edinburgh print strike that followed in its wake. As William Blackwood III, one of the directors of the Edinburgh publishing firm William Blackwood and Sons, commented on behalf of the trade when confronted with striking workers later in the year, 'Unless a bold front is now shown it will be a mill stone hanging round our necks and our office will be conducted on their will not ours.'[18] What this conveniently elided was the differences that could exist between individual workplace structures—where the Chapel was often central to managing shop floor interactions, and where union and non-unionized workers might sit beside each other adhering to agreed local codes of conduct—and general trade union structures, where negotiations over working conditions across the sector for members was often based on general principles of equity and shared social contracts.

A central board meeting in Glasgow rubberstamped union support for the strike that was now being launched, while noting that quick action was needed to counteract moves by *Scotsman* management to recruit non-union 'rat' workers to fill the impending vacancies. Union representatives were sent to Belfast, Dublin, Liverpool, London, and key northern towns to keep apprised of recruitment activities and to actively persuade colleagues to resist the blandishments of *Scotsman* representatives. Reports were fed back of where the *Scotsman* was actively recruiting non-union labour: Ireland, it was reported, 'had not been tampered with', but in London and Liverpool agents had been advertising and signing up strike-breaking recruits. Several of these recruits had subsequently been located and successfully induced 'to think better of their intentions', but not all, and printed material and general information was circulated around city centre trade locations to alert others to the issues at stake and urge resistance to agency incentives.[19]

---

[17] 'The "Scotsman" and Its Late Compositors', *The Scotsman*, 10 August 1872, p. 4.

[18] 'Correspondence', in *Blackwood Papers* (National Library of Scotland). William Blackwood III to John Blackwood, 17 October 1872.

[19] 'Edinburgh Typographical Society Minute Books', pp. 161–2, 5 August 1872.

VIGILANCE COMMITTEES

On 21 August 1872, after consultation with main union representatives in Glasgow, the Edinburgh union committee met to approve setting up and funding a Vigilance Committee. The Vigilance Committee's role was to monitor trade activity from within affected printing establishments, to encourage strike-breakers to abandon their posts and support union goals, and to work with external trade contacts to share information, monitor and act on Master Printer recruitment attempts. Members appointed to the committee were to be awarded an extra 2s 6d a week on top of any wages or strike allowances garnered.

The widespread use of Vigilance Committees by British and overseas print trade unions throughout the latter part of the nineteenth century has not been acknowledged or noticed in past labour history chronicles of the sector. As later sections of this piece note, such committees were in use not just in Edinburgh and London, but also in Dublin and Toronto, among other sites. Their mode of operation ranged from offering financial inducements to leave employment ('treating', as the Edinburgh union termed it), propagandizing in recruitment centres, infiltrating targeted firms with spies posing as 'rat' workers, through in more extreme cases to direct confrontations and battles with strike breakers and print employers. In Britain, such methods were classed as illegal for a good portion of the early 1870s, prosecutable under the Masters and Servants Acts of 1823 and 1867 and the 1871 Criminal Law Amendment Act, which criminalized union activity that could be classed as intimidating or coercive in intent. Similar restrictions existed in Canada and the USA.

One of the first acts of the Vigilance Committee was to quietly recruit individuals to act as 'dummies', posing as strikebreaking recruits and infiltrating the *Scotsman* with the aim of informing on management actions and of subverting recruitment and retention of rat labour where possible. Henry Self, secretary of the London Society of Compositors, recommended two veteran London strike spies, Messrs Austin and Elliott, who took up positions in the *Scotsman* in September 1872. Questions over adequate remuneration threatened to put an end to the plan, however, as Austin and Elliot, who were married with families in London, demanded extra funding in order to offset costs of maintaining rooms in Edinburgh and to cover domestic costs back home. Strike breakers were being paid over the odds to man the *Scotsman* shop floor (an average of 38 shillings a week, 8 shillings more than the standard wage of the striking hands), but Austin and Elliott demanded an extra 30 shillings a week each from the local union to cover their general costs. A compromise offer of 15 shillings a week extra was rejected, with the suggestion that past work in London had netted them each £2 a week. After consultation with London colleagues, the Vigilance Committee settled on an offer of £1 (or 20 shillings) a week, which Austin and Elliott accepted. They were joined by a third recruit, an Anglo-Irish compositor named J. Ryan recently arrived and pulled over from the Constable firm as support.[20] The subsidy was maintained

[20] 'Edinburgh Typographical Society Outgoing Letter Books', pp. 466–7, 17 October 1872.

through to mid-November, past when the strike was conceded as lost, and the union commenced its second, trade wide general strike.[21]

The job of the *Scotsman* spies was to monitor and pass on relevant trade information, to entertain key management figures for information gathering purposes, and to 'treat' selected strike-breakers to meals and drinks in an attempt to convince them of the error of their ways and to gather trade information. Edinburgh society minutes record snippets of news gleaned in this fashion, as for example an alarming report in early October on a dinner hosted for the *Scotsman's* London based recruiter (Mr J. Cross), where he had boasted of signing up 200 potential recruits from London. The Edinburgh branch secretary duly contacted his London Society of Compositors counterpart to confirm whether unemployment in London was severe enough to warrant such high recruitment.[22] It is not clear what was reported back, but the subsequent number of replacement staff brought in and retained by the *Scotsman* suggest there was no shortage of volunteers willing to take up work in a non-union space.

When union spies spotted likely waverers in the *Scotsman* ranks, details were passed on to the Vigilance Committee, who in several cases sanctioned offers of 'leaving money' to encourage mass defections from the workplace. How much was on offer depended on who was reporting on the matter. The *Scotsman* reported sneeringly that the union seemed happy to waste up to £5 per person on securing such dismissals, but this seems unlikely.[23] The union did offer the original 53 *Scotsman* strikers up to £4 each if they were forced to leave town to find work elsewhere, as well as full membership cards to similarly affected apprentices who had gone out with them.[24]

The *Scotsman* management took a dim view of such workplace intrusions, and robustly pursued and prosecuted suspected spies, and strike breakers who were induced to leave their employment, as well as contesting cases against alleged union agitators under the various employment acts. One example demonstrating the way in which the infamous Masters and Servants Act (and its equivalent in Scotland) could be mobilized against workers occurred in late August 1872, when the compositor George Gardener sued the *Scotsman* proprietors for £10 damages on the grounds of unfair dismissal. The case, reported in the *Scotsman* on 29 August 1872, was a classic example of innuendo and hearsay being used to punish those supposedly working against an employer's interests. In Gardener's case, he had been recruited by the *Scotsman's* London agents to take up employment in Edinburgh starting 7 August, but was dismissed twelve days later without the

---

[21] Society ledgers record several payments for spying services: on 2 November 1872, £14 was expended on 'expenses of Dummies, in Scotsman to date', while between 15 and 20 November 1872 a total of £7.8.6 was paid to Austin and Elliott for their work. See 'Edinburgh Typographical Society Income and Expenditure Account, 1 July 1846–2 Jan 1879', in *Edinburgh Typographical Society* (National Library of Scotland), ff. 221–223.

[22] 'Edinburgh Typographical Society Outgoing Letter Books', p. 470. John S. Common to Henry Self, 30 October 1872.

[23] 'Scotsman Office: Action by a Compositor for Dismissal without Notice', *The Scotsman*, August 29 1872, p. 6.

[24] 'Edinburgh Typographical Society Minute Books', pp. 162–3, 14 August 1872.

usual two weeks' notice on grounds he had been acting on behalf of the union to undermine the strike. More specifically, Gardener was accused of speaking in favour of the union, and of offering workers union backed financial 'inducements' (bribes) to leave *Scotsman* employment. The *Scotsman's* assistant editor testified he had witnessed Gardener acting shiftily, accompanying newly hired men to the pub with the intention of speaking on behalf of the union, loitering in the firm's smoking room when work was on to agitate against the firm, and against regulations allegedly smuggling in a flask of brandy. ('I never brought in any bottle of brandy', protested Gardener, 'I only brought in half a mutchkin of brandy, and it was filled with water.'[25]) Other workmen were wheeled in to testify that Gardener had been seen in conversation with the secretary of the Glasgow union branch (who happened to be lodging in the same hostel), had stood his colleagues a suspicious number of expensive rounds of ale in the pub, and had spoken in favour of taking union money to leave the *Scotsman*. The *Scotsman* management had sought but failed to uncover substantial connections between Gardener and the union, but Gardener's pub talk was enough to convince the judge that the *Scotsman* management was entirely within its rights to dismiss Gardener without notice. Gardener protested that he faced a conspiracy and a company intent on crushing dissent within its ranks. No hard evidence had been presented to indicate his being a member of the union or linked to it in any way, and the hearsay offered in substantiating such a charge was just idle talk in pubs, not active campaigning on the union's behalf. It did not matter. In dismissing the case and assessing £1 expenses in favour of the defendants, the judge's conclusions made clear how political and business establishments could successfully use such legal spaces to assert and reinforce unequal power relationships in the workplace. 'One can hardly conceive in ordinary commercial life a circumstance more noxious to the interests of masters', he growled, 'than that of one of their own servants, brought here (as the pursuer has been) from a distance for a certain purpose, should be undermining their influences by his conduct in the office – trying to do what might have been to them an irreparable and certainly was a serious injury'.[26]

Actions were also taken against three of the original *Scotsman* strikers for abandoning work prior to the legally required fourteen-day notice period. The union responded by instructing its legal counsel to defend John Johnstone, Daniel Polson and Alexander Williams in court, with minutes recording, 'summonses having been served upon three of the late <u>Scotsman</u> companionship at the instance of the proprietor for alleged desertion of employment, it was resolved to instruct the Society's agent to defend the actions; and further agreed that, in the event of an adverse decision, the men be instructed to return to the office and complete their engagement'.[27] The case was heard in the Edinburgh Sheriff Court on 22 August, with Johnstone being found guilty of absconding from work without proper notice

[25] 'Scotsman Office: Action by a Compositor for Dismissal without Notice'. A mutchkin was an old Scottish term referring either to a measurement of liquid equivalent to 0.9 of a pint (424 ml), or to a container that would hold the same amount.
[26] Ibid., p. 8.
[27] 'Edinburgh Typographical Society Minute Books', pp. 162–3, 14 August 1872.

and fined £5, and the other cases being declared 'not proven' (the most Scottish of verdicts, indicating probable cause but lack of corroborating evidence to fully prove the charges).[28]

Similarly, workers who had left employment rather than strike break were brought to court, often in London from where they had originally been recruited. The *Manchester Guardian* and the *Daily News* recorded court actions brought in the Lambeth Police Court against F. Perring, a compositor who had been paid 43 shillings for travel and general expenses to take up work in the *Scotsman*, but who a few days later had subsequently and abruptly departed with two other workers without giving the statutory two weeks' notice. 'I know we have done wrong', he admitted, 'but prefer being punished in London than being punished in Edinburgh.'[29] £20 damages were sought; the judge awarded the *Scotsman* representative £5 compensation and 23 shillings in legal expenses, or six months in jail for the defendant if he failed to post payment.

Whilst pursuing union members and errant workers through the courts, the *Scotsman* conducted a vigorous public relations campaign via its news pages. It reported assiduously on the court cases pursued and the judgements rendered on its behalf, and issued leaders and editorials justifying its conduct, which were picked up and reprinted in allied newspapers in Birmingham, Dundee, London, and Sheffield, among others. When *Scotsman* reporters were barred from union meetings, editorials were run castigating the workers and the union for misrepresenting the situation, and for offering support for union members who could not be bothered to work due to dereliction of duty and drunkenness. 'The principle asserted by the strike', one editorial averred, was 'that the employed themselves are alone to be the judges of the proper length of absence from duty, and the proper degree of drunkenness.'[30] The *Scotsman* editorials commented that, in having to seek replacement workers (notably strike breakers from outside Scotland), 'we found that there were throughout England many respectable men and excellent workmen who had retained their liberty', that is, were non-unionized and likely to remain so.[31] But alas, lamented the editors, such noble workers were not allowed to work freely, instead facing union intimidation as well as workplace tampering and bribery. 'Then came bullying, "picketing," bribing, and latterly the smuggling into the premises of equivocal or peculiarly soporific whisky', the editors fumed.[32] These comments were picked up and reprinted in other newspapers, such as the *Birmingham Daily Post,* becoming the de facto public narrative deployed by the *Scotsman* in later legal prosecutions (such as the Gardener case referred to earlier), and in future justifications of its decision to close the shop floor to union members.[33]

The trade union fraternity did not view such journalistic interventions kindly, and early on sought to bar *Scotsman* reporters from Trade Council and print union

---

[28] 'Desertion of Service by Compositors'.
[29] 'The Strike at the "Scotsman" Office', *The Manchester Guardian*, 29 August 1872; 'The "Scotsman" and Its Compositors', *Daily News*, 29 August 1872.
[30] 'The "Scotsman" and Its Late Compositors', *The Scotsman*, 21 August 1872.
[31] Ibid.   [32] Ibid.
[33] 'The "Scotsman" and Its Late Compositors', *Birmingham Daily Post*, 13 August 1872.

meetings, while encouraging more sympathetic papers to attend. For example, representatives from the *Edinburgh Evening Courant* and the *Review* were invited to an open meeting of the Edinburgh Trades Council on 10 August 1872 at the Printers Hall at 50 South Bridge. When three *Scotsman* reporters also appeared, members voted to bar them from the hall, wary of how matters would be reported in the next day's *Scotsman*. It was not the reporters themselves who were at fault, agreed the delegates, but the *Scotsman* management, whom they blamed for skewing reportage of union matters through vigorous editing and hostile editorials. The former Father of the *Scotsman* Chapel (J. Crawford) offered first hand testimony on the matter: 'I think I speak for every one of my fellow workmen when I say that we cannot but have seen in the *Scotsman* offices how some reports are cooked up, very seldom to the advantage of the working-man.' In demanding the *Scotsman* representatives be escorted from the premises, he concluded pointedly, 'We have no faith in the reports of the *Scotsman* – that is to say, in those who overhaul the work of the reporters.'[34] The *Scotsman*'s editors allowed a faithful reporting of the matter in even tone, but could not help adding a sharp rebuttal at the end of the news item refuting what they saw as slander. 'It cannot be necessary to say that the statement made above by the compositor Crawford is, as can be testified by every reporter that is or ever was in our office, an utter falsehood.'[35]

Given the *Scotsman* stance, and its ability to recruit non-unionized workers to fill the vacant posts, defeat for the unions was inevitable. Throughout October 1872, union leaders clung vainly to the hope that the strike would succeed, though by the end of the month it was clear this position was untenable. As late as 30 October John Common, Edinburgh union secretary, was writing rather unconvincingly to his London counterpart Henry Self that there was nothing to worry about. 'Things are really looking well for us in the <u>Scotsman</u>', he claimed, 'if their row can only be prevented maturing into something serious.'[36] Though it continued to pay expenses for union 'dummy' spies into November, by then the union had effectively conceded defeat at the *Scotsman*, realizing that despite their efforts, the *Scotsman* had managed to recruit and retain a stable number of non-union workers.

The union emerged substantially weakened financially from this encounter, expending £793 in defence of the *Scotsman* hands, which swallowed up most of the £844 in membership fees raised during the year.[37] To the trade's credit, the Scottish Typographical Association's Central Board contributed £606 from its reserves, softening the financial blow.[38] The union had entered this battle unwillingly, and in defeat lost union influence in a key Edinburgh press office. Fifty years later, in editorials penned during the General Strike of 1926, the *Scotsman* reached back to the events of 1872 to claim vindication for its anti-union stance, which underpinned its general antipathy to the demands of the labouring classes then manifesting

---

[34] 'Dispute in the Scotsman', *The Scotsman*, 10 August 1872, p. 4.   [35] Ibid.
[36] 'Edinburgh Typographical Society Outgoing Letter Books', p. 470, John S. Common to Henry Self, 30 October 1872.
[37] The total expended by the Union in support of the *Scotsman* strike was £793.8.9. 'Edinburgh Typographical Society Income and Expenditure Account, 1 July 1846–2 Jan 1879', ff. 224.
[38] Ibid., ff. 224.

itself on British streets. 'To the proprietors it brought peace, which has already lasted a couple of generations – a peace that has been equally beneficial and appreciated by employers and employed, and that, as has been seen, has now come triumphantly through the ordeal to which it has been subjected.'[39]

THE EDINBURGH GENERAL STRIKE OF 1872–1873

The results of this workplace skirmish would significantly influence Edinburgh print employer tactics and approaches when the union began its delayed campaign for a reduction in working hours in mid-October 1872. Success or failure of such trade strikes often depended on employers' views of a union's financial viability. As the pioneering economic and social historians Beatrice and Sydney Webb astutely noted,

> It was soon found that the immediate success of the applications depended on the estimate formed by the employers of the men's financial resources, and their capacity to withhold their labour for a time sufficient to cause embarrassment to business. Wherever the employers were assured of this fact, they usually gave way without a conflict.[40]

In Edinburgh, determined resistance by local employers occurred in a way that took account of the union's weakened position when the union issued a Memorial to the Master Printers Association on 12 October 1872. The Memorial called for an increase in piece rate wages of $\frac{1}{2}$ pence per 1000 ens, a rise to 30 shillings in the weekly 'stab' wage, and a reduction from a fifty-four- to a fifty-one-hour working week. The Edinburgh employers who comprised the Master Printers Association, founded in 1846 with the express aim of fighting union demands, felt they had compromised enough on hours when they had agreed to a fifty-four-hour working week in August 1871, which was implemented in January 1872. Thirty-seven firms who made up most of the Master Printers Association (MPA), met to consider the new demands, and feeling they had conceded enough in January, refused the terms, and responded accordingly on 18 October.

The Edinburgh union had anticipated resistance, but as the union secretary John Common acknowledged at the commencement of the strike, it suspected the backlash would be based not on the merits of the case put forward, but on assumptions of union weakness. 'We have reason to know', he wrote on 5 November to a member of the Glasgow Trades Council, 'that the opposition of the employers is based not so much upon the plea that our demands are unreasonable (we have a fifty-four-hour week at present), as upon a determination to crush our union, which they suppose has had its resources seriously crippled by the expense attending the late Scotsman strike'.[41] This was indeed true.

---

[39] 'The "Scotsman" Strike of 1872: Reason for Non-Union Basis'.
[40] Webb and Webb, *The History of Trade Unionism*, p. 316.
[41] 'Edinburgh Typographical Society Outgoing Letter Books', p. 478, John S Common to Mr Bennett, 5 November 1872.

In the last weeks of October, meetings were held on both sides and compromise offers made to the Union to accept small increases in overtime rates and 'stab' wages (from 27/6 to 30/- a week). The MPA, while willing to compromise on such wage demands, baulked at simultaneously introducing a decreased working week in whatever form.[42] This was tantamount to suggesting paying more for less, and to their mind undermined their traditional authority in the workplace. Faced with this opposition, the union gave two weeks' strike notice at the beginning of November, signalling its membership would leave the workplace in an open-ended strike on 15 November 1872. Further discussions were held in the run-up to the deadline, with compromise proposals from the Union to phase in working hour reductions over the course of a year, and compromises offered on overtime payments, established wages and piece rates. The sticking point over working hour reductions refused to go away. The stage was now set for the commencement of a full strike.

On 15 November 1872, 750 men representing apprentices, journeymen, readers and compositors walked out of thirty-seven Edinburgh offices. The union took a robust stance on the matter, expressing strong conviction in the righteousness of their cause and the need to stand firmly united: 'It is high time we should teach them our real marketable value', wrote John Common to his Newcastle union counterpart TW Boag, 'and probably the dispute will not terminate until an additional half crown has been added to our demands.'[43] Nine of the major Edinburgh firms, however, had made plans to fill the anticipated gaps.[44] Banding together to create a strike contingency fund of £1000, they engaged sixteen agents to advertise for non-union 'rat' labour; within a fortnight 150 men had been recruited and distributed amongst the offices involved.[45] They also drew on a list of recruits compiled earlier in the year by the *Scotsman's* recruiting agent J. Cross to secure further replacement workers. Ads in major town newspapers and active agency recruitment drives saw workers arrive from Glasgow, Hull, Manchester and London.[46] Their success in attracting external labour stiffened the MPA's resolve to reject further union compromises. 'If the Masters hold firm today', William Blackwood III predicted on 15 November, 'we will break the back of the Union line at all events.'[47]

---

[42] Sarah C. Gillespie, *A Hundred Years of Progress. The Record of the Scottish Typographical Association, 1853 to 1952* (Glasgow: Printed for the Scottish Typographical Association by Robert Maclehose & Co., 1953), p. 118.

[43] 'Edinburgh Typographical Society Outgoing Letter Books', p. 473, John S. Common to TW Boag, 2 November 1872.

[44] 'Correspondence 1871-1880', in *Oliver and Boyd Papers* (National Library of Scotland). Thomas Nelson to John Boyd, October 31, 1872. Among key subscribers to the fund were William Blackwood and Sons, Burness, W&R Chambers, T&T Clark, T&A Constable, Murray and Gibb, Neill & Co., and Thomas Nelson.

[45] 'Trade Disputes: The Edinburgh Printers' Strike', *The Scotsman*, 13 December 1872. 'Trade Disputes. Great Strike of Printers in Edinburgh', *The Sheffield Daily Telegraph*, 16 November 1872.

[46] 'Correspondence'. William Blackwood to John Blackwood, 15 November 1872, MS. 4286, ff. 216–17.

[47] Ibid. William Blackwood to John Blackwood, 15 November 1872, MS. 4286, f. 215.

Attempts by workers to support the strike position were swiftly dealt with. In one case, two readers from the Blackwood publishing firm who refused to 'go to case' to reset type for a magazine proof were threatened with dismissal if they did not comply. When one did not, he was promptly dismissed.[48] The Blackwood firm, like several others, equally engaged in moral pressure, sending management figures to the homes of apprentices 'to give them a few words of counsel and warning' as to the likely effect upon their careers and their families of joining such strike action.[49]

William Blackwood III and Thomas Nelson were key leaders of the MPA resistance to workers. William and his uncle John were among the first to declare their firm non-unionized after the strike began. On 25 October 1872, William and John, in conjunction with their office manager John Simpson, produced a joint statement that was read out to shop floor staff, declaring the firm closed to union members. All future hires would be conducted based on wages and hours determined by the firm alone. As John would report to G. H. Lewes in late November 1872, the decision was not taken lightly, but done as a move against what was external interference. 'We have found it necessary to declare that we will not take a Union man into our office and we are determined to stand to our ground', he wrote, continuing, 'It will not put us about much and will do good.'[50] He concluded that he felt sorry for the men, 'but they yield like slaves to the tyranny of the Union'.[51] Although the official stance was to bar new recruits who declared themselves members of the union, after the strike Blackwood overseers quietly overlooked union connections of returning staff. Nevertheless, the result was a precipitous drop in union membership within the Blackwood firm, from 120 men registered in 1873 to thirteen listed in 1881.[52]

Not all Master Printers were so anti-union. John and Thomas Boyd of Oliver and Boyd were among those who remained sympathetic to the Union cause. Throughout the strike, their conciliatory stances alienated both Nelson and Blackwood, who saw them as threatening the unified image being projected by the Association's public statements. Approached by Thomas Nelson to contribute to the anti-strike fund, John Boyd declined, and at various meetings both he and Thomas made clear the family view that strike demands should be met at least in part. As William Blackwood III exclaimed to John Blackwood after a fractious MPA meeting centred round Thomas Boyd's commentary, 'Boyd again tried to break up our Union, the firmness of which was very sore to the men & giving them

---

[48] This is confirmed in the Minute Books of the Edinburgh Typographical Association strike committee, which records on 25 November 1872: 'Letter read from Mr. A. Wilson, Reader, Blackwood's, thanking Executives of Society for offering him pecuniary reward on receiving his notice for refusing to go to case.' 'Edinburgh Typographical Society Minute Books'. Accession 4068, #39, p. 20.

[49] 'Correspondence'. William Blackwood to John Blackwood, 11 November 1872, MS. 4286, ff. 207–8.

[50] 'Outgoing Correspondence', in *Blackwood Papers* (National Library of Scotland). John Blackwood to G. H. Lewes, 22 November 1872, pp. 206–7.

[51] Ibid. John Blackwood to G. H. Lewes, 22 November 1872, pp. 206–7.

[52] 'Edinburgh Typographical Society Index to Members of the Society, 1871–1880', in *Edinburgh Typographical Society Records* (National Library of Scotland).

more annoyance than our rejecting their demands almost.'[53] When John Boyd showed signs of wavering from the MPA's hardline stance, Nelson wrote a stern letter on behalf of the committee advising Boyd to stick to the agreed position. 'Some one told me today that you had expressed some doubts about the course that is being taken in the present dispute with the printers', Nelson commented, going on to caution: 'As that course was decided on after very careful consideration and with the view of trying to secure peace in the trade for years to come, I hope you will do nothing that will tend in any way to weaken the hands of the Masters' Association.'[54] He concluded tellingly, 'It is essential we remain united and go through with this matter.'[55] This did not stop the MPA providing help to the Oliver and Boyd office when print work of strategic importance required it. In the same letter, Nelson extended an offer from the MPA Committee to supply men to help complete work on Oliver and Boyd's annual *New Edinburgh Almanac and National Repository*. 'We all have pressing work in hand', Nelson added, 'but your Almanac was considered entitled to a preference if help should be required.'[56] It is not clear whether that offer was taken up.

THE NON-UNION FRIENDLY SOCIETY

Those who steered the Master Printers Association during the strike period privately and publicly disparaged the value of trade unions in the workplace. Nevertheless, they could not ignore the key role unions played in offering social welfare benefits that most employers were either unwilling or unable to fund or support themselves. One such area of support was sickness and unemployment benefits. These benefits, like death and burial costs, pensions and other family support mechanisms, had throughout the nineteenth century fallen under the province of a patchwork network of cooperative trade unions. They would remain so until replaced by twentieth-century state social welfare infrastructures.

It is instructive, therefore to find evidence of Edinburgh print employers initiating a short-lived social welfare organization for the benefit of its strikebreaking staff that mimicked trade union structures. An MPA supported meeting at Hogg's Temperance Hotel on 4 December 1872 announced the launch of an Edinburgh Non-Union Printers' Friendly Society. The Society's aim was to 'provide a fund for the relief of members who, through sickness or other circumstances over which they had no control may be rendered temporarily incapable of working'.[57] The tone of the meeting was needlessly patronizing: workers were encouraged to thank

---

[53] 'Correspondence'. William Blackwood III to John Blackwood, 12 November 1872, MS. 4286, ff. 209–10.

[54] 'Correspondence 1871–1880'. Thomas Nelson to John Boyd, 4 November 1872, Accession 5000, no 215.

[55] Ibid.   [56] Ibid.

[57] 'Trade Disputes: Edinburgh Printers' Strike and the Non-Society Hands', *The Scotsman*, 5 December 1872; 'Trade Movements. Edinburgh Printers' Strike and the Non-Society Hands', *Dundee Courier & Argus*, 6 December 1872.

their employers for treating workers in a very gentlemanlike manner, and in return all that was asked for was that men 'give satisfaction', and so 'reap the reward of their labour'.[58] The society was declared a safe space for incomers to 'come together and make themselves one'.[59] The Society assumed the same structure as a union society, appointing office bearers, trustees, auditors and committee members to manage and run its affairs in good order. No evidence exists to suggest this organization survived beyond the strike's conclusion a few months later.

UNION CANVASSING

As was becoming standard practice in these circumstances, the union sent committee members to key UK print centres to canvas for support, raise awareness and raise funds. Cities canvased throughout November included Aberdeen, Dundee, Glasgow, London, Newcastle, Perth, and London.[60] In December, deputations canvased the Scottish border towns of Galashiels, Hawick and Kelso, and travelled to Dublin to petition for support.[61] Other trade societies were also pursued for financial and moral support. In late November, a deputation spent three days in Glasgow canvassing over thirty trade society meetings, including those related to pipemakers, bricklayers, plumbers and tailors, while a parallel group in Edinburgh spoke to plate workers, joiners, typefounders and 'employees of Rubber and Vulcanite works'.[62] Two weeks later a deputation presented their case to meetings of the Perth masons, joiners and engineering societies.[63]

Support was generous and frequent, and came in several forms. Several fundraising events and rallies were held in aid of the strikers. Aberdeen, Edinburgh, and Perth print union committees, among others, organized public concerts throughout

---

[58] 'Trade Disputes: Edinburgh Printers' Strike and the Non-Society Hands'.

[59] Ibid.

[60] 'Edinburgh Typographical Society Minute Books'. Accession 4068, #39, p. 20; Perth Typographical Society committee minutes of 30 November 1872 record discussions with Edinburgh print workers and subsequent circulations of material related to the Edinburgh strike with a resolution passed to support the men, and 'with the view of raising subscriptions a Committee was appointed to wait on the various trade secretaries in town and request their assistance.' 'Perth Typographical Society Minute Books', in *Perth Typographical Society Records* (AK Bell Library).

[61] 'Edinburgh Typographical Society Minute Books'. Accession 4068, #39, p. 20, 2 December 1872; Following a donation from the Dublin print union of £20 in early December, Edinburgh representatives followed through with a visit later that month. Dublin union minutes note that on 23 December 1872, 'Messrs Sandilands and Brough attended as a deputation from the Edinburgh Society, and the Secretary placed before the Committee a resolution which had been adopted at the Council on Saturday evening, calling on them to take further steps with a view to assisting the Edinburgh Society. The delegates stated at some length the facts in reference to the Strike and matters in connection therewith, and ultimately the matter was adjourned until next meeting.' 'Dublin Typographical Provident Society Committee Minute Books'. OL Microfilm 703, 90/40 Committee Minute book, August 1872–July 1875.

[62] 'Edinburgh Typographical Society Minute Books'. Accession 4068, #39, p. 20, 25 November 1872.

[63] 'Perth Typographical Society Minute Books'. Special Meeting, 14 December 1872. My thanks to Helen Williams for uncovering relevant commentary on the Edinburgh strike in the Perth minutes.

December 1872 to raise strike funds.[64] Others provided long-term loans, grants, and donations via individual subscription calls. The London Society of Compositors sent £500, half as a gift, half as a loan; donations of between £5 and £50 arrived from print unions in Bradford, Cardiff, Dublin, Leeds, Liverpool, Manchester, Oxford, Sheffield, and Newcastle, among other.[65] By far the largest contributor was the Scottish Typographical Association's Central Board, who donated £2,708, 45 per cent of the total strike fund eventually raised (£4,890).[66] Every penny counted, as the union absorbed staggering expenditures of £5,321 over the three-month strike period, of which strike pay costs alone accounted for £4,607 (£300 was expended in strike allowances in the first fortnight), and associated costs amounted to over £700.[67]

In addition to fund raisers and supported social events, union branches organized public rallies and marches, arranged for officials to canvas opinion through public appearances and speeches, and ensured sympathetic coverage of their actions in allied newspapers. During the three-month strike, the Edinburgh union also produced a strike newsletter, entitled initially *Out on Strike*, then *The Craftsman*, which was circulated widely amongst Scottish print trade to inform and to boost morale. The unit charged with producing the newsletter was later spun out post-strike into a co-operative printing company that made effective interventions in the Edinburgh print trade for several decades after.[68]

WOMEN COMPOSITORS ENTER THE FRAME

One unanticipated by-product of the strike was the opportunity it gave women to enter the trade as compositors. Prior to 1873, print employers and print unions had paid little attention to women interested in taking up typesetting as an occupation. There had been a few initiatives in the mid-century to test women's abilities in this area. The best known of these was the Victoria Press, set up in London in 1860 by Emily Faithfull with 14 female compositor trainees and two journeymen overseers. It served as a model for similar initiatives in Dublin, Edinburgh and

---

[64] 1 December 1872 Aberdeen committee minutes record a motion to arrange a concert later that month to benefit the Edinburgh strike; Perth committee minutes note a commitment to running a concert in mid-December, while in Edinburgh three concerts were held on consecutive Saturdays in December at the Waverley and Literary Institute Halls: 'Scottish Typographical Association (Aberdeen Branch) Minute Books', (Aberdeen University Library). MS2471/3; 'Perth Typographical Society Minute Books'. Special Meeting, 14 December 1872; 'Edinburgh Typographical Society Minute Books'. Accession 4068, #39, 19 November 1872. My thanks to Iain Beavan for uncovering relevant commentary on the Edinburgh strike in the Aberdeen minutes.

[65] *Scottish Typographical Association: A Fifty Years' Record, 1853–1903*, p. 63; 'Edinburgh Typographical Society Minute Books'. Accession 4068, #39, 19 November 1872, 25 November 1872, 4 December 1872; 23 January 1873; 'Dublin Typographical Provident Society Council Minutes', in *Dublin Typographical Provident Society Records* (Trinity College, Dublin); 'Dublin Typographical Provident Society Committee Minute Books'. OL Microfilm 703, 90/40, 10 December 1872.

[66] 'Edinburgh Typographical Society Income and Expenditure Account, 1 July 1846–2 Jan 1879'.

[67] 'Edinburgh Typographical Society Income and Expenditure Account, 1 July 1846–2 Jan 1879'.

[68] Gillespie, *A Hundred Years of Progress*, pp. 119–20. The Edinburgh Cooperative Printing Company would later restructure and rename itself the Darien Press.

London, gained Queen Victoria's patronage, and survived for several decades by undertaking jobbing and general printing work.[69] An Edinburgh equivalent was launched in 1861, inspired by a speech given by Faithfull in Glasgow in October 1860. Funded by local philanthropists and reform minded families, the Caledonian Press was set up in May 1861 at No 4 South Saint David's Street, just off Princes Street.[70] It began with eight apprentice girls and three journeymen tutors, and its first publication was a political pamphlet on the Marquis of Bute, advertised for sale in the *Scotsman* on 23 May 1861.[71] By November 1861 the Caledonian Press was touting for work in legal areas, advertising its ability to print Court of Session law papers, and in 1863 it had expanded its workforce to include fourteen women compositors.[72] However, in face of fierce opposition from local unions and the print fraternity, lacking in consistent sales and profitable printing accounts, and dependent on dwindling philanthropic donations, it ceased operations in 1865.[73]

Seven years later, the Edinburgh strike created space for women's re-entry into the composing room. It would be a foothold that Edinburgh print unions spent decades trying to dislodge. As Sian Reynolds has outlined in her elegant study of Edinburgh women compositors, key employers saw value in drawing on the pool of young, educated women living in the capital city for replacement labour once the strike had taken full effect.[74] They began bringing them into the case room. An 1898 account published in *The Women's Industrial News* recounts that the impetus for this move came from an unnamed head of a printing firm (likely to have been Ballantyne or Constable). The company head recruited six young women from one of The Merchant Company's schools in Edinburgh, secretly trained them to set type, then demonstrated the results to a cohort of print firms affected by the strike.[75] Impressed by the results, several firms began discreetly advertising for young female workers to join the ranks. In late January 1873, union members reported to the strike committee that Constable had issued a circular to boarding schools calling for young male apprentices and girls to train as compositors.[76] W&R Chambers subsequently placed ads on 8 February 1873 in the *Edinburgh Evening Courant* and the *Scotsman* seeking 'young women of good education and

[69] Emily Faithfull, 'Women and Work', *Women and Work*, no. 19 (1874). See also William E Fredeman, 'Emily Faithfull and the Victoria Press: An Experiment in Sociological Bibliography', *The Library* 29, no. 2 (1974); For interesting background details on several of the women employed at the Victoria Press, see Marianne Van Remoortel, *Women, Work and the Victorian Periodical: Living by the Press* (Basingstoke: Palgrave Macmillan, 2015), pp. 115–32.

[70] 'Classified Ad 94'.

[71] Sian Reynolds, *Britannica's Typesetters: Women Compositors in Edinburgh* (Edinburgh: Edinburgh University Press, 1989), pp. 32–3.; 'Classified Ad 66', *The Scotsman*, 23 May 1861. The full title of the work was 'The Marquis of Bute. The Future Guardianship During His Lordship's Minority. The Judgment of the House of Lords'.

[72] Reynolds, *Britannica's Typesetters*, p. 34; 'Classified Ad 139', *The Scotsman*, 9 November 1861.

[73] Reynolds, *Britannica's Typesetters*, p. 35.   [74] Ibid.

[75] L. Barbara Bradby, 'Edinburgh Compositors and Women's Work', *The Women's Industrial News*, no. New Series, 6 (1898).

[76] 'Edinburgh Typographical Society Minute Books'. 'Strike Minute Book', January 25, 1872; Reynolds, p. 42.

character, to act as compositors', while later in the year, Neill & Co. quietly advertised for a 'Girl (Respectable), above 13 for a Printing Office. Must be a good reader.'[77]

In June 1873, sixty-three women were working in Edinburgh firms.[78] By 1875, 114 women were reportedly employed in nine firms across Edinburgh.[79] Among the most notable employers of women compositors were Neill & Co. and Murray and Gibb, two large print firms alternately contracted to do government printing work during the 1870s and 1880s, and whom we will see featured in the 1878 Dublin print strike discussed later in this chapter. They had the highest concentration of women compositors working in Edinburgh in 1875, with Murray and Gibb employing thirty-five women working alongside sixty-eight journeymen and apprentice compositors and press machinists, and Neill and Co. employing eighteen women alongside 135 journeymen and apprentice compositors and press machinists.[80] By 1891, at least eight firms were known still to employ women compositors, and that year's census recorded a total of 659 women registered as compositors in Edinburgh.[81] In 1910, however, a major strike was instigated by the printers' union with the specific aim of restricting further entry of female workers and apprentices into the Edinburgh printing trade. The result was an agreement by Master Printers to keep current numbers of women employed in the trade but observe a five-year moratorium on further hiring of female compositors.[82] The effect was to freeze and ultimately squeeze out women from the Edinburgh composing space.

THE STRIKE ENDS

Three months into the strike, union positions began to crumble, as it became apparent that the strike was having little effect on Edinburgh printing activity. Widely reported outbreaks of violence between strikers and 'rats' were also damaging the union's reputation. In early January 1873 a strikebreaker (William Rylett) was brought to trial and fined 30 shillings for lashing out at a group of striking printers who had surrounded him on Hunter's Square, near the town's High Street, for throwing a printer down the stairs of Mrs Doig's Public House, and for assaulting James McLaren, an out-of-work printer.[83] That there had been probable cause for acting in self-defence was possible, given that one of the players in this scenario, James McLaren, would himself appear in court a few weeks later accused of assaulting a strikebreaker 'rat' in the same venue. The union, though it deplored such actions by its members, reluctantly funded McLaren's defence costs, though not

---

[77] Reynolds, *Britannica's Typesetters*, p. 43; 'Classified Ad 25', *The Scotsman*, 8 February 1873. 'Classified Ad 1', *The Scotsman*, 6 June 1873.

[78] Reynolds, *Britannica's Typesetters*, p. 45.

[79] 'Compositors, Pressmen, Machine-Minders (Journeymen and Apprentices), and Female Compositors, in Edinburgh, Sept 1875', in *Edinburgh Typographical Society Records* (National Library of Scotland). Acc. 4068, no. 16–17.

[80] Ibid. Acc. 4068, no. 16–17.

[81] Bradby, 'Edinburgh Compositors and Women's Work'.

[82] Gillespie, *A Hundred Years of Progress*, pp. 67–87.

[83] 'The Printers' Strike. Alleged Intimidation', *The Scotsman*, 4 January 1873, p. 4.

without issuing a stern warning to all concerned 'that such parties must not look for sympathy or support from the committee in averting the consequences'.[84] After much contradictory testimony as to who was there and what had occurred, the judge concluded that McLaren had probably thrown Michael Whitson down the stairs of Doig's public house (a popular place for such acts, it would seem), and sentenced him to twenty days in prison.[85] The *Scotsman* was quick to circulate the results as a news item in its pages, following which it was picked up and reprinted by other regional papers, adding to the general negative publicity surrounding union actions.[86]

By mid-February 1873, it was clear that the number of strikebreakers in use throughout Edinburgh had remained constant and high, despite vigorous union action. A survey of print establishments at this stage suggested that the number of strike breakers on the books that month had reached 404: 253 'foreign comps', presumably recruited from outside Scotland, seventy 'home comps' recruited from Scotland, forty-three 'foreign machine men' and thirty-nine 'home machine men'.[87] Official histories of the union put the total number who'd crossed strike lines over the three-month period as fully 700 'unreliables'.[88] The 'rat' labour recruited, along with newly involved women compositors, enabled employers to carry on day-to-day operations and general business with little difficulty. With the union haemorrhaging strike funds, they conceded the battle was lost.

Based on the outcome of a meeting and vote held on 6 February, union leaders sent a letter on 7 February to the MPA noting their intention to end the strike, and proposing submitting the matter to arbitration. The MPA responded on 11 February rejecting the proposal, but agreeing to allow workers to return to their positions under the terms offered in the run-up to the 15 November strike, whereby small concessions were made on increases to overtime and stab wages.[89] On 13 February 1873 union members voted by 200 to 131 to return to work based on the original compromise offer of slightly better wages but no concessions on working hours.[90] As John Blackwood gleefully announced to his nephew William in regards to their particular interests, former employees 'have surrendered at discretion & come back to <u>Blackwoods</u> throwing up the Union in fact on any terms back'.[91]

Of the 750 original union strikers, 450 remained in Edinburgh after the strike. Within two months, all but twenty of these had returned to work.[92] The printing unions emerged extremely weakened from the loss, burdened by accumulated debts and a devastating drop in membership. In mid-1872, Union membership

[84] 'Edinburgh Typographical Society Minute Books', 1 February 1873; 4 February 1873.

[85] 'Another Alleged Outrage by a Printer on Strike', *The Scotsman*, 4 February 1873.

[86] 'The Outrage by a Unionist Printer', *The Scotsman*, 6 February 1873; 'A Unionist Sent to Prison', *The Sheffield Daily Telegraph*, 6 February 1873.

[87] 'Edinburgh Typographical Society Minute Books', No. 40, 13 February 1873.

[88] *Scottish Typographical Association: A Fifty Years' Record, 1853–1903*, p. 63.

[89] 'Trade Disputes: Edinburgh Printers' Strike', *The Scotsman*, 11 February 1873.

[90] Reynolds, p. 42; 'Classified Ad 25', *The Scotsman*, 8 February 1873; 'Classified Ad 5', *The Scotsman*, 20 October 1873.

[91] 'Correspondence'. John Blackwood to William Blackwood III, Feb 21, 1873, MS 4299, f. 172.

[92] Reynolds, *Britannica's Typesetters*, pp. 42–3.

stood at 1000 members.[93] Within a year of the strike's end, union membership had reduced by 10 per cent to 900, and by 1880 membership had dwindled a further 55 per cent to 342.[94]

TORONTO BATTLES, 1872

Three thousand miles away and almost concurrently in time, a similar battle raged in Toronto over print wages, working hours, union status and print floor control. The printers' strike of March–June 1872 has been well documented, given its significance in Canadian labour history.[95] Much like in Edinburgh, the Canadian confrontation pitted the Toronto Typographical Union against a virulently anti-unionist politician and kingpin newspaper proprietor. It featured union spies and vigilance committees. It saw strikes, arrests, prosecutions for conspiracy and a union defeat that left it wounded and stripped of funds and members. But it also featured an unlikely political intervention that galvanized and subsequently protected labour organizations across Canada from the crude and destructive tactics used against the Toronto printers. A print trade worker defeat ultimately became celebrated as a victory for general labour organization in Canada. The circumstances of this key labour strike offer interesting parallels with the other strikes documented in this chapter.

The Toronto Typographical Union (TTU) began as the York Typographical Society (YTS) in 1832. Though formed by a group of twenty-four printers to 'meet industrial problems, not social and benevolent needs', it did on occasion act along the more traditional lines of a benevolent society.[96] For example, shortly after amalgamation it provided financial assistance in accordance with the tradition of the trade-wide tramping system to a Scotsman named Baird from the Cork Typographical Society, who petitioned for help to travel to the United States in search of employment.[97] The YTS changed its name to the Toronto Typographical Society (TTS) in 1835, but collapsed and disbanded in 1837 after a failed city-wide strike for enhanced wages.[98] In 1844 the TTS was resurrected in response to actions by George Brown, publisher of the *Globe* and the *Banner*, who sought to organize Master Printers to push through a reduction in wages across the Toronto

---

[93] 'Edinburgh Typographical Society Contributor Records, 1861–1900'; 'Edinburgh Typographical Society Index to Members of the Society, 1871–1880'. The membership total was derived from a hand count made of members listed in union records at the end of May 1872.

[94] Reynolds, *Britannica's Typesetters*, pp. 45–6.

[95] Christina Burr, 'Class and Gender in the Toronto Printing Trade, 1870–1914' (PhD thesis, Memorial University of Newfoundland, 1992); Kealey, '"The Honest Workingman" and Workers' Control: The Experience of Toronto Skilled Workers, 1860–1892'; *Toronto Workers Respond to Industrial Capitalism, 1867–1892*; Sally F. Zerker, 'A History of the Toronto Typographical Union, 1832–1925' (Ph.D. thesis, University of Toronto, 1972); 'The Development of Collective Bargaining in the Toronto Printing Industry in the Nineteenth Century', *Relations industrielles/Industrial Relations* 30, no. 1 (1975); 'George Brown and the Printers' Union', *Journal of Canadian Studies/Revue d'etudes canadiennes* 10, no. 1 (1975); *The Rise and Fall of the Toronto Typographical Union, 1832–1972*.

[96] *The Rise and Fall of the Toronto Typographical Union, 1832–1972*, p. 20.

[97] Ibid, pp. 21–2, 54.   [98] Ibid, pp. 26–9.

print sector. This led to bitter relations between Brown and his employees, and the TTS called for a boycott of his shop. Three years later, the Master Printers success-fully negotiated a wage reduction with the TTS. To protect their own interests, more journeyman printers joined the society, thus ameliorating its financial situ-ation. As a result, the TTS could offer its members a guaranteed wage, sick and unemployment benefits, relocation assistance, and a burial fund of £2 10s for deceased members. By 1851, forty-nine printers had joined the TTS, and by 1871 the TTS has almost quadrupled in membership to 190.[99]

In 1866, the TTS affiliated itself with the American National Typographical Union (NTU), which in 1869 was renamed the International Typographical Union (ITU), in part because of the incorporation of Canadian branches into its general network. Initial impetus for joining was mobility for TTS members: mem-bership of the NTU brought with it the ability to circulate freely within the US print network tramping system. NTU/ITU branches retained a fair degree of autonomy. When the TTS embarked on strike action in late March 1872, the par-ent organization paid little attention, though the results were recorded in a short aside by the ITU president in his annual report for 1872. 'With the aid and sym-pathy of other trades organizations', President W.J. Hammond concluded, 'the strike was vigorously prosecuted, and I learn with partial if not complete success.'[100] To gauge how true was this statement, we need to review the history of the con-frontation between Toronto printers and employees.

The nine-hour working movement which had galvanized organized labour in Britain throughout 1871 filtered through to Canada in early 1872. Similar working week movements were also ongoing in the USA. The NTU/ITU fought unsuccess-fully throughout the 1860s and 1870s to implement an eight-hour working day. Lobbying for a nine-hour working day proved more successful in local circum-stances: for example, in 1864, the largest branch in the ITU, the New York Typographical Union No. 6, negotiated lowering the working time of morning press printers to nine hours a day.[101] However, it would take another 35 years before the nine-hour system was agreed across the ITU national network to include book and jobbing printers.[102]

The first Canadian nine-hour week initiative was launched in Hamilton, Ontario on 27 January 1872 at the local Mechanics' Institute.[103] A meeting involving

---

[99] Ibid, p. 326.

[100] International Typographical Union, *A Study of the History of the International Typographical Union, 1852–1963*, 2 vols. (Colorado Springs, Colorado: International Typographical Union Executive Council, 1964), vol. 2, p. 76.

[101] G. A. Stevens, *New York Typographical Union No. 6; Study of a Modern Trade Union and Its Predecessors* (Albany, NY: J. B. Lyon Co., State printers, 1913), p. 368.

[102] Ibid, pp. 372–6. George Stevens in his history of the NYTU dates the change to late 1899, when three key print unions (the International Typographical Union, the International Printing Pressmen and Assistants' Union, and the International Brotherhood of Bookbinders) agreed with the Typothetae, the national print employers' federation, to adopt a standardized nine-hour working day. At this stage, Stevens comments, 'So far as New York was concerned President Delaney on December 3, 1899, informed the union that the nine-hour law had been successfully instituted without any trouble' (p. 376).

[103] Details that follow are drawn from John Battye, 'The Nine Hour Pioneers: The Genesis of the Canadian Labour Movement', *Labour/Le Travail* 4 (1979).

carpenters, blacksmiths, machinists, and other trade union representatives concluded with a resolution to create Canada's first nine-hour League. The resolution was officially sanctioned at a mass meeting the following week involving representatives from across Hamilton's trades and manufacturing bases. Early successes in convincing Hamilton employers to grant reductions in working hours emboldened key League members to write to other trade organizations across Ontario urging them to adopt similar proposals. Few heeded the call, though the recently established Toronto Trades Assembly, representing skilled labour interests across the city, picked up news of the Hamilton movement, and at a meeting on 2 February endorsed campaigning for a nine-hour working day across Toronto labour sectors. They appointed a general committee to rent a hall for a public meeting at which to 'agitate the nine hour system'.[104] On 14 February the first of such meetings was held in the Toronto Music Hall, chaired by trade unionist J. S. Williams, head of the Toronto Typographical Union, and attended by a packed audience drawn from representative trade sectors in the city. Here, and at subsequent meetings, speeches in favour of the movement were interspersed with nebulous plans for action, culminating in an agreement at another mass meeting on 15 March 1872 to press for a fifty-four-hour week to be implemented across the trades in early June, letting labour unions lobby separately for such concessions in their respective trade areas. The result was a fragmented and diluted approach to what should have been a collective discussion.

TORONTO PRINT WORKERS ACT

The Toronto print union, impatient with the slow pace of collective action, unilaterally set in motion plans to 'memorialize' employers for a reduction in hours, along with an increase in piece rate wage scales. On 17 February, the union met and approved demands for increases in piece rate wages and a reduction from sixty to fifty-four in weekly working hours.[105] On 29 February the union issued a general circular to Toronto printers and newspaper proprietors setting out demands for the reduced hours and new piece wages scale (a 10 per cent increase in piece rates from 30 to 33⅓cents per 1,000 ems, and $10 wages for a fifty-four-hour week). Union representatives felt confident they would gain some concessions. Earlier in the week they had successfully lobbied the managing director of the *Globe*'s newsroom to apply the piece rate increases (but not the working hour reductions) to newsroom night compositors, who set the type for the next day's

[104] Ibid., p. 32.

[105] Strike details outlined here are derived from J. M. S. Careless, *Brown of the Globe*, vol. 2: *Statesman of Confederation, 1860–1880* (Toronto: The Macmillan Company of Canada, Ltd, 1963), pp. 287–98; D. F. Creighton, 'George Brown, Sir John Macdonald, and the "Workingman": An Episode in the History of the Canadian Labour Movement', *Canadian Historical Review* 24, no. 4 (1943); Bernard Ostry, 'Conservatives, Liberals, and Labour in the 1870s', *Canadian Historical Review* 41, no. 2 (1960), pp. 93–127; Zerker, *The Rise and Fall of the Toronto Typographical Union, 1832–1972: A Case Study of Foreign Domination* (Toronto, Buffalo, NY, and London: University of Toronto Press, 1982), pp. 78–88.

news, and agree a system of shortening the daily attendance hours of day compositors.[106] Other master printers in the city then accepted these terms. However, the successful application of these demands to other sectors of the print trade, chiefly book and jobbing printers, was less certain. Some employers conceded the demands, including James Beaty (proprietor of the Conservative newspaper the *Leader*), the *Mail* newspaper and eight other printing firms.[107] Beaty would go on to become a leading supporter of the print strikers, opening his newspaper pages to editorials promoting the nine-hour movement and reporting from a union perspective on the shifting events of the print strike. As he acknowledged at a nine-hour rally in St Lawrence Hall on 3 April, where he was guest of honour, to disavow such demands was to deny how capitalist profits were built on the back of labour's efforts. 'What has produced the capital?' he exclaimed. 'Why, the labouring classes! It is the labour put on raw material which gives all value.'[108]

Most Toronto print employers, however, baulked at the idea of conceding a 10 per cent increase in wages alongside a 10 per cent decrease in working hours. The Master Printers Association, responded to the initial request negatively. Their communiqué was received and debated at a union meeting on 13 March. The master printers agreed to concede the wage rise of 33 1/3 cents for night compositors, but rejected the other demands. The union issued their ultimatum reiterating their demands and threatening a general strike if they were not met. On 19 March the master printers reiterated their terms, which were to agree the raise for night compositors, but maintain day rates at 30 cents per 1,000 ems and $10 for a sixty-hour working week. Six days later, on 25 March 1872, the Toronto Typographical Union members went out on strike.

At the heart of the employers' refusal was an ideological rejection of the union position. In addition to objecting to the increased costs to their business, the Master Printers, much like their counterparts in Britain and Ireland, found threatening the incursion of organized labour into decisions about productivity and working conditions, which they felt they alone were qualified to decide upon. This was made clear in a manifesto published by Brown in the *Globe* on 8 April on behalf of a group of 50 employers drawn from a range of trades, including painters, glaziers, boot, and shoe manufacturers, harnessmakers, tinsmiths and printers. The manifesto had emerged from a meeting Brown organized to create a cross-sector anti-union movement. In arguments echoing those deployed against similar strikes in London, Edinburgh and Dublin, the anti-union federation saw nothing but harm in the labour demands. The nine-hour movement, they argued, posed a fundamental threat to industrial expansion and capitalist growth, undermined the employers' authority in the workplace, and raised the spectre of a Communist overthrow of Canadian capitalist systems. 'Any attempt on the part of the Employees

---

[106] Ostry, 'Conservatives, Liberals, and Labour in the 1870s', p. 95.

[107] Zerker, 'A History of the Toronto Typographical Union, 1832–1925', p. 87. Zerker lists those who conceded union demands as follows: *The Irish Canadian;* McLeish and Co.; *The Canadian Freeman;* Messrs Rowsell and Hutchinson; Messrs Copp, Clark and Co.; *The Express;* the Church Herald Printing Company; and Messrs Bell and Co.

[108] Quoted in Careless, *Brown of the Globe*, vol. 2, p. 294.

to dictate to them in what way, or to what extent they shall lawfully use their own resources', they stated in robust fashion, 'is not only an unwarranted interference with the rights of others, but a very transparent attempt to introduce amongst us the Communistic system of levelling.'[109] Therefore, employers had to stand firm, maintain the ten-hour day and 'resist any attempts on the part of our Employees to dictate to us by what rules we shall govern our business'.[110]

James Beaty argued in the *Leader* that working classes would be more productive if given the right incentives to cooperate with capitalist intentions. For him, the union demands seemed reasonable requests in face of challenging working weeks. The *Leader* was not the only newspaper to present the union viewpoint. On 18 April 1872, almost four weeks into the strike, the TTS launched its own newspaper, the weekly *Ontario Workman*. Until its demise in 1875 it was run on cooperative lines by key members of the strike committee, and initially edited by the TTS president J. S. Williams. The *Workman* addressed workers' issues in didactic and informative manner, offering a mix of news, reportage, poetry, and fiction in a weekly, five-column broadsheet format. It also used its pages to directly address other trade unionists, including its sister counterparts in Britain, to whom was directed a letter in late April 1872, signed by leaders of the Canadian trade union movement, calling for help and asking that overseas branches discourage printer emigration to Canada until the movement had successfully achieved its objective. The union also sought donations from allies to support strike costs: contributions duly arrived from fellow trade unionists in Hamilton, Montreal, Oshawa, St. Catharines and Ottawa.[111]

VIGILANCE COMMITTEES AND MASTER PRINTER COUNTERMOVES

The strike lasted just over two months, and attracted international press attention: news reports appeared in Connecticut, New York, Philadelphia, and Scotland, among others, chronicling the ebb and flow of the dispute between 25 March and 1 June 1872.[112] Much like Edinburgh employers would later in the year, and Dublin firms would in 1878, once the strike was in progress Brown led the master printers in aggressive moves against the union. Brown hired a government officer, a detective by the name of O'Neil, to keep track of individual strike committee members, and had on his payroll at least one informer reporting from the shop

---

[109] Quoted in John Battye, 'The Nine Hour Pioneers: The Genesis of the Canadian Labour Movement', *Labour/Le Travail* 4 (1979), p. 46.

[110] Ostry, 'Conservatives, Liberals, and Labour in the 1870s', pp. 98–9.

[111] Battye, 'The Nine Hour Pioneers', p. 45.

[112] 'Telegraph Item', *Hartford Daily Courant*, 26 March 1872. 'The Toronto Printers' Strike: Arresting the Malcontents'; 'The Labourers' "Sweet Voices"', *New York Herald*, 7 August 1872; 'Threatened Typographical Strike in Canada', *New York Herald*, 23 March 1872. 'Strike of the Journeymen Printers', *Philadelphia Inquirer*, 26 March 1872; 'Dominion of Canada', *The Scotsman*, 23 April 1872; 'Dominion of Canada', *The Scotsman*, May 11 1872; 'Our Own Correspondent', *The Scotsman*, 19 September 1872.

floor on union developments.[113] He and fellow Master Printers advertised assiduously and widely in the *Globe* and allied newspapers for non-union labour to fill their vacancies. The Master Printers pooled resources (as did their Edinburgh counterparts later that year) to share facilities, sent recruiting agents to non-unionized strongholds in London, Hamilton and Woodstock, and distributed workers who responded across relevant printing establishments.[114] Even George Brown reputedly 'set to work at the "case" in his shirt sleeves, and all the staff who knew anything about handling "a stick" turned to type-setting'.[115] There were also reports that, as occurred in Edinburgh later that year, some printing firms began training girls to work on the shop floor. 'The [striking] men stand out firm to their purposes', one Scottish correspondent reported, 'and their places are being supplied as far as possible with country hands and girls who have been taken in hand to learn the business.'[116] The inaugural issue of the *Ontario Workman* made similar allegations against the *Globe*, referring to its hypocrisy in supporting the British nine-hour movement the year before, then denying its introduction in Canada and importing female labour to staff the composing rooms. 'During the Newcastle strike the *Globe* spoke of the "ill-advised attempt of the Newcastle capitalists to import labour from the Continent"', the *Workman* editorial complained. 'What has it to say on the ill-advised attempt of Mr Geo Brown and the Master Printers Association to import all the simple country lads and lasses who have a knowledge of printing to Toronto, to keep back that same nine-hour movement that he then advocated?'[117] The country hands brought in surreptitiously from unorganized parts of Ontario would disparagingly be labelled 'country mice' by sympathetic labour commentators tracking their entrance.[118]

A union Vigilance Committee, set up by the strike organizers to monitor and mitigate strikebreaking efforts, also tracked the strikebreakers. Toronto unions utilized similar strike management tactics seen at play in London, Edinburgh, and later Dublin. They drew on a network of informants to keep apprised of incoming workers, with conductors and trainmen on the Great Western, Northern, and Grand Trunk rail lines recruited to report on strikebreaker arrivals. Union reception committees then met incoming workers to try and persuade them to take the next

---

[113] Careless, *Brown of the Globe*, vol. 2, p. 294; Ostry, 'Conservatives, Liberals, and Labour in the 1870s', p. 97; D. F. Creighton, 'George Brown, Sir John Macdonald, and the "Workingman"', p. 369. Eric Tucker identifies Brown's hired detective as a Detective O'Neil from the diary records of Robert Harrison, the barrister who provided George Brown with legal assistance in framing his legal case against the striking printers, and who interviewed O'Neil in the course of preparing notes for the prosecution. Eric Tucker, '"That Indefinite Area of Toleration": Criminal Conspiracy and Trade Unions in Ontario, 1837–77', *Labour/Le Travail* 27 (1991), p. 44. He was also named in the *Ontario Workman*, who commented, 'It is something rather strange, that members of the Government secret service are allowed to work up private interests at the people's expense, as in the case of Mr O'Neil, a Government officer, whom Mr Brown of the *Globe* has secured to procure him help.' 'The Arrest', *Ontario Workman*, 18 April 1872.

[114] Careless, *Brown of the Globe*, vol. 2, pp. 292–4.

[115] 'Dominion of Canada', *The Scotsman*, 23 April 1872, p. 3.   [116] Ibid.

[117] 'Our Mission', *Ontario Workman*, 18 April 1872.

[118] Zerker, *The Rise and Fall of the Toronto Typographical Union, 1832–1972: A Case Study of Foreign Domination*, p. 83.

train back.[119] The Vigilance Committee also had members actively encouraging men who had signed contracts to resign and leave the city, offering incentives such as travel funds and money to stay away from work. How much was offered varied according to whom you spoke to. An apprentice printer was said to have been paid $1.50 out of strike funds to support himself during the industrial action. Another printer testified later in a court deposition that a union representative had offered him four dollars a week 'to work for him and do nothing but walk about the streets', while another claimed to have been offered a dollar, then later $14 a week plus board.[120] Such tactics infuriated Brown, who in a *Globe* editorial on 29 March 1872 railed against such actions, for 'the law is perfectly clear and most effective in its operation against everything in the shape of molestation, coercion, or intimidation'.[121] Brown continued: 'Strenuous efforts continue to be made by the emissaries of the Typographical Society to intimidate or bribe the men from fulfilling their engagements; and in too many cases they have been successful in their illegal and reprehensible work.' He concluded ominously: 'This can however, no longer be submitted to, and steps have been taken for the detection and prompt prosecution of all guilty of indictable offences.'[122]

A demonstration in central Toronto on 15 April 1872 attracted upwards of 10,000 participants, who gathered in Queen's Park to hear speeches from union leaders arguing in favour of the nine-hour movement. The event was said to have enraged Brown. In an anti-union employers' gathering ten days later, he rallied the congregants with a full-throated cry: 'Crush out the aspirations of employees! Stamp out the movement! Ostracize union men! Drive them out of Canada!'[123] On Brown's instigation, on 16 April 1872, twenty-four warrants were issued for the arrest of key typographical Vigilance Committee members, though of these only fourteen were pursued and arrested.

The committee members were brought to trial on charges that they had 'conspired with divers others to lessen the usual time of work in the Art and occupation of Printers'.[124] The initial arraignment took place on 18 April 1872 in front of Police Magistrate MacNabb, an irascible and obtuse personality. The prosecution drew on a position paper produced for George Brown by Barrister Harrison to support their case, arguing that union members, in striking and then interfering with the workplace, were guilty of an 'indictable conspiracy'. They offered documentary material and depositions from ten witnesses (including four ex-union members) who were willing to testify to the various infractions that amounted to conspiracy to coerce and intimidate other workers. MacNabb didn't take long to conclude that matters should be progressed to full trial: trade unions were illegal, he concluded

---

[119] Careless, *Brown of the Globe*, vol. 2, p. 294.

[120] Paul Craven, 'Workers' Conspiracies in Toronto, 1854–1872', *Labour/Le Travail* 14 (1984), p. 66.

[121] Quoted in Careless, *Brown of the Globe, Vol. Two*, p. 294.

[122] Quoted in D. F. Creighton, *John A. Macdonald: The Young Politician, the Old Chieftain* (Toronto: University of Toronto Press, 1998), p. 369; Zerker, *The Rise and Fall of the Toronto Typographical Union, 1832–1972*, p. 84.

[123] Quoted in Battye, 'The Nine Hour Pioneers', p. 47.

[124] Quoted in Paul Craven, 'Workers' Conspiracies in Toronto, 1854–1872', 65.

bluntly, so merely proving the existence of a workmen's association dedicated to organization in the workplace was enough to bring forward a prosecution. MacNabb peremptorily adjourned the case for a second hearing on 7 May, which was adjourned again for a decision on 18 May. (The latter in any case were overtaken by subsequent political decisions and never held.) Bail was set at $400 and the strikers walked out of the courtroom cast as martyrs of a miscarriage of justice, perpetrated by the Master Printers, led by a ruthless George Brown dubbed the 'Czar of King Street'.[125]

CANADIAN TRADE UNION AND CRIMINAL LAW ACTS INTRODUCED

Canada's premier John MacDonald reacted quickly when news broke of the criminal prosecutions of the strike leaders. Taking his lead from the British Trade Union and Criminal Law Acts that had been passed in 1871, he presented similar acts to the Canadian House of Commons for discussion and approval on 7 May 1872. This also happened to be the date set for trials of the union Vigilance Committee 'conspirators'. Considering the legislation, which had a direct bearing on the underlying legality of the prosecution and rendered the issues moot, the trials were abandoned.

Shifts in labour and trade capital underpinned in part the argument for enacting political change. The growth of trade unions in Canada, their increasing power as Canadian business needs expanded and grew, and the sharpening battles over wages and working conditions made clear the legal inconsistencies by which such relations were now bound. The prosecution of the Toronto print strikers for criminal conspiracy highlighted the anachronistic and oppressive means by which a legal hodgepodge of statutes could be used to suppress legitimate social protests.

MacDonald's interest in the matter has been extensively analysed and debated over the past fifty years.[126] What seems clear from these analyses is that MacDonald's main goal in enacting protective union measures was not to solve the plight of trade unions per se, but rather to negotiate a complex series of political and economic challenges. A key issue, as Bernard Ostry has pointed out, was immigration, and the need to attract and retain the skilled working classes required to meet nation-building demands.[127] Much needed and substantial inward flows of British and American skilled workers between 1868 and 1870, driven by economic downturns in the UK and US markets, 'chain migration' pulls from successfully emigrated and integrated family and friends, and targeted efforts by emigration agents, diminished as economic opportunities improved in the UK and the USA in the early 1870s. In response, in early 1872 the Canadian Parliament passed two Immigration Acts and set up assisted passage schemes designed to bolster inward

---

[125] Careless, *Brown of the Globe*, vol. 2, p. 296.
[126] Mark Chartrand, 'The First Canadian Trade Union Legislation: An Historical Perspective', *Ottawa Law Review* 16 (1984); Creighton. *John A. Macdonald*, pp. 125–7. Ostry, 'Conservatives, Liberals, and Labour in the 1870s'.
[127] Ostry, 'Conservatives, Liberals, and Labour in the 1870s', pp. 107–9.

migration. General protection of workers' rights, as enshrined in the British Trade Union Act of 1871, demanded similar responses if Canada wished to promote itself as equally welcoming to British skilled workers.

MacDonald's union manoeuvering was transacted also against a need to steer through Parliament other controversial trade and economic initiatives. The first was the Washington Treaty, a bilateral trade agreement tortuously negotiated between Britain and the USA with Canadian involvement as junior partner, whose key outcomes were the settling of border claims, the offering to Canadians of access to US fishing grounds, and the legislative enshrining of US fishing rights in Canadian waters. The second involved the incorporation of British Columbia into the Canadian federation, the price of which was a promise to complete the Canadian Pacific Railway within ten years, so offering a transcontinental railway link to the Pacific and opening the territory to new settlement. Key Conservative and opposition Liberal politicians strenuously opposed these proposals as threats to Canadian fishing industries and general financial stability. Joseph Howe, a Conservative Cabinet minister, nearly lost his position for publicly denouncing the former as England's attempt to 'buy her own peace at the sacrifice of our interests', while Liberal voices argued against the latter 'as being reckless and improvident, and far beyond the resources of the Dominion'.[128] Upcoming federal elections in which the Conservative party faced strong Liberal campaigns also preoccupied MacDonald. The Trade Union Act, therefore, represented a powerful mechanism by which to connect with over 50,000 industrial working-class citizens across the Canadian provinces and to discomfit Liberal opposition. It also allowed Macdonald to tweak the Liberals' irascible leader George Brown, MacDonald gadfly and key anti-unionist opponent of the Toronto printers. MacDonald drew on British legislation passed under the premiership of Liberal icon Gladstone, allowing him also to annoy Canadian Liberals by appropriating a political arena they considered to be their own.

While politically the battle for union recognition had been won, the print strike itself petered out into failure. Strikebreakers were still being recruited to fill vacated positions, strike funds were running out, and employers were refusing to give ground beyond the concessions offered in late March. By the end of May, the union conceded that their working hour demands would not be met, and on 1 June union members voted by thirty-seven to five to cease the strike, suspend strike levies and payments, reopen closed offices, and regain where possible their former positions. In return for conceding the fight, the Master Printers agreed to wage increases for day hands, and also agreed to shorten the working hours on Saturday, bringing the working week total close to the fifty-four hours demanded.[129] In addition, the union had reached agreement for a fifty-four-hour working week with several key print employers who had broken with George Brown, and had been joined by the Bookbinders Union, whose parallel strike had resulted in all Toronto bookbinder employers agreeing to implement the fifty-four hour week by late May.

---

[128] Quoted in Creighton, *John A. Macdonald*, p. 125; Quoted in Chartrand, p. 293.
[129] Careless, *Brown of the Globe*, vol. 2, pp. 296–7.

AFTERMATH

As in almost every other print strike example from this decade, the nine-hour movement exacted a heavy toll on union membership and finances. TTS membership more than halved as a result, dropping from 190 in 1871 to ninety in 1872, though the end of 1873 saw the union recuperate some ground, with membership rising to 135.[130] Skilled members did leave in search of work elsewhere, some of whom 'were regarded as…the *best* men in their various departments of the craft'.[131] It took several years for union funds to be rebuilt to their previous healthy standing. Nevertheless, the Toronto printers enabled other unions to draw on their example to argue for similar working hour concessions. It would take their US print counterparts several decades to achieve such reductions in their own working hours.

Other parties took note of the results. The *Scotsman* reported extensively on the Toronto strike over the months it ran. When its own men struck that summer, it drew interesting parallels between the two events. The Canadian premier John MacDonald's rapturous welcome at a trade union testimonial event in September 1872, in which he was praised for coming to the aid of the workers and presented with a gold mounted ebony walking stick, was followed by a speech in which he alluded to his role in introducing the Trade Union Act, vindicating the rights of the imprisoned print trade unionists. The *Scotsman*'s Canadian correspondent noted the parallels between the two events, concluding, 'The labour question, however, with all due deference to the Premier, is a dangerous matter to introduce into political speeches for, like Faust of old, those handling the subject might eventually find they had raised a Frankenstein that all the Parliamentary legislation in the world cannot allay.'[132] Yet by the end of the decade, other gains would be recorded in a number of print centres, as well as significant defeats.

CONFRONTATION AND UNION ACTION IN DUBLIN, 1877–1878

Similar trade battles would surface in Dublin five years later. Local concerns around wages would lead to several strikes coalescing around working hours and debates in the British parliament over national print boundaries and gender issues. The events pitted the Dublin Typographical Provident Society against Dublin printers, led by yet another print mogul, Alexander Thom. Debates and outcomes like those seen in Edinburgh and Toronto awaited Dublin print union counterparts, but with interesting political dynamics becoming intertwined in the strike narrative.

The development of printing unions in Ireland had its start in the early nineteenth century, with the founding of the Dublin Typographical Provident Society

---

[130] Zerker, *The Rise and Fall of the Toronto Typographical Union, 1832–1972*, p. 87.
[131] *The Ontario Workman*, 20 June 1872, quoted in ibid, p. 87.
[132] 'From Our Own Correspondent', *The Scotsman*, 19 September 1872.

(DTPS) in 1809, and on which scholars like Charles Benson, Mary Pollard and Vincent Kinane have written.[133] A short-lived regional union, the Irish Typographical Union, was also extant between 1836 and 1841. In the 1850s and 1860s, Irish union activity began gathering momentum and strength, with the revitalization of the Dublin Typographical Provident Society, the absorption of Irish regional printing union clusters into the English based Typographical Association, and the parallel development of its Scottish counterpart, the Scottish Typographical Association (STA). The DTPS was representative of most members of the trade at the time, though exact numbers of print workers in Dublin during the latter half of the 19th century are hard to come by. One source quotes a total of 899 letterpress printers employed in the 1860s, while union records for 1870 show letterpress membership standing at just over 690, or roughly 77 per cent of Dublin's estimated total print trade workforce.[134]

As in the rest of the United Kingdom, the early 1870s was a boom period for the Irish print trade; but 1877 and 1878 were less kind to key Irish print centres, as worldwide recession began to affect trade activity. Attempts to improve wages and working conditions were less well received. Thus, print union strikes for wage increases during this period, such as one between July and November 1877 in Limerick, were fiercely resisted and often defeated by employers. Consequently, large numbers of strike hands subsequently spread across Ireland, Scotland, England, and the USA in search of work.

As in Edinburgh, Dublin unions could find themselves dragged into internal disputes over individual firm practices instigated by local Chapels. From mid- to late 1877, for example, the Dublin Typographical Providential Society faced an ongoing dispute with the printers M.H. Gill & Son over font sizes used to set work for the firm. Following the takeover of the printing firm by James McGlashan in 1875, the firm had begun to install cheaper font types and to insist their men use them. Longstanding M.H. Gill workers complained they were forced to set type with fonts thinner than the normal standard, and being paid less as a result in comparison to other print houses. If your pay was based on these scales, as opposed to 'stab', or established weekly wages, size of fonts mattered. The larger the font, the more lines were needed to complete texts, the more you earned. Thinner fonts meant more words crammed into each line set. Wages decreased accordingly.

Correspondence flowed back and forth between January 1877 and May 1878 disputing whether these fonts were fair, average standard size or 'bastard', that is, a fraudulent non-standard size. The union upheld the case-room's view that they were thinner than normal standards and so required payment at the rate of 26 ens per alphabet, while Gill disputed this and refused to pay more than 24 ens per alphabet. At a meeting between the Union and the Master Printers' Association on

---

[133] See for example Charles Benson, 'The Dublin Book Trade 1801–1850, 4 Volumes', PhD thesis, Trinity College, Dublin, 2000; Kinane, *A History of the Dublin University Press, 1734–1976* (Dublin: Gill and Macmillan, 1994); Mary Pollard, *A Dictionary of the Members of the Dublin Book Trade, 1550–1800* (London: Bibliographical Society, 2000).

[134] Nicholas McGrath, 'Meandering through the Past'. In *Dublin Typographical Provident Society records*: Trinity College Dublin, p. 1870.

1 March 1877 it was agreed that a survey would be done of other firms and their rates of pay and the results would inform whether Gill agreed to the demands. It was found that most Dublin firms were indeed paying higher rates for the thinner fonts, and so Gill agreed to the rise. This would be undone in March 1878, when Gill used the pretext of the strike then engulfing the Dublin print trade to cease such extra payments.

Labour disputes over wage calculations determined by font and typeface sizes were common over the nineteenth century, particularly given the finely attuned manner in which such piece rate system of payments effectively dis-incentivised efficiency in working practices. The most striking example of strike action over font sizes during the 1870s was the walkout in Stuttgart, Germany in January 1872, when newly unionized compositors and journeymen printers (293 in total) downed tools over a wage decline caused by new payment calculations based on wider typefaces. As Reinhold Reith notes, Stuttgart workers argued for a shift to the so-called 'Alphabetrechnung' system, where the whole alphabet was the basis for wage calculations.[135] This ran counter to general practices in Stuttgart that used either the 'Tausenderpreis' system, where composers were paid for the amount of type that was set in a week, or the '1000 n-Rechnung' system, where wages were calculated based on the size of the lower case 'n' in the relevant typeface. Printing firms in other cities such as Berlin and Hanover had agreed to wages based on the 'Alphabetrechnung' system. Stuttgart workers sought parity. They were met with robust resistance: the master printers locked them out, brought in strike-breaking workers (though contemporary reports suggest not more than thirty were induced to risk the wrath of printer colleagues), and also drafted in soldiers to help run the printing works.[136] More than half the strikers left with union backing to seek work elsewhere, part of union strategies to tactically manage the flow of workers across regional borders in moments of crisis and trade disputes.[137]

In Dublin, as the union began debating payment scales at Gill, more militant union members declared it was time to demand wage increases for both established and casual or line employment across the Dublin print trade. A committee meeting was called on 17 November 1877 to consider the matter, with one office bearer missing. Two of the four office bearers present favoured moving forward with a Memorial to employers requesting wage rises and increases in line work rates. Two argued for deferring action. At a full committee meeting on 20 November 1877, the committee swung round and unanimously decided to implement a plan of action. The committee sent Dublin print employers warning that a Memorial would be issued on 3 December 'seeking an advance on the present Scale of Prices'. Two separate Memorials were issued addressing related matters, one to firms operating Book and Press Departments, the other to firms running Newspaper

---

[135] Reinhold Reith, *Lohn Und Leistung. Lohnformen Im Gewerbe 1450–1900* (Stuttgart: Franz Steiner Verlag, 1999), s. 228f.

[136] Anon, *The Newspaper Press*, 1 February 1872.

[137] My thanks to Jan Alessandrini, Paul van Capelleveen, John P. Chalmers, David Oels, and Bernhard Wirth for their help in locating and interpreting relevant Dutch, English, and German language sources on this subject.

Departments. Print employers were given a month to respond, with strike action planned in early February if the requests were not honoured. Both Memorials requested an increase of two shillings in established weekly wages ('stab' rates) to £1.15.0 (or 35 shillings), an increase of one halfpenny to 6d per 1,000 ens for line work, and other pro rata increases. Newsprint workers also requested increases in the differential wages for work on daily, evening, and weekly papers, as well as a reduction to fifty-four working hours a week.[138]

This was a high-risk strategy. At the time, though union members might have disputed this, Dublin wage rates (33 shillings per week stab wages and 5½d per 1,000 ens) were high in comparison with other print centres in Britain. Comparable rates across Britain at the time varied, with the lowest rates in regional print centres such as Birmingham (27 shillings a week) and Dundee (22 shillings a week, 5½ pence per ens, negotiated in 1866 and in force through to 1880).[139] London was the only major centre that operated a weekly 'stab' rate higher than Dublin, with comparable employees in Edinburgh, Glasgow, Liverpool and Manchester averaging lesser rates of between 28 to 31 shillings per week.[140] Thus raising the 'stab' rate would have brought Dublin print worker wages in line with the highest earners in London, but not many others.

Likewise, working hours were a constant area of contention between employers and workers. General hours in Dublin had reduced in the early part of the decade because of negotiations by the DTPS, shifting from an average sixty hours a week in 1870 to fifty-seven hours a week in 1872, though some firms still operated a fifty-nine-hour week in 1877.[141] In other regional centres, battles over working weeks became a key feature of trade action during this period, part of the nine-hour day movement increasingly advocated by general trade unions. Between 1870 and 1880 many print trade associations were successful in lowering working hours from between fifty-seven and sixty hours to fifty-one to fifty-four hours. As noted already, in London and Edinburgh negotiations had led to working hours shifting from sixty hours a week in 1869 to fifty-four a week by 1872.[142] Dublin workers therefore felt justified in demanding parity with other trade colleagues.

The union argued that despite it having been a good period for the print trade, wages across the sector in Dublin had not increased since 1870. Living costs had

---

[138] 'Dublin Typographical Provident Society Committee Minute Books'. OL Microfilm 704, roll 90/34, July 1875–December 1877.

[139] Alloway, 'Appendix A: Personnel in the Print and Allied Trades', p. 485; 'Dundee Typographical Society Minute Books, 1858–1877', in *Dundee Typographical Society Records* (Dundee City Archives). MS 2322, 16 December 1865. Dundee Union Committee notes record agreement after several months of negotiation of the following rates across the city's printing houses: 'Resolved that the rate of wages on and after the first week of January 1866 for the profession in Dundee, must stand as follows: Newspaper Day Work 5½d per thousand; Newspaper Night Work 7d per thousand; Jobbing Offices not less than 22/- per week.'

[140] Alloway, 'Appendix A: Personnel in the Print and Allied Trades', p. 485.

[141] Kinane, *A History of the Dublin University Press*, pp. 177–9. DTPS committee minutes from 30 January 1878 note, for example, that a fifty-nine-hour week was still in place in the printing firm Alley & Reilly (OL Microfilm 704, roll 90/34, Committee Minute book Jan 1878–Feb 1879, 30 January 1878).

[142] E. Howe and H. Waite, *The London Society of Compositors (Re-Established 1848): A Centenary History* (London: Cassell and Company, 1948), pp. 214–18.

risen substantially and other trade sectors had gained wage increases to compensate. Likewise, other trade centres across the UK had seen fairer working hours negotiated, acknowledging also the higher productivity resulting from the installation of more efficient equipment and rearrangement of working spaces. It was only fair that these factors should be considered, and wage increases applied equally to printers in Dublin's book, jobbing and newspaper printing industries.

MASTER PRINTERS RESPOND

A consortium of print employers met on 11 December 1877 to consider the union's demands. 35 firms signed a statement rejecting the requests, which was communicated on 8 January 1878. Union delegates met on 10 and 19 January 1878 to discuss the collective employers' responses to the separate book and newspaper memorials. On both occasions, chapel representatives from twenty-seven print and twenty-five newspaper establishments respectively voted unanimously to take 'extreme measures' to force the issue, and ballots were issued to society members in both sectors. By 22 January, voting results had come in: 375 members of book and press departments in favour, with fifty against, while on the newspaper press side, 366 were in favour and eight against. Employers met with union delegates in the weeks following and offered small compromises on piece, token and newspaper rates, but refused to accede to the key demand of a two-shilling increase in the 'stab' rate.

The results were robustly debated at a fractious general delegates meeting held at the Rotunda Exhibition Room on 16 February 1878, attended by over 400 members. The din was extraordinary and few could get a word in edgewise. Individual house delegates fought each other over whether to accept the compromises or not, with militant sections shouting down those who favoured a more conciliatory approach. When a delegate from the University Press advocated accepting the compromise, other members responded furiously. 'The uproar was tremendous, it was impossible to hear the sense of what he was speaking', recorded the Secretary at that stage. A second delegate called for the postponement of the meeting to give chapels more time to consult individually and was shouted down with loud cries of 'no, no'.[143] At one point, with three fights going on simultaneously in different parts of the room, the frustrated Chairman 'wanted to know if anything but boxing was to be done'.[144] He left the room in face of the chaos, and was only persuaded to return once a modicum of order had been restored. Ultimately, further arbitration with the employers was rejected, and a vote on implementing full strike action was taken, with 300 in favour and 42 against. The secretary, not normally given to personal commentary on proceedings, concluded his report in damning fashion that the meeting would 'live in memory as one of great disorder, caused solely by about six members appearing in a state of intoxication'.[145] Later meetings

---

[143] 'Dublin Typographical Provident Society Committee Minute Books', 16 February 1878.
[144] Ibid., 16 February 1878.   [145] Ibid., 16 February 1878.

would prove no less fractious, with one memorable incident involving a *Nation* chapel delegate being fined 2 shillings and 6 pence for slurs made against a *Freeman* delegate, and as he was being tossed out of the room defiantly challenging the *Freeman* delegate to accompany him to the yard 'to have it out'.[146]

The unions gave notice on 18 February that strike action would commence in two weeks' time. Some firms saw justice in the union's requests, and after various negotiations and meetings, agreed to honour the terms. Most were either small firms or ones that had strong links with the union through former membership or through high ratios of union employees. On 3 March 1878, as the strike was due to commence, the strike committee welcomed a report that twenty-one newspaper, book and jobbing print firms had acceded to the memorial, including Falconers, Freemans, Porteous, and Dollards.[147]

Larger employers remained opposed to negotiations. And as in the other strikes examined in this section, one employer played a key role in shaping responses to union demands. Union representatives soon realized that many of the large employers took their lead from Alexander Thom, the most important printing firm in Dublin, in opposing wage rises. As one owner explained, the issue wasn't about fair wages; it was about competition and survival, with Thom key to how matters were conducted in Dublin. 'That gentleman's establishment was the *sui qua non* [sic]', the head of R. D. Webb & Son told a union delegation. 'If he gave the advance all would have to give it. Up to the present he had refused, and he [Webb] must do likewise.'[148]

Alexander Thom (1801-1879) had built a thriving business from 1824 onwards through securing printing contracts for the Post Office of Ireland and for Irish Royal Commission work. In 1844, he founded the work by which he was subsequently known, the *Irish Almanack and Official Directory*, which in a short time, as Charles Benson notes, 'superseded all other publications of the kind in the Irish capital'.[149] Other important developments included taking over the printing of the official *Dublin Gazette* in 1851, and in March 1876 becoming appointed the Queen's Printer for Ireland. Thom's firm was one of the largest in Dublin, in 1878 employing over 160 individuals in various supporting positions, of which around sixty to seventy were journeymen printers tasked with composing, setting and

---

[146] 'Dublin Typographical Provident Society Council Minutes'. OL Microfilm 708, roll 90/14, July 1877–Mar 1883, 20 April 1878.

[147] Ibid. A council minute dated 2 March 1878 lists the following houses 'having conceded the prayer of the Memorial: Atkinsons, Carrolls, Chambers, College, Dollards, Droughts, Falconers, Freeman, Forsters, Gills, Irishman, Kings, Leckies, Piries, Porteous, Powells, Sportsman, Underwood, Whites, Mara's, Martin & Co.' This was a small percentage of the total number of print trade employers in Dublin at the time. The 1880 Kelly's Stationers directory lists 164 newspapers, printers, booksellers, lithographers and stationers operating in Dublin at that period, though how many of these were purely jobbing printers or letterpress firms is not clear.

[148] 'Dublin Typographical Provident Society Committee Minute Books'. OL Microfilm 704, roll 90/34, 29 January 1878.

[149] Charles Benson and C. J. Falkiner, 'Thom, Alexander (1801–1879)', *Oxford Dictionary of National Biography* (Oxford: Oxford University Press, 2004), http://www.oxforddnb.com/view/article/27189, accessed 14 May 2015.

producing print material required.[150] Though contemporary chroniclers may have suggested otherwise, Thom was, as one recent union historian notes, an 'inveterate enemy of trade unionism', whose firm was for many years deemed 'unfair' due to its anti-union stand.[151] Yet given its significance as an employer in the city, it was one of the few in which members were permitted by the DTPS to accept employment without automatic ejection from union membership for working in a 'closed' house.

In February 1878 Thom appointed Edward Thomas Lefroy as manager of his print works. Lefroy was a controversial figure with a background in journalism. He had worked for several years as sub-editor for the *Irish Times*, and for eleven years prior to his appointment had been the leader writer for the *Freeman's Journal*.[152] LeFroy stepped in just as the strike motion was being carried out. Like Thom, Lefroy had little sympathy for unions, and he expressed this through direct means, using the strike as an excuse to reshape the shop-floor into a fully non-unionized space. His decisions and actions, according to a contemporary account, supposedly caused Thom's much distress and perhaps apocryphally led to his early demise, though given Thom's general stance this must be taken with a pinch of salt.

> Mr. Thom's closing years were clouded by labour troubles, and his death is said to have been hastened by the results of a strike in the printing trade in 1878–the first experience of its kind in his long and successful business career. He is believed to have fretted too much over the loss of his old staff of competent craftsmen, when compared with the strike-breakers brought in by his newly-appointed manager, who had ill-advised him to resist the men's demands for an increase of two shillings per week, and who was afterwards cashiered for incompetence. Most of the strike-breakers imported by the manager were unskilled men of poor experience, and the results of their handiwork disorganised Mr. Thom's systematic plant and equipment.[153]

Lefroy did leave the firm in late 1878, though not due to incompetence but rather to ill health.[154] Alexander Thom had held him in great esteem and much trust until that point, attested to by the adding in March 1878 of a codicil to his last will and testament making Lefroy his executor and apportioning LeFroy two-fifths of his interest in his printing and publishing firm.[155] LeFroy passed away from an unspecified illness on 1 September 1879, and Thom was among the mourners at his funeral.[156] Thom would pass away four months later on 22 December 1879.[157]

---

[150] Kinane, *A History of the Dublin University Press*, p. 209; 'The Board of Works Report: Criminal Information against Saunders Irish Daily News', *The Irish Times*, 5 August 1878, p. 5.

[151] McGrath, 'Meandering through the Past', p. 15.

[152] 'The Board of Works Report: Criminal Information against Saunders Irish Daily News', *Irish Times*, 29 July 1878, p. 4.

[153] Joseph W. Hammond, 'The Founder of "Thom's Directory"', *Dublin Historical Record* 8, no. 2 (1946), p. 55.

[154] Obituaries in the following year hinted that Lefroy's long term ill health had impeded his ability to work in his final years, suggesting other factors than incompetence may indeed have been at work in connection with his stepping down from running the print works. See for example 'Death of Mr E. T. Lefroy', *Irish Times*, 1 September 1879, p. 6.

[155] Transcriptions of Alexander Thom's Last Will and Testament from 1877, as well as of the codicils added in 1878, are featured in Colin W. Thom, *Bervie and Beyond* (n.p.: Xlibris Corporation, 2013), pp. 62–6.

[156] 'Funeral of Mr E. T. Lefroy', *Irish Times*, 3 September 1879, p. 6.

[157] Thom, *Bervie and Beyond*, p. 66.

COMMUNICATION NETWORKS IN ACTION

The strike committee knew its survival depended on mobilizing support for its cause. It also needed trade information to anticipate difficulties and negotiate effectively against Dublin print owners. The DTPS minute books record a complex information network in action as the strike unfolded, encompassing local, regional, and national interests.

As many of its counterparts had done in the past, the DTPS turned to 'vigilance committees' to target non-striking workers and send in spies to report on shop-floor activity. Those who uncovered valuable intelligence were rewarded accordingly. Three such spies included Joseph Doyle and Joseph Smith, awarded 10/- and 5/- respectively in March and April 1878 for 'services rendered' as part of the Dublin Steam Printing Company 'Vigilance Committee', and William McCormack, who was commissioned to join the *Irish Times* shop-floor and 'report, in writing, the state of that establishment to the Committee'.[158] Similarly, George Ducker, who petitioned in late April 1878 for his union card and support from the union's emigration fund to seek work in England (for which he was initially awarded £2), was asked by the committee to change his plans and instead join the *Irish Times* to 'work in the interests of the Society'.[159] Patrick O'Brien joined Ducker in June, tasked with providing 'information relating to the internal workings of that establishment'.[160]

At key moments, the strike committee also sent out delegations to benevolent societies and trade unions across the UK to solicit strike funds to sustain its strikers and their families. Two DTPS members made flying visits to London and Birmingham in April 1878 to meet with representatives from the London Society of Compositors and the Provincial Typographical Association, while members of the strike committee visited local trade associations and communicated with sister unions in Cork, Belfast, Glasgow, and Edinburgh. All responded as best they could: by late June the DTPS had received £928 in donations from aligned typographical union branches, including £200 in donations (and a further £300 in loans) from London, £250 in donations and loans from Edinburgh and Glasgow, and sums ranging from £10 to £23 from Belfast, Birmingham, Cork, Leeds, Manchester, and Sheffield typographical branches.[161]

Such gestures were indicative of the way common ground via shared skilled trade identity could cross transnational borders. As the Secretary of the Scottish Typographical Association, John Battersby, remarked in a note to his counterpart in Dublin,

> Be firm and united in your actions, and your efforts, even if not successful, will at least merit the approval and commendation of the printing profession all over the country. We are all men and printers, and may the day soon dawn when one grand national

---

[158] 'Dublin Typographical Provident Society Committee Minute Books'. OL Microfilm 704, roll 90/34, Tuesday 26 March 1878; 16 April 1878.

[159] Ibid., Tuesday 30 April 1878.   [160] Ibid., 11 June 1879.

[161] 'Dublin Typographical Provident Society Council Minutes'. OL Microfilm 708, roll 90/14, 18 May–5 June 1878.

organization will bind us hand in hand together; and while each of us feels the fire of patriotism which longs for freedom and is the outcome of an ardent love of country, let us love each other with the devotion which springs from a true principle on which unionism alone can hope to rest and flourish.[162]

Patterns of support from other trade sectors give valuable insight into the layers of social networks and social capital in operation amongst benevolent trade organizations at the time. In addition to funds from aligned print-trade units, the DTPS received a mixture of support from other technical trades. Many of these took the form of small donations from groups equally engaged in wage and employment struggles, with some coming because of benevolent societies voting to provide general funds or to generate funds from agreed membership levies. Among the most affecting examples from the committee's point of view were several donations received from the Dublin Regular Gentlemen's Bootmakers Association, and the Amalgamated Tailors of Dublin, at the end of June. Each donated £5 and £11.19.0 respectively, raised from levies on their members, and done in recognition of 'kindness and assistance in former years'.[163] The Bootmakers representative added that despite their numbers having halved as a result of past strikes and the depressed state of the trade, 'what was now given was given cheerfully', and further support was promised as best as could be mustered from their reduced membership.[164]

Valuable trade information was also gleaned from allied print union sources on the UK mainland. When the Dublin master printers made moves to recruit strike-breakers from Scotland, Scottish union secretaries quickly reported the news to the Dublin strike committee. Thus, on 4 March 1878, the Edinburgh union secretary wrote warning that an Irish recruitment agent had begun operating out of the *Scotsman* premises. This was an irony not lost on the correspondents, given as noted earlier that the *Scotsman* newspaper had been the source of a bruising, epic and ultimately unsuccessful print strike in 1872 that had led to the ejection of labour organizers and to the news print-room becoming a fully non-unionized, 'closed' shop. Glasgow sent word between January and July 1878 of 'rat' labourers setting out from the city to strike-break in Dublin, and Glasgow membership lists note at least six 'rat' members who left town for Dublin positions during this period.[165]

---

[162] 'Dublin Typographical Provident Society Committee Minute Books'. OL Microfilm 704, roll 90/34, 19 May 1878.

[163] Ibid., 25 June 1878.

[164] Ibid., 25 June 1878. The Bootmakers did come through with further support, handing in another £5 donation raised from membership levies at the end of July.

[165] Ibid. An example of this information circuit includes a note in minutes from 29 January 1878, recording receipt of a telegram from the Glasgow Secretary rapping out: 'Six compositors, non-society men preferred for Saunders News Letter. What relation does it stand to Society? Telegraph reply at once.' To which the answer was: 'Rupture imminent. Six under notice. Relationship unfriendly some time past. Use influence keep back union and non-union men particularly.' Likewise, 20 June 1878 minutes record news from Glasgow 'that two machinemen (Messrs James M'Fadyen and Robert Farquhar were about to start from that town to "rat" it in Dublin.' Glasgow Typographical Union membership lists stridently affixed RAT labels against the following members who left for Dublin during this period: January 1878, James Dowris, William Oliver; March 1878, Joseph Collins; June 1878, Robert Farqhuar, Thomas M'Fadyen, James M'Fadyen. 'Glasgow Typographical Association Membership Lists'. T-GTS 1/2/3-5).

In late April 1878, news arrived from Scottish union sources that a portion of Thom's government contract work was being sent to Government printing office counterparts in Edinburgh. It was an arrangement negotiated by the London government printing office as a means of circumventing strike action in Dublin. Responding to requests for further information, Edinburgh union sources swung into action, scouting out matters and reporting which firms were involved (in this case the previous Scottish Government Printing Office contractor Murray and Gibb and the current contract holder Neill & Co). Pressed on what was being produced and by what means, they noted the firms had split work on a much-delayed title, the 'Index of Births Registered in Ireland in 1868', and that it was 'being entrusted to non-union men and girls, who will probably be able to blunder through it some way'.[166]

PARLIAMENTARY INTERVENTION

Concerned at this new turn of events, and the possibility that in this way Dublin print work would be dispersed to cross-border competitors, the strike committee sought help from supportive Irish Members of Parliament. A two-page printed memorial dated 10 May 1878 was sent to various Home Rule supporting MPs summarizing the situation to date: workers had sought a small two shilling per week increase on established wages and a 1.5 per cent rise in piece work rates; a number of firms had agreed but major establishments, not least the Queen's Printing Office (Thom's), had rejected the request; the resulting strike had been ongoing for almost three months; key firms such as Thom's had sought to hire non-union Scottish and English strike-breaking labourers, and Thom's was sending Government work across to Scotland to be completed 'by non-society men and women' at the expense of the hard working Irish print-trade worker.[167]

Charles Stewart Parnell, Frank H O'Donnell and Alexander Martin Sullivan agreed to raise the matter in Parliament where possible, though as Sullivan pointed out in a private response, there was little hope much could be achieved, given Parliament was unlikely to interfere in an internal trade dispute. As they could not directly sponsor a bill on a strike related issue, Sullivan, Parnell, and O'Donnell decided the best strategy was to attack Thom's response to the crisis, and so question the propriety and legality of sending Irish government work across to Scotland. Surely, they tried to reason, Irish workers, not mainland collaborators, should print Irish documents in Ireland? Such arguments were in line with their general strategy of fighting for Irish control over domestic matters, a strategy that underpinned much of the 'obstructionist' Home Rule discussions that occupied parliamentary debates at the time.

---

[166] 'Dublin Typographical Provident Society Committee Minute Books'. OL Microfilm 704, roll 90/34, Letters dated 27 April 1878, 14 May 1878.
[167] Ibid. Printed Memorial dated 10 May 1878.

The Irish MP trio made their first attempt at a Parliamentary intervention during a debate on 13 May 1878 on a proposed £3,000 subsidy for Hansard's reporting of Parliamentary discussions, and a £298 stationery allocation to the Queen's Universities of Ireland contained within a £376,545 allocation for general government printing needs. Why should Hansard get a subsidy for reporting on Parliamentary matters, they demanded, given its reliance on English press sources for corrections and insertions, and the discrimination inflicted upon the Irish press, who were not permitted to observe Parliamentary proceedings, so denying accurate reflection on Irish issues. Such a point seemed an exceedingly slender reed from which to launch an inquiry into the injustices being suffered by Dublin printers, but Sullivan was the first to try, sidetracking the conversation for a moment. 'Referring to the item for Printing', he began, alluding to the £376,500 budget proposed for Government printing, 'the printers of Dublin had recently made an effort to increase their rate of wages; and, while successful to some extent, it had not altogether succeeded.'[168] He then outlined briefly the attempt to import external workers, and the subsequent move by Thom to outsource material to Scotland, but the point became lost in subsequent heated discussions about the significance of £289 for stationery costs assigned to the Queen's Colleges and Queen's University in Ireland, to which several Irish MPs objected. Why should stationery costs of universities in Ireland, they argued, be subsidized by the government, given the way these institutions discriminated against the Catholic majority? The fact that approval for a printing budget of £376,500 was in danger of being derailed by arguments over a single item of less than £300 did not impress those present, and as the session dragged on past its allotted time, a decision was made to hold over the budget statement for final discussion three days later.

Discussions resumed on 16 May over the proposed printing budget, and much heat and energy was again dedicated to the matter of stationery costs for the Queen's Colleges and University. Threats were made to veto the budget unless the sum was taken out. Questions were asked as to whether the sum was even a valid expense. Could it not be funded through other means? Back and forth the debates raged. Then Parnell and O'Donnell made their move, on a minor note regarding salaries paid to those awarded contracts as official Government printers. Thom's salary came under scrutiny briefly, and with it the opportunity to lay out the union's case: how it had sought a small rise in establishment wages and piece rates, how several print establishments had acceded but not Thom, and how Thom's had subsequently begun outsourcing Irish material to Scottish government printing houses. Dublin livelihoods were being threatened, O'Donnell exclaimed, because of the use of cheap female labour in Edinburgh.

As Sullivan subsequently reported to the DTPS strike committee, this point was not well received, and threatened to undermine all that was being argued for. 'I feared, at one moment at all events', he commented, 'that <u>harm</u> instead of <u>good</u>

---

[168] 'Hansard House of Commons Debates', (London 1878), 13 May 1878, vol. 239, cc1761–1812.

would be done.'[169] Hansard does not record the interjections at this stage, but O'Donnell's explicit gender bias provoked strong negative reactions, for there were many in the debating chamber who objected to this line of argument. 'And why not?' shouted several MPs, while others muttered, 'Quite right, women should get a chance.'[170] In the 1870s, as previously noted, Edinburgh had seen printing houses opened to female workers, following the 1872–73 strike during which many women had been hired and trained to replace unionized male compositors.

By contrast, Irish unions fought fiercely against women entering the profession, though census records show that women were able to advance in other allied trades such as bookbinding, papermaking, bookselling, and stationers offices. In 1861 not a single woman was registered in the Irish census as working in the printing or letterpress trade. By 1871, twenty-five were recorded, most likely based in Dublin, given that the 1881 Dublin census listed nineteen women employed in printing. Which Dublin firms employed them is not clear, though there are suggestions that Thom's may have staffed a composing room with women recruits on the outskirts of Dublin near the Maynooth railway station.[171]

Seeing this argument was not working, Parnell switched tack to concentrate on the issue of national interests and regional printing contracts. In this he was aided by Mitchell Henry, Irish nationalist MP for Galway County, who rose to comment that Thom's monopoly on government printing in Ireland should not form an excuse to oppress employees by shifting work out of the country when it suited. Parnell added that his understanding was that Parliament awarded government printing contracts on the basis that matters referring to Scotland would be printed in Edinburgh, documents referring to Ireland should be produced in Dublin, and printing referring to England should be done in London. It was clear in the papers put forward for Parliamentary vote that this was the principle involved in allocating current funding. National and regional interests were thus being abrogated through Thom's actions. He concluded:

> If a Glasgow printer could do the printing cheaper than anyone else, by all means let the House of Commons, if it desired, give him the work. But, in this instance, the House of Commons had not chosen to do that, the Vote being presented in an entirely different way; and as long as they appeared in that shape, and a Dublin contractor sent his work to Scotland, he (Mr. Parnell) would protest against it.[172]

The Irish MPs pressed the Secretary to the Treasury, Sir Henry Selwyn-Ibbetson, to investigate the matter accordingly, which he grudgingly agreed to do. Buoyed by this turn of events, Parnell wrote to the DTPS on 23 May requesting they put together a statement for the proposed enquiry, which was duly completed and sent on 30 May, and then forwarded by Parnell to Sir Henry.

---

[169] 'Dublin Typographical Provident Society Council Minutes', OL Microfilm 708, roll 90/14, 1 May 1878.
[170] Ibid., 18 May 1878.
[171] Kinane, 'Irish Booklore: A Galley of Pie: Women in the Irish Book Trades', *The Linen Hall Review* 8, no. 4 (1991), pp. 11–12.
[172] 'Hansard House of Commons Debates'. 16 May 1878, vol. 240, cc41–95.

Selwyn-Ibbetson took several weeks to review the material, responding with a formal letter on 12 July 1878. The response was to be expected. In regard to wage demands, it was not the government's business to interfere with an internal matter. Regarding the removal of printing work from Dublin to Scotland, he argued that this had been a decision taken by a central government body (the government printing office) because of the strike's effects on government business. UK government interests trumped regional printing demands. In other words, Thom's could not be blamed for instigating this shift, as he was a mere sub-contractor to central government departments, who had ultimate authority on where relevant printing was undertaken. 'The removal of the work was due to the Public Department in charge of the printing business of the Government, not to the Contractor of the Government', he concluded, 'and that, if it had the effect of temporarily reducing the amount of printing work done for the Government in Dublin, this was a necessary consequence of the unsettled state of the labour market at the time and the delay resulting therefrom.'[173] As Edinburgh union sources confirmed, by this stage London had taken full control of the process and was bypassing Dublin printing circuits, as 'proofs go and come directly from H.M. Stationery Office in London without going near Dublin'.[174]

THE TIDE EBBS

With no relief to be gained from official sources, DTPS members' morale began to collapse, not coincidentally reflected in the utter depletion of union funds in the face of continued employer resistance. Dublin union members were far from united in the militant stance originally proposed; tempers flared, robust language abounded, and as noted earlier brawls punctuated many evening gatherings.

One group caused great aggravation amongst strike members, namely representatives from Thom's Chapel. From the start, aware of the significance of Thom's to the Dublin print economy, its members had consistently opposed radical strike action. They had advocated against stab wage demands and supported compromising for lesser piece rate increases; they had sought to submit a separate memorial to Thom's rather than join the general demands; and on occasion they had suggested steps to support partial lifting of the strike to benefit workers in dire straits. Their conservative approach to negotiations and strike action irritated other members, and in several fractious meetings Thom's delegates were railed against, accused of being 'white torpedoes' intent on scuttling union progress, and on occasion dragged into fracas when tempers overheated to dangerous levels. Their suggestion at a committee meeting in April 1878 that a limited number of union members be allowed to enter employment in 'closed houses', so as to prevent non-union labour taking these jobs and diluting the future position of the union in such places, was thoroughly condemned. A stern notice was subsequently issued to all members

---

[173] 'Dublin Typographical Provident Society Committee Minute Books', OL Microfilm 704, roll 90/34, 12 July 1878.
[174] Ibid., 18 May 1878.

from the Secretary directing 'that on no consideration will members of the Dublin Typographical Society be permitted to work in any Closed House, unless the matter in dispute is finally and satisfactorily arranged between the Society and the employers who still hold out against the moderate increase sought for in the Memorial of December last.'[175] A rehashing of the idea by Thom delegates at a subsequent meeting saw a shout from the Chairman of 'preposterous', followed by 'a scene of great disorder' caused by individuals refusing to sit down or leave the room as the Chair attempted to maintain order.[176]

At the start of the strike, the union had a cash balance of £1135 in reserves. By June, this had dwindled to £354 due to the burden of strike relief payments to out-of-work members. Despite significant donations and loans from allied trade organizations, by 19 October, eight months into the strike, delegates were informed that the union had just enough funds to support a further week's strike benefits. Delegates were instructed to consult colleagues on future steps and return for further talks on 28 October. At that stage striking hands agreed they would settle for returning to the old scale of 33 shillings per week stab wages, but seek reinstatement of the compromise offered of 1 shilling and twopence raise per 1,000 ens on piece rates. Inconclusive negotiations with uncompromising employers dragged on for three weeks, and at a special delegates meeting on 22 November defeat was finally admitted, with a vote of 171 versus 76 in favour of returning to work at pre-strike wages. Members returned to work where they could on 25 November, so ending a bitterly contested and ruinous trade dispute from which little was gained and much was lost.

DUBLIN SUBSIDES

The DTPS emerged from the strike weakened in strength and ability to shape future employment conditions. It would take several decades to pay off the accumulated debts and loans negotiated from sister organizations and to build up union membership to healthy numbers. One major concern was that the large number of 'non-amicables' who had been brought in to strike break would remain *in situ* for years to come. In response to this, though reneging on wage concessions agreed to initially in line with the general employers' position, the sympathetic head of Porteous and Gibb advised the union to strategically 'go back to the old scale, send their men into closed houses and gradually work the non-amicables out'.[177] Given the transient and fluid nature of print worker engagement during this period, over time many scab workers were indeed 'worked out'.

CONCLUSION

As a study in information flow across national borders, these strikes offer a valuable perspective on the strategic development of social capital and trade networks to

---

[175] Ibid., 12 April 1878.   [176] Ibid., 20 April 1878.   [177] Ibid., 21 November 1878.

shape and direct responses to trade struggles and print economies in flux. As events unfolded over a decade-long period of intensive struggle between employers and employees, one can see similar patterns of strike ebbs and flows, as well as common tactics used by opponents: much use was made of trade informants to gather intelligence on employers; there were concerted drives to draw in 'non-amicables' to choke union effectiveness; great use was made of effective links between regional networks to provide financial, moral, and trade backing to strike actions; and political agencies were drawn in to force strategic debates and enquiries in Parliament over gender, labour roles, and national identity issues. The 1870s was an important decade in terms of print trade relations, and while it witnessed many defeats, it also pushed forward debates over labour conditions and working hours that underpinned strategies adopted in future by other trade organization seeking improvements in trade working conditions.

3

Creative Printers
Labour Laureates and the Typographical Trade Press, 1840–1900

From the 1840s, newly emerging print trade unions backed the launch of typographical trade journals in the USA, UK, South Africa, and Australia. Many were short-lived, or underwent multiple transformations of title, frequency, and format throughout their lifespan. Among the first of such print trade journals were London-based ones such as the monthly *Compositors' Chronicle* (1840–3), succeeded by *The Printer* (1843–5); the monthly *Typographical Gazette* (1846–7), revived in 1849 as the *Typographical Protection Circular* (1849–53), relaunched as the *Typographical Circular* (1854–8), then run as the short lived fortnightly *London Press Journal and General Trade Advocate* (November 1858–January 1859), and succeeded by *The Printers' Journal and Typographical Magazine* (1865–7). An Australian trade union sponsored counterpart was the short-lived Melbourne-based *Australian Typographical Circular* (1858–60). Longer lasting were trade union supported or union sympathetic journals such as the New York-based *The Printer* (1852–75), the London-based *Bookbinders' Trade Circular* (1850–77), the Edinburgh run *Scottish Typographical Circular* (1857–1909), recast as the *Scottish Typographical Journal* in 1909, and the Manchester-based *Typographical Societies' Monthly Circular* (1852–74), relaunched as the *Provincial Typographical Society Circular and Monthly* in 1875, then transformed into the *Typographical Circular* in 1877.

MISCELLANY FORMS

The aim of these journals was to inform, entertain, and support the development of a cooperative, shared professional trade identity. As the *Compositors' Chronicle* announced in its launch issue of 7 September 1840, 'Our principal object is to promote a better understanding in regard to the general interests of the trade, and to ensure a more perfect and sincere co-operation on the part of its members, whether in town or country, or whether connected or disconnected with societies.'[1] The editor singled out creative contributions and trade communication from across the United Kingdom as key components of planned journal content: 'The columns of

---

[1] 'Address', *Compositors' Chronicle*, 7 September 1840.

the "Chronicle" will be open to all correspondents whose aim is to promote the interests of the professions', he noted, 'to the secretaries of the various societies in England, Ireland, and Scotland, and to the literary effusions of the members of the trade upon all subjects.'[2]

When the London-based *Typographical Circular* launched in 1854, the editors equally encouraged self-expressive written contributions from its readers and trade members. Such work was vital and relevant to the advancement of the trade, they argued, encouraging communication and intellectual endeavours amongst members, as well as offering space for debate and discussion for those less inclined to oratorical flourishes in public meetings. 'As, however, there are many who, although not calculated to shine at a general meeting (through timidity or want of nerve)', they pronounced, 'yet possess the ability of putting their thoughts into intelligible sentences, the columns of the *Typographical Circular* will afford them the means of doing so, with satisfaction to themselves and benefit to the trade.'[3] The written word was seen as a powerful tool for engagement with fellow members, more so even than the windy words of public speakers – they were not evanescent and quickly forgotten, but thought through, permanently available for considered review and more likely therefore to influence trade views. Contributions from readers were to be welcomed, 'because it is the epitome of such men – thoughtful, studious, and well-informed – which generally sway the decisions of the Trade Delegates in chapel, and are of more importance than the windy speeches of empty orators'.[4]

The *Scottish Typographical Circular* (*STC*), a Scottish union-backed version of the London-based *Typographical Circular,* was launched on 5 September 1857 as a monthly, priced at one-penny with similar commitments to print trade concerns. Financially supported by the Edinburgh Typographical Society, the *STC* closely modelled itself on its London counterpart. When the *Typographical Circular* began publication in 1854, Scottish unions had watched with close interest: the Edinburgh branch committee, for example, immediately put in a subscription for a dozen copies a month, 'given to the Members of the Committee to show the same to their respective Chapels, and one or two copies to be kept at the Committee rooms, for the perusal of any Member that may be present on a Saturday evening'.[5] The *Typographical Circular* proved popular enough that by October the committee had raised its subscription to two-dozen copies a month.

Receipt of the London journal sparked interest in a Scottish version, and through a slow, three-year period of meetings and correspondence, the Scottish Typographical Association (STA) in Glasgow and its Edinburgh branch counterparts worked out relevant details. Unwilling to shoulder the financial editorial and production costs, the STA passed journal responsibilities onto the Edinburgh branch, who duly delivered the first issue of the *STC* in September 1857. Much like its London counterpart, the leading article declared the journal would be devoted to 'the legitimate benefit of the working printer in Scotland, by the dissemination of printing intelligence, and the consideration of the various measures likely to affect

[2] Ibid.   [3] 'Address', *Typographical Circular* 1, New Series (1854).   [4] Ibid.
[5] 'Edinburgh Typographical Society Minute Books'. MS 4068, Vol. 1, 6 April 1854.

his position for better or worse'. This was to be accomplished not only through news articles and trade reports, but also through creative self-expression reflecting the opinions of the print worker, done through featured original verse, prose memoirs and serial fiction.[6]

Likewise, when the London-based *Typographical Circular* was revived in January 1865 as the monthly *The Printers' Journal and Typographical Magazine*, the lead editorial announced its mission would, like its predecessors, include chronicling trade news, commenting on health and safety issues and interestingly, highlighting the art of typography. 'Our chief duties', it noted,

> will be to chronicle the progress of the various department of typography (so far as art itself is concerned); register the current state of business; report the proceedings of our trade and benefit societies; urge the necessity of proper ventilation and improved sanitary arrangements in our workrooms; point out the indispensability of recreation and manly exercise as conservative of health; and afford to printers themselves the opportunity of discussing and ventilating those arrangements which may be most beneficial for them to adopt in the development of their various institutions.[7]

Creative material of interest to readers would also form part of the journal's contents, with the editor promising, 'when space permits, to insert, as cheerful and entertaining company with our budget of news, sketches of a lighter character or short extracts from our best authors'.[8] Owned, edited and mainly written by Thomas Plackett, who had previously been a journeyman compositor on *The Sporting Life*, the journal lasted until 1868, when Plackett's firm went bankrupt as a result of debts accrued in running a short lived, loss making French language evening newspaper.[9]

The early issues of the *Scottish Typographical Circular*, the London-based *Typographical Circular*, the *Australian Typographical Circular*, and the New York-based *The Printer*, demonstrate close affinities with other literary miscellanies of the 1840s and 1850s. The layouts and mixtures of reportage and literary material of the *Australian Typographical Circular*, the *Scottish Typographical Circular*, and the *Typographical Circular*, for example, consciously echoed the formula established by *Chambers' Edinburgh Journal*, and in particular its New Series octavo format of 1844 onwards (see Figure 3.1).

Chambers' Edinburgh Journal originated in 1832, the brainchild of William and Robert Chambers. Its initial format, three columns laid out in a broadsheet format, was revised for a New Series in 1844. The new look *Chambers' Edinburgh Journal* was tightly organized, with a layout in boxed, double column duodecimo octavo form. Gone was the broadsheet formula, replaced by a compact periodical journal size. Each page featured a double column of text enclosed by a double line edge; each column was separated by a thin edged line; the journal title stood at the top, centred and bound within the double line edge; immediately below, two horizontal double lines framed a horizontal column in which was located the issue number on the left-hand side, the day and date centred, and the price on the

---

[6] 'Our Views and Intentions', *Scottish Typographical Circular*, September 1857.
[7] 'Address', *The Printers' Journal and Typographical Magazine*, 2 January 1865.　　[8] Ibid.
[9] 'Forty Years Ago', *London Typographical Journal*, October 1907.

CONDUCTED BY WILLIAM AND ROBERT CHAMBERS, EDITORS OF " CHAMBERS'S INFORMATION FOR THE PEOPLE," " CHAMBERS'S EDUCATIONAL COURSE," &c.

No. 1. New Series.   SATURDAY, JANUARY 6, 1844.   Price 1½d.

THE HOUSE OF NUMBERS.

NATURE nowhere shows her partiality more remarkably than in the very different proportions in which she deals out the ever-succeeding new generation of our race amongst those who are to bring them up. Her average is ascertained to be four and a half children—for statisticians are Solomons in this respect at least, that they never scruple to halve a child—her average, I say, is four and a half children to each couple, and a very fair and reasonable burden this would make, if it were a uniform case, barring, indeed, that the half-child, even though not quite left without a single leg to stand upon, might be rather troublesome to set up in life. But anything like this happy medium—by which I mean four or five—is unfortunately not more frequent of occurrence than almost any other number under twice the amount. Nature, indeed, evidently despises the average of the statisticians. To some she gives six, seven, eight, and so on; to others, three, two, one. Nay, it is not uncommon for her—though this is what a friend of mine, who has twelve, never *could* understand—to give *not even one*. This friend and I once reckoned up above a dozen couples of our common acquaintance who were in this state of double blessedness; all of them professedly most happy and contented in their having been spared the cares, toil, and expense of a family, although vexed every day of their lives at the way in which their friends managed their young flocks, so different from the way in which they knew children *ought* to be managed; so that it might be said their only source of regret was in the accident which had placed the rising generation in the hands of the only people not qualified to rear them. But this again is nothing. The strange thing is, that nature should keep our dozen friends so perfectly exempt from their share of this duty towards society, while to others she deals such a tissue of issue, as make poor men think of such quotations as—

> " Another and another ! Will they stretch on
> Unto the crack of doom"—

or of such venerable and veritable proverbs as, "It never rains but it pours," and all that sort of thing.

My friend—I may as well say at once that it is my cousin John Balderstone—sometimes groans under what he calls his visitation of children; but he is such a happy-tempered fellow, that I cannot doubt that his groans are much more in jest than in earnest. Indeed, I rather think he likes to have a joke now and then at himself and his spouse on the score, as he himself would say, of their score. For instance, he professes that they are pelted with children. He speaks of the *population* of his house. The very children themselves, he alleges, wonder at their own numbers. He had a feeling of alarm, he declares, at every fresh addition up to the sixth; but after that, custom hardened him a little; and ever since the eighth, he has been perfectly indurated. Mrs John, for her part, takes things quite as easily, being entirely of that quiet good temper which one somehow expects in a lady who has had a large family. John often raises a laugh about her anti-Malthusian qualifications, at which she only turns to him one of those placid smiles which speak so much more than words between such as are happily united, and then peaceably resumes her attention to a nameless little garment, which I half believe she has never ceased hemming for the last ten years.

One of John's jokes about his multitudinous state is, that he and other persons in the like circumstances are designed as beacons to give young men in their quadrilling days a salutary caution on the subject of matrimony—at least not to enter upon their matrimonial, till they are pretty sure about their patrimonial state. It is, he says, a kind of final cause for enormous families. Nature—so runs his argument—desires that the population should not increase too fast for subsistence. Were all families moderate in number, thoughtless youth might be encouraged to rush to the temple of Hymen in too great numbers. As a warning, she here and there plants a couple whom she oppresses with a burden of blessings absolutely overwhelming. Young men, seeing such a tremendous risk before them, think it best to keep cool, and go out to India. Syllogistic as this appears, I suspect it to be fallacious at bottom, for, as far as I can see, John and Susan are anything but miserable under their load. Whenever I happen to be in their house, I find it the seat of good humour and comfort; nor is there even more noise or confusion than (let me speak good-naturedly) is bearable. My reasoning rather is, that the polypedic state, as John sometimes calls it, is in itself an evidence (though the converse of the rule may not hold) of the presence of the chief elements of happiness in a house, as health, good temper, sufficiency; for it is never found in any station of life where these do not exist; so that the idea of its being a source of vexation or an oppression may be said to be self-refuted. And I think I shall be able to make good this point before quitting my pen.

John's own constant jocularity on the subject serves to convince me that he at least feels his charge but lightly. Spending a night lately in his house, and getting up rather early, I met him in the staircase, when he told me he would show me a sight. He then led me along a passage, at the end of which was an apartment which I recognised as the nursery, from the school-like murmur of little voices which proceeded from it. There, upon a long table, was ranged, in two rows, a series of shoes of almost all sizes, reminding me very much of the stalls for the sale of such articles second-hand, which are to be seen in the humbler parts of our city. " John, what a bill this speaks of," said I. He only laughed, and then led me to a window commanding a view of his washing-green, where I saw such ropefuls of little petticoats, and little stockings, as were perfectly bewildering. I held up my hands in astonishment: John only laughed once more. We took a short walk, and returned to breakfast, when my ears were saluted by a confused noise proceeding from a side-room. "What is that?" said I. " Oh," said he, " only the meal mob." The mystery and the phrase were explained together, when he opened a door and showed me a multitude of little

right-hand side. It is unclear whether this layout was original to Chambers or an adaptation of competitor penny press publications. What is certain is that it influenced key literary periodicals and miscellanies that followed. These included *Sharpe's London Magazine* (later *Sharpe's London Journal*), launched in November 1845 as a 1½ penny weekly, and Dickens's *Household Words*, started in 1850 (see Figures 3.2 and 3.3).

The launch of the *Typographical Circular* in 1854 (see Figure 3.4) saw adoption of the *Chambers' Edinburgh Journal* format, copying layout, size, and price (one penny), and a similar miscellany formula of news items, book reviews, creative fiction and poetry that echoed textual conversations across genres found in both *Chambers' Edinburgh Journal* and *Household Words*.

The *Scottish Typographical Circular*'s first six issues, published between September 1857 and January 1858 on a probationary basis, were not dissimilar to the original unrevised format of *Chambers's Edinburgh Journal*, in this case issued as a four-page broadsheet on blue paper. In March 1858, however, the journal was expanded to eight pages royal Octavo style, and revised to closely align with the miscellany style used in the 1844 *Chambers' Edinburgh Journal* relaunch and subsequently adopted by the *Typographic Circular*, as per Figure 3.5. The *STC* used this format until September 1861, when a new editor simplified its layout and adopted a similar sized but boxed, one column format.

The *Australian Typographical Circular* (Figure 3.6), launched in January 1858 by the Victoria Typographical Association, followed the lead of the *Typographical Circular*, adopting the same octavo size and two columned, boxed layout, and featuring a similar mixture of commentary, readers' correspondence, poetry, news and miscellany material. Its mission was, like its counterparts and predecessors, to offer a space for the practical printer 'because he has something to say which he earnestly believes to be worthy of utterance'.[10] The journal, though ostensibly conducted on behalf of the general Australian typographical and print trade community, was like its Scottish counterpart edited and run by a regional branch of the typographical trade association. The Melbourne-based Victoria branch shouldered the costs and labour of production, though it was careful from the onset to suggest the journal was meant to be a resource for everyone involved in Australian printing. 'It will be sufficient to say, here', noted the editor, 'that in its design it is intended to be the receptacle of information forwarded by the authorized contributors of the various districts, and not at all with the view to enforce the individuality or editorial eccentricities of it conductor upon the members of the profession.'[11]

The goal, as the initial editorial made clear, was to be as comprehensive as possible, extending beyond the regional boundaries of the trade in Victoria: 'We disclaim any desire on our part to limit its sphere of usefulness to this colony', though its comprehensiveness had to then rely on the willingness of regional correspondents to supply the journal with relevant material.[12] It would be greeted with pleasure both at home and overseas, with international counterparts welcoming this partner in international trade news exchange. 'We wish to our

---

[10] Anon, *The Australian Typographical Circular*, January 1858.   [11] Ibid.   [12] Ibid.

among millions of beings. The earth is poorly tilled, and vast tracts of it are left totally wild. Mines remain unworked, and immense natural treasures wholly undeveloped. Rivers, towns, tribes, hills, lakes, and even kingdoms exist here unknown to Europeans, and only described in the reports of the barbarian traders. It is evident that civilization has found few resting-places on this " wild and swarthy shore."

On the borders of the Atlantic and the Eastern Oceans, the Red and the Mediterranean Seas, as well as around the Nubian Deserts, lie kingdoms which we cannot enumerate. At the extreme south is our flourishing and important colony of the Cape of Good Hope, whose prosperity will shortly receive such an impulse from steam communication with Great Britain. Rounding the famous promontory of Rams, and sailing northward, we reach the newly settled district of Natal. Of these settlements we shall have more to say, especially of the latter, which has recently been much misrepresented.

On the shores of the Mediterranean lies Algeria, the scene of French conquest, which presents some curious facts for our contemplation in another notice. At a few other points on the coast European flags have been fixed, but principally as naval stations. It will be remembered that Gordon Cumming, who displayed so much manly valour in his conflicts with the gazelles and giraffes of South Africa, penetrated further into the countries beyond Kaffirland than any previous traveller. He crossed extensive tracts north of the Bamangwato Mountains, among the boundless elephant forests. He found them inhabited by numerous tribes, and densely swarming with the nobler orders of the animal creation. Many other gentlemen have, within a few years, visited different parts of Africa, obtaining a knowledge of their resources and their social state. One has just returned with an interesting picture of life in Dahomey, another has described his visit to Algeria, another has accompanied a French expedition among the wild tribes of the Kabylie. Mr. Richardson, with several companions, is, as we have said, exploring the interior. Bayle St. John lately visited the little-known Oases of Garah and Siwahah, and is now prosecuting his researches on the banks of the Nile, though we know not whether he may be enabled to reach the White River and explore it even so far as Werne went.

With this slight glance at the aspect of Africa, and the recent endeavours to improve our knowledge of its geography, we conclude our first notice of the great continent. We shall next sketch, briefly, the present state of the slave trade, the foreign and domestic commerce, the condition of our settlements, and the French possessions. A plan has been proposed for extirpating by the roots the inhuman traffic in negroes. This we shall briefly describe and submit it to discussion. Many projects have been started, but all have, hitherto, failed, though our African squadron does good service by checking what it cannot destroy. It will be a melancholy day for Africa, if ever this check should be withdrawn. We

are advancing towards success in the great object which humanity has in view, and it will be poor policy now to abandon the African coasts to the undisputed reign of slavers, that they may run riot in their hideous occupation. The Americans are anxious to abolish the vile traffic. Let it be remembered we gave it to them. It is an inheritance they received from Great Britain, but their landed proprietors, the aristocratic lords of the soil, in the southern states, cling to it, and it is only by civilizing Africa that we can cut off their supply of slaves.

LOVE GIFTS.

(FROM THE ITALIAN.)

BY S. LEY WOLMER.

Two gentle lovers to an absent friend
Some gifts of love's remembrance fain would send.
The youth an off'ring of a rose-bud bore,
The damsel on her breast a lily wore;
This rose, he said, her clustering hair shall deck,
And this fair gem shall sparkle on her neck.
And this lily send, the girl replied;
My chasten'd flower shall be thy rose's bride.
Sweet love, the youth replied, Oh ! never spare
From thy fair breast the lily—guard it there.

AUTOBIOGRAPHY OF EMINENT MEN.

BENJAMIN FRANKLIN.

EVERYBODY has heard of Benjamin Franklin, how from a poor printer's boy he raised himself, by following out his own maxims of thrift and perseverance, to be one of the first citizens of Philadelphia; that he took an important part in the struggle which ensured the independence of America, became her representative in foreign courts, and died full of years and honours, embalmed in the hearts of his countrymen, and venerated by the whole civilized world. In the intervals of leisure he left behind him an Autobiography, certainly one of the most delectable as well as the most instructive ever penned by mortal. As the whole may now be bought for a shilling, we shall allow ourselves but a few racy extracts, which will serve however to convey a distinct idea of the moral idiosyncrasy of the man.

In proposing to write his memoirs, Franklin sets out in the peculiar vein of pleasantry that runs through all his writings:—

" In thus employing myself, I shall yield to the inclination so natural to old men, of talking of themselves and their own actions; and I shall indulge it without being tiresome to those who, from respect to my age, might conceive themselves obliged to listen to me, since they will be always free to read me or not. And, lastly (I may as well confess it, as the denial of it would be believed by nobody), I shall, perhaps, not a little gratify my own vanity. Indeed, I never heard or saw the introductory words, 'Without vanity I may

Figure 3.2. *Sharpe's London Journal,* 1845

"*Familiar in their Mouths as HOUSEHOLD WORDS.*"—Shakespeare.

HOUSEHOLD WORDS.

A WEEKLY JOURNAL.

CONDUCTED BY CHARLES DICKENS.

Nº· 204.]　　　SATURDAY, FEBRUARY 18, 1854.　　　[Price 2d.

BIRTH OF PLANTS.

The Vegetable World bears inscribed upon its glorious front, a threefold purpose. The first, implies that which Emerson would delight to call the culinary use of plants. Under this aspect we regard the plant as ministering to the sustenance of the whole animal world, and above all, of mankind : not alone furnishing the basis of the existence of the human race, but affording the materials for boundless appliances of comfort and convenience. This material relation of the vegetable world, although most important, socially considered, æsthetically must be regarded as the meanest ; since it ultimately concerns the animal requirements of each individual, however much these may be glossed over by refinement. Far more lofty is the part which the plant world plays in the regulation of the all-embracing operations of the universe. The scorched and rainless desolation of the Sahara, and the overflowing wealth of vitality in the humid forests of the gorgeously clothed tropics, partly owe their characteristic peculiarities to the action of the plant creation. Varying states of climate, dry or humid atmosphere, parched or moist soil, scanty or abundant development of animal, and especially of human, life, in the mass, find their mastering conditions in the nature and extent of local vegetation. Herein the vegetable world is related to the well-being and actual existence of whole races, and the great physical features of entire regions.

But the most sublime and exalted mission of the vegetable creation is as the material interpreter of the spiritual ; the veil which conceals but yet declares the mighty Author and Sustainer—the gorgeous tapestry of God's great temple ; the emblem of the Eternal; teaching us to look for the permanent through the mutable and fleeting. The spiritual ordinance of eternal being is nobly symbolised to us in the immutable law of vegetable nature, which decrees that death shall proceed out of life, and life out of death ; that the living animal shall feed its vitality upon the dead plant, and the living plant upon the dead animal ; that decomposition shall be but the commencement of recomposition ; and putrefaction but the symbol of renewed production.

" For though to every draught of vital breath,
Renewed throughout the bounds of earth or ocean,
The melancholy gates of death
Respond with sympathetic motion ;
Though all that feeds on nether air,
Howe'er magnificent or fair,
Grows but to perish and entrust
Its ruins to their kindred dust ;
Yet, by the Almighty's ever-during care
Her procreant vigils nature keeps
Amid the unfathomable deeps,
And saves the peopled fields of earth
From dread of emptiness or dearth."

The inexhaustible fertility of the vegetable world affords matter for profound wonder and admiration to the naturalist. Does a volcanic island rise from the ocean, bare and devoid of aught that can allure man to take up his habitation on its soil, or that can furnish food for his sustenance or implements for his use, yet when years have rolled on, it will be covered by a peculiar form of vegetation, to which will succeed others more perfect ; and the sun that glared upon a smoking rocky mass may smile upon an earthly paradise. What have been the weapons which nature has here employed to battle against want and desolation, to cast out death and implant the germs of life ? The waves have wafted the seeds of vegetation, and the winds have carried them on their wings. Strangely fashioned insects and brilliantly plumed birds have paused in their flight to wonder or to rest, and, pursuing their careless way, have left precious traces of their visit—the seeds of a teeming host of plants.

" Thus in the earth, in water, and in air,
In moisture and in drought, in heat and cold,
Thousands of germs their energies unfold."

To us, then, it is of the deepest interest to investigate the means by which the limits of the vegetable kingdom are extended, and the multiplication of plants is effected. And even if the relation which this all-important process bears to the life of the universe were less lofty than we have seen it to be, the phenomena accompanying it might well arrest our attention. The function of reproduction is performed in all flowering plants, by the aid of the blossom. In nature everything has a meaning and a purpose : nothing which is

Figure 3.3. *Household Words*, 1854

THE

TYPOGRAPHICAL CIRCULAR.

𝔄 Journal devoted to the Interests of the Printing Profession.

No. 11.—New Series.]   FEBRUARY 1, 1855.   [Price 1*d.*

THE PRINTERS' LIBRARY AND NEWS ROOM.

In our last number we called the attention of the trade to the evils attendant upon the present system of the "call slate," and briefly adverted to the advantages that would result from the establishing of a library and reading room, for the use of the trade, which might, we believe, be carried into operation, were the Society house removed from its present undignified situation; and we deem the subject one of such extreme importance that we venture again to call the attention of our readers to the proposed library and news room.

There is probably no class of working men who in their daily employment so much require information from books as compositors; to them reading and instruction are not merely matters of amusement but of necessity—without them a man can scarcely be otherwise than an incompetent workman, a bore to readers, who are often exasperated (but sometimes amused) at the foolish errors which are committed, for want of that intelligence which only a comparatively small amount of reading would have conferred. Such a man is also of little value to an overseer, who finds himself harassed and the work impeded, by the mass of corrections which have to be made in the "first proof," which frequently causes disappointment and vexation to authors, who cannot get their proofs at the time appointed, and are even then subjected to the annoyance of finding errors which have escaped the reader, owing to his attention being so much diverted. No wonder, then, that when a period of slackness arrives, the overseer makes a selection, and discharges first those who have given so much trouble, and who thus suffer severely from the neglect of mental culture.

Yet, under present circumstances, how difficult it is for one whose early education has been neglected to raise himself to that standard which is so essential; for while we are ever ready to blame those who fall into bad habits, we yet take no steps to provide the means of usefully occupying their leisure time, but leave the matter in the hands of the publican, who, more alive to his own interest, provides for his customers every species of gaming, generally ending in quarrelling or fighting, and thus the time which might be employed in mental culture is spent in debasing and enervating both mind and body. If, on the other hand, a suitable room in a central situation were provided, supplied with newspapers and periodicals, and with a library stored with books of an instructive and entertaining character, well conducted and made comfortable, we are confident that it would be highly appreciated and well attended, and would lead to a great improvement in the habits of the members of the trade, who would become more elevated and refined, and, from being better informed, would bring a higher degree of intelligence to the discussion of trade questions, and thus avoid those errors which have been so fatal to the best interests of many other trades. And in proportion as an improvement took place, should we advance in the social scale, and by showing that we possessed a fair share of self-respect, command the respect of others.

We do not deny that in carrying out the proposed arrangement some difficulties would have to be encountered; but they are only in matters of detail, and would certainly be overcome if set about in earnest; and we could at once point to a number of men who take the deepest interest in the subject, to whom the trouble to be taken would indeed be a "labour of love,"—men who possess sufficient energy and influence to carry to a successful issue whatever they undertake, and by whom the gratification of benefiting their fellow men would be deemed a sufficient reward.

Where, then, is the difficulty that could not be overcome? It cannot be the expense; for surely no one will assert that a society numbering nearly 3000 members, with a large sum in hand, which, in spite of the amount voted to other trades, has during the past year been increased by upwards of 400*l.*, cannot afford to pay the additional ten or twenty pounds a year for rent which would be required. The only reason for transacting the Society business at a public house was on account of want of funds, and, the use of the secretary's room being at that time given gratuitously, the saving was an object; but as 20*l.* a year is now charged, and the society is in a highly flourishing condition, circumstances are wholly changed, and reasons which were all-powerful at one time are now unworthy of consideration.

If, then, the trade is convinced that the object to be attained is a good one, let us not be deterred by seeming difficulties, but set about the matter with vigour, and with a determination to overcome every obstacle. The only real difficulty lies in the supineness of the members of the trade, who appear to have fallen into a kind of lethargy, from which it is exceedingly difficult to arouse them. It is an old proverb, that "What is everybody's business is nobody's business;" but we trust that some

Figure 3.4. *Typographical Circular*, 1855. (© St Bride's Library)

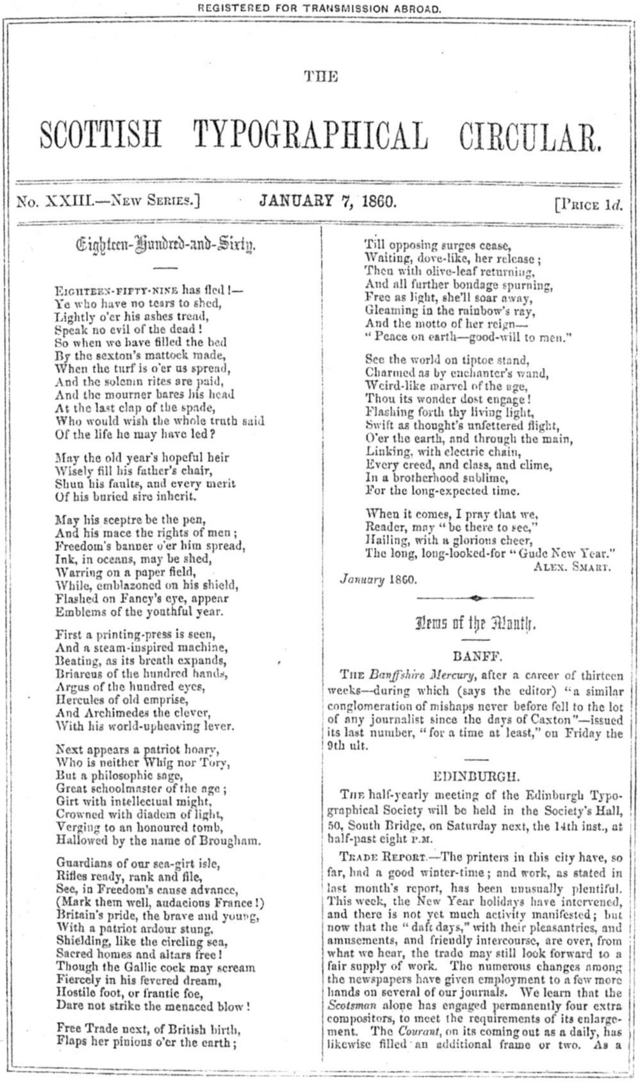

REGISTERED FOR TRANSMISSION ABROAD.

THE

SCOTTISH TYPOGRAPHICAL CIRCULAR.

No. XXIII.—New Series.] JANUARY 7, 1860. [Price 1*d*.

Eighteen-Hundred-and-Sixty.

Eighteen-fifty-nine has fled!—
Ye who have no tears to shed,
Lightly o'er his ashes tread,
Speak no evil of the dead!
So when we have filled the bed
By the sexton's mattock made,
When the turf is o'er us spread,
And the solemn rites are paid,
And the mourner bares his head
At the last clap of the spade,
Who would wish the whole truth said
Of the life he may have led?

May the old year's hopeful heir
Wisely fill his father's chair,
Shun his faults, and every merit
Of his buried sire inherit.

May his sceptre be the pen,
And his mace the rights of men;
Freedom's banner o'er him spread,
Ink, in oceans, may be shed,
Warring on a paper field,
While, emblazoned on his shield,
Flashed on Fancy's eye, appear
Emblems of the youthful year.

First a printing-press is seen,
And a steam-inspired machine,
Beating, as its breath expands,
Briareus of the hundred hands,
Argus of the hundred eyes,
Hercules of old emprise,
And Archimedes the clever,
With his world-upheaving lever.

Next appears a patriot hoary,
Who is neither Whig nor Tory,
But a philosophic sage,
Great schoolmaster of the age;
Girt with intellectual might,
Crowned with diadem of light,
Verging to an honoured tomb,
Hallowed by the name of Brougham.

Guardians of our sea-girt isle,
Rifles ready, rank and file,
See, in Freedom's cause advance,
(Mark them well, audacious France!)
Britain's pride, the brave and young,
With a patriot ardour stung,
Shielding, like the circling sea,
Sacred homes and altars free!
Though the Gallic cock may scream
Fiercely in his fevered dream,
Hostile foot, or frantic foe,
Dare not strike the menaced blow!

Free Trade next, of British birth,
Flaps her pinions o'er the earth;
Till opposing surges cease,
Waiting, dove-like, her release;
Then with olive-leaf returning,
And all further bondage spurning,
Free as light, she'll soar away,
Gleaming in the rainbow's ray,
And the motto of her reign—
"Peace on earth—good-will to men."

See the world on tiptoe stand,
Charmed as by enchanter's wand,
Weird-like marvel of the age,
Thou its wonder dost engage!
Flashing forth thy living light,
Swift as thought's unfettered flight,
O'er the earth, and through the main,
Linking, with electric chain,
Every creed, and class, and clime,
In a brotherhood sublime,
For the long-expected time.

When it comes, I pray that we,
Reader, may "be there to see,"
Hailing, with a glorious cheer,
The long, long-looked-for "Gude New Year."

Alex. Smart.

January 1860.

News of the Month.

BANFF.

The *Banffshire Mercury*, after a career of thirteen weeks—during which (says the editor) "a similar conglomeration of mishaps never before fell to the lot of any journalist since the days of Caxton"—issued its last number, "for a time at least," on Friday the 9th ult.

EDINBURGH.

The half-yearly meeting of the Edinburgh Typographical Society will be held in the Society's Hall, 50, South Bridge, on Saturday next, the 14th inst., at half-past eight P.M.

Trade Report.—The printers in this city have, so far, had a good winter-time; and work, as stated in last month's report, has been unusually plentiful. This week, the New Year holidays have intervened, and there is not yet much activity manifested; but now that the "daft days," with their pleasantries, and amusements, and friendly intercourse, are over, from what we hear, the trade may still look forward to a fair supply of work. The numerous changes among the newspapers have given employment to a few more hands on several of our journals. We learn that the *Scotsman* alone has engaged permanently four extra compositors, to meet the requirements of its enlargement. The *Courant*, on its coming out as a daily, has likewise filled an additional frame or two. As a

Figure 3.5. *Scottish Typographical Circular*, 1860. (© National Library of Scotland)

contemporary a useful and a successful career', declared the *Scottish Typographical Circular* on receiving its copy.[13] The journal's overseers, however, soon found that initial, local enthusiasm for a national 'trade organ' failed to be matched by enough paid subscriptions to sustain production costs. By April 1860, the situation

[13] 'Book Notices. The Australian Typographical Circular', *Scottish Typographical Circular*, no. 4, New Series (1858).

THE

AUSTRALIAN

𝕿𝖞𝖕𝖔𝖌𝖗𝖆𝖕𝖍𝖎𝖈𝖆𝖑 𝕮𝖎𝖗𝖈𝖚𝖑𝖆𝖗.

PUBLISHED, UNDER THE SANCTION OF THE AUSTRALIAN TRADE, BY THE
BOARD OF THE VICTORIA TYPOGRAPHICAL ASSOCIATION.

No. I.   "WE MUST STEM THE TORRENT IF WE WOULD   **Price 6d.;**
January, 1858.   NOT BE CARRIED DOWN BY IT."   **6s. per annum.**

COMMUNICATIONS intended to appear in the next issue of the *Circular* should be to hand not later than the first of the month.

The *Circular* is published on the fifth of each Month, and despatched by first mail to its subscribers.

Original correspondence on interesting trade questions invited.

All correspondence relating to the *Circular*, or to the Trade of Melbourne, should be addressed to Wm. Clarson, 94 Bourke Street East.

Advertisements in the *Circular* are charged at the rate of four shillings per inch.

OF all men in the world, perhaps, the practical printer is the least likely to rush into print merely from the love of being seen there. The novelty of the thing has no charm for him. If, then, he occasionally be found there, we may conclude it is not from the indulgence of any propensity, but because he has something to say which he earnestly believes to be worthy of utterance.

Without offering any apology for our appearance, it may reasonably be expected that, on the first issue of a work of this character, some general plan of the course intended to be pursued in its conduct should be sketched out. While, perhaps, to those who have read our prospectus this will scarcely be needed, we know there are many others to whom an avowal of our views will be acceptable, and even necessary. We cheerfully run over the matter from the time when the notion was first mooted to the present moment when the original crude and immature ideas as to its establishment are assuming something of reality and orderly arrangement.

Some eighteen months ago, on the reorganisation of the Association in

Melbourne, no little difficulty was experienced in approaching the Trade of the sister colonies, and the up-country districts. It was frequently a source of annoyance to the Board that it could not reply to the many questions seeking information respecting the state of the business in these localities; and there seemed to be no possibility of improving matters beyond the casual information received from private members of the profession, and whose observation must generally be of a limited character. Things remained pretty much in this condition until about four months ago, when, on issuing a circular to the Trade, the Board asked for an expression of opinion as to the advisability of publishing a monthly medium of communication, and to what extent the various districts were prepared to support it in the event of its being issued. To this most favorable replies poured in, and they were induced to lose no time in issuing its prospectus, to which we must refer our readers as containing, at greater length than we can now find space for, our views and intentions in the establishment of the Circular.

It will be sufficient to say, here, that in its design it is intended to be the receptacle of information forwarded by the authorised contributors of the various districts, and not at all with the view to enforce the individuality or editorial eccentricities of its conductor upon the members of the profession. We are not without a policy, nor shall we refrain from occasionally insisting on

Figure 3.6. *Australian Typographical Circular*, 1858. (© The British Library Board, Shelfmark P.P. 1622 be)

had reached a tipping point. The quarterly accounts from that month revealed that it cost £37 16s 9d to print and distribute the *Circular*, against subscription receipts of £23 9s 10d. A quarterly loss of £14 6s 11d was not sustainable in the long term. The Victoria branch debated the viability of continuing to support a loss-making enterprise, and concluded they would not continue with it. The *Circular* quietly announced in its May 1860 issue that it would be the last issued by its editorial team, and the Australian print industry would not see the re-establishment of a typographical trade journal until the 1870s.

An important point raised by the development and demise of the *Australian Typographical Circular* was the crucial role of local unions in managing and ensuring viability of these types of journals. In the case of the *Australian Typographical Circular*, general trade ambivalence to the value of such a trade wide resource led to unsustainable losses for the regional trade union branch managing the editing, production, and circulation of the journal. As the *Scottish Typographical Circular* noted about its Antipodean counterpart,

> After a useful and honourable existence of twenty-nine months, its career was brought to a sudden termination by the refusal of the Victoria Typographical Association to continue to provide against the losses of that periodical. The *Circular* was started by the Society in Melbourne for the use and benefit of the whole Australian trade; and although the venture was heartily applauded at the outset, the trade did not continue to support it throughout as it ought to have done. There were exceptions; but we are informed that 'a very large number of individuals confined their exertions to making objections to this and that course.' It is a pity that such extreme littlenesses should have interfered with the prosecution of those valuable labours which are bound up with the publication of even a monthly *Circular*.[14]

The *Australian Typographical Circular's* struggle between commercial imperatives (making a journal pay its way) and social value (informing and entertaining its print trade readers) was not unique. Others such as the *Scottish Typographical Circular* survived through a reliance on union subsidies. Those that did not have such support had to find relevant ways of reducing costs and extending their circulation to remain solvent.

One contemporary journal that did manage to thrive for a period was the New York-based *The Printer* (Figure 3.7), launched in May 1858 with extensive backing of local printers, type foundries and allied print trade owners and proprietors. It was an impressive and lavishly illustrated twenty-four paged monthly, imperial quarto sized, three columned and costed at a dollar an issue. A majority of the production costs were covered by the illustrated advertising at the back, which occupied up to eight pages of each issue, and featured in particular type specimens and illustrated examples from the printing firm James Conner and Sons. 'Messrs Conner & Sons furnish promptly', the introductory editorial puffed brashly, 'in large or small quantities, every article that the most extensive printing establishments may require.'[15] The goal of the journal was to offer 'an elegant paper devoted

---

[14] 'News', *Scottish Typographical Circular*, no. 33 (1860).
[15] 'Ourselves and Our New Enterprise. A Few First Words', *The Printer* 1, no. 1 (1858).

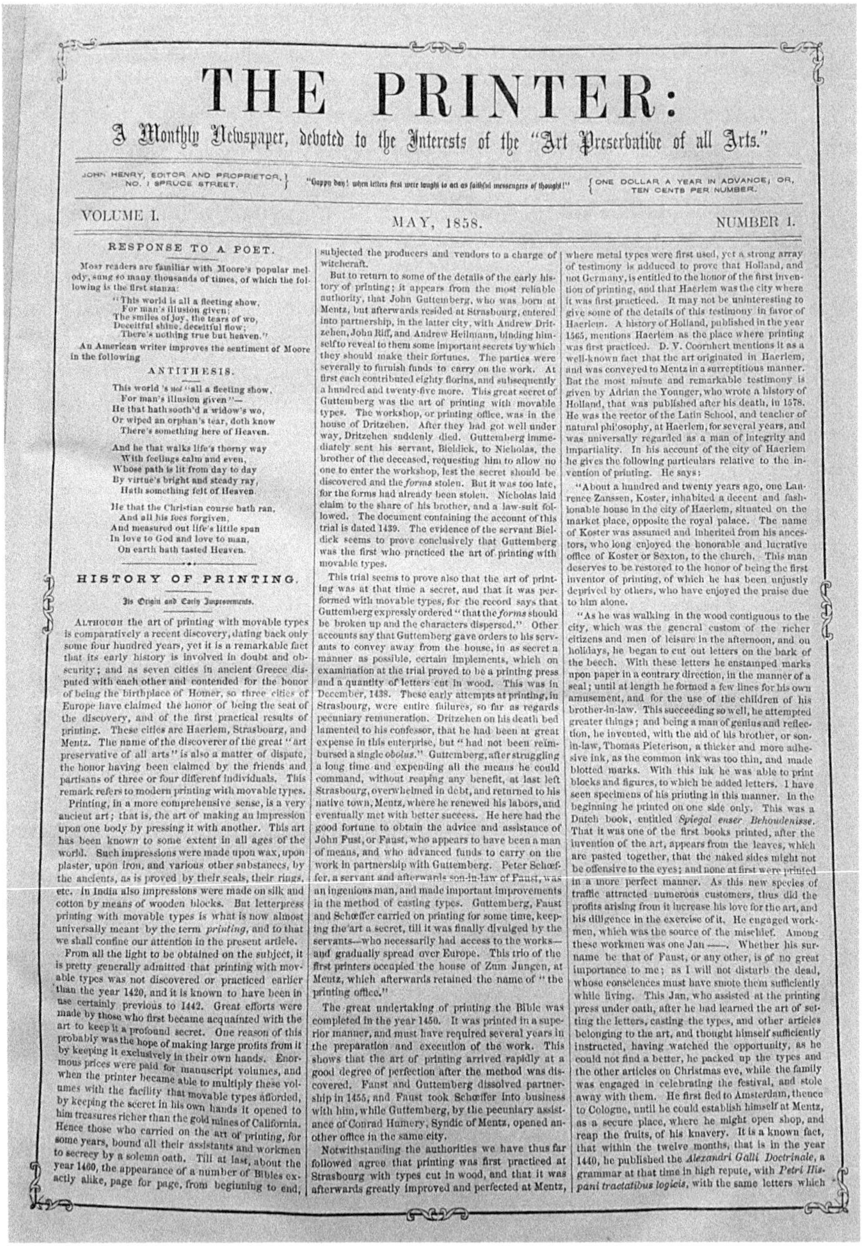

THE PRINTER:

A Monthly Newspaper, devoted to the Interests of the "Art Preservative of all Arts."

JOHN HENRY, EDITOR AND PROPRIETOR, NO. 1 SPRUCE STREET.

"Happy day! when letters first were taught to act as faithful messengers of thought!"

ONE DOLLAR A YEAR IN ADVANCE; OR, TEN CENTS PER NUMBER.

VOLUME I. MAY, 1858. NUMBER 1.

RESPONSE TO A POET.

Most readers are familiar with Moore's popular melody, sung so many thousands of times, of which the following is the first stanza:

"This world is all a fleeting show,
For man's illusion given;
The smiles of joy, the tears of wo,
Deceitful shine, deceitful flow;
There's nothing true but heaven."

An American writer improves the sentiment of Moore in the following

ANTITHESIS.

This world 's *not* "all a fleeting show,
For man's illusion given"—
He that hath sooth'd a widow's wo,
Or wiped an orphan's tear, doth know
There's something here of Heaven.

And he that walks life's thorny way
With feelings calm and even,
Whose path is lit from day to day
By virtue's bright and steady ray,
Hath something felt of Heaven.

He that the Christian course hath ran,
And all his foes forgiven,
And measured out life's little span
In love to God and love to man,
On earth hath tasted Heaven.

HISTORY OF PRINTING.

Its Origin and Early Improvements.

Although the art of printing with movable types is comparatively a recent discovery, dating back only some four hundred years, yet it is a remarkable fact that its early history is involved in doubt and obscurity; and as seven cities in ancient Greece disputed with each other and contended for the honor of being the birthplace of Homer, so three cities of Europe have claimed the honor of being the seat of the discovery, and of the first practical results of printing. These cities are Haerlem, Strasbourg, and Mentz. The name of the discoverer of the great "art preservative of all arts" is also a matter of dispute, the honor having been claimed by the friends and partisans of three or four different individuals. This remark refers to modern printing with movable types.

Printing, in a more comprehensive sense, is a very ancient art; that is, the art of making an impression upon one body by pressing it with another. This art has been known to some extent in all ages of the world. Such impressions were made upon wax, upon plaster, upon iron, and various other substances, by the ancients, as is proved by their seals, their rings, etc. In India also impressions were made on silk and cotton by means of wooden blocks. But letterpress printing with movable types is what is now almost universally meant by the term *printing*, and to that we shall confine our attention in the present article.

From all the light to be obtained on the subject, it is pretty generally admitted that printing with movable types was not discovered or practiced earlier than the year 1420, and it is known to have been in use certainly previous to 1442. Great efforts were made by those who first became acquainted with the art to keep it a profound secret. One reason of this probably was the hope of making large profits from it by keeping it exclusively in their own hands. Enormous prices were paid for manuscript volumes, and when the printer became able to multiply these volumes with the facility that movable types afforded, by keeping the secret in his own hands it opened to him treasures richer than the gold mines of California. Hence those who carried on the art of printing, for some years, bound all their assistants and workmen to secrecy by a solemn oath. Till at last, about the year 1460, the appearance of a number of Bibles exactly alike, page for page, from beginning to end, subjected the producers and vendors to a charge of witchcraft.

But to return to some of the details of the early history of printing; it appears from the most reliable authority, that John Guttemberg, who was born at Mentz, but afterwards resided at Strasbourg, entered into partnership, in the latter city, with Andrew Dritzehen, John Riff, and Andrew Heilmann, binding himself to reveal to them some important secrets by which they should make their fortunes. The parties were severally to furnish funds to carry on the work. At first each contributed eighty florins, and subsequently a hundred and twenty-five more. This great secret of Guttemberg was the art of printing with movable types. The workshop, or printing office, was in the house of Dritzehen. After they had got well under way, Dritzehen suddenly died. Guttemberg immediately sent his servant, Bieldick, to Nicholas, the brother of the deceased, requesting him to allow no one to enter the workshop, lest the secret should be discovered and the *forms* stolen. But it was too late, for the forms had already been stolen. Nicholas laid claim to the share of his brother, and a law-suit followed. The document containing the account of this trial is dated 1439. The evidence of the servant Bieldick seems to prove conclusively that Guttemberg was the first who practiced the art of printing with movable types.

This trial seems to prove also that the art of printing was at that time a secret, and that it was performed with movable types, for the record says that Guttemberg expressly ordered "that the *forms* should be broken up and the characters dispersed." Other accounts say that Guttemberg gave orders to his servants to convey away from the house, in as secret a manner as possible, certain implements, which on examination at the trial proved to be a printing press and a quantity of letters cut in wood. This was in December, 1438. These early attempts at printing, in Strasbourg, were entire failures, so far as regards pecuniary remuneration. Dritzehen on his death bed lamented to his confessor, that he had been at great expense in this enterprise, but "had not been reimbursed a single *obolus*." Guttemberg, after struggling a long time and expending all the means he could command, without reaping any benefit, at last left Strasbourg, overwhelmed in debt, and returned to his native town, Mentz, where he renewed his labors, and eventually met with better success. He here had the good fortune to obtain the advice and assistance of John Fust, or Faust, who appears to have been a man of means, and who advanced funds to carry on the work in partnership with Guttemberg. Peter Schœffer, a servant and afterwards son-in-law of Faust, was an ingenious man, and made important improvements in the method of casting types. Guttemberg, Faust and Schœffer carried on printing for some time, keeping the art a secret, till it was finally divulged by the servants—who necessarily had access to the works—and gradually spread over Europe. This trio of the first printers occupied the house of Zum Jungen, at Mentz, which afterwards retained the name of "the printing office."

The great undertaking of printing the Bible was completed in the year 1450. It was printed in a superior manner, and must have required several years in the preparation and execution of the work. This shows that the art of printing arrived rapidly at a good degree of perfection after the method was discovered. Faust and Guttemberg dissolved partnership in 1455, and Faust took Schœffer into business with him, while Guttemberg, by the pecuniary assistance of Conrad Humery, Syndic of Mentz, opened another office in the same city.

Notwithstanding the authorities we have thus far followed agree that printing was first practiced at Strasbourg with types cut in wood, and that it was afterwards greatly improved and perfected at Mentz, where metal types were first used, yet a strong array of testimony is adduced to prove that Holland, and not Germany, is entitled to the honor of the first invention of printing, and that Haerlem was the city where it was first practiced. It may not be uninteresting to give some of the details of this testimony in favor of Haerlem. A history of Holland, published in the year 1565, mentions Haerlem as the place where printing was first practiced. D. V. Coornhert mentions it as a well-known fact that the art originated in Haerlem, and was conveyed to Mentz in a surreptitious manner. But the most minute and remarkable testimony is given by Adrian the Younger, who wrote a history of Holland, that was published after his death, in 1578. He was the rector of the Latin School, and teacher of natural philosophy, at Haerlem, for several years, and was universally regarded as a man of integrity and impartiality. In his account of the city of Haerlem he gives the following particulars relative to the invention of printing. He says:

"About a hundred and twenty years ago, one Laurence Zanssen, Koster, inhabited a decent and fashionable house in the city of Haerlem, situated on the market place, opposite the royal palace. The name of Koster was assumed and inherited from his ancestors, who long enjoyed the honorable and lucrative office of Koster or Sexton, to the church. This man deserves to be restored to the honor of being the first inventor of printing, of which he has been unjustly deprived by others, who have enjoyed the praise due to him alone.

"As he was walking in the wood contiguous to the city, which was the general custom of the richer citizens and men of leisure in the afternoon, and on holidays, he began to cut out letters on the bark of the beech. With these letters he enstamped marks upon paper in a contrary direction, in the manner of a seal; until at length he formed a few lines for his own amusement, and for the use of the children of his brother-in-law. This succeeding so well, he attempted greater things; and being a man of genius and reflection, he invented, with the aid of his brother, or son-in-law, Thomas Pieterison, a thicker and more adhesive ink, as the common ink was too thin, and made blotted marks. With this ink he was able to print blocks and figures, to which he added letters. I have seen specimens of his printing in this manner. In the beginning he printed on one side only. This was a Dutch book, entitled *Spiegal enser Behoudenisse.* That it was one of the first books printed, after the invention of the art, appears from the leaves, which are pasted together, that the naked sides might not be offensive to the eyes; and none at first were printed in a more perfect manner. As this new species of traffic attracted numerous customers, thus did the profits arising from it increase his love for the art, and his diligence in the exercise of it. He engaged workmen, which was the source of the mischief. Among these workmen was one Jan ——. Whether his surname be that of Faust, or any other, is of no great importance to me; as I will not disturb the dead, whose consciences must have smote them sufficiently while living. This Jan, who assisted at the printing press under oath, after he had learned the art of setting the letters, casting the types, and other articles belonging to the art, and thought himself sufficiently instructed, having watched the opportunity, as he could not find a better, he packed up the types and the other articles on Christmas eve, while the family was engaged in celebrating the festival, and stole away with them. He first fled to Amsterdam, thence to Cologne, until he could establish himself at Mentz, as a secure place, where he might open shop, and reap the fruits, of his knavery. It is a known fact, that within the twelve months, that is in the year 1440, he published the *Alexandri Galli Doctrinale*, a grammar at that time in high repute, with *Petri Hispani tractatibus logicis*, with the same letters which

Figure 3.7. *The Printer*, 1858

exclusively to the art of printing, and those arts immediately connected with it…'[16] The list that followed of topics to be covered was exhaustive, taking in everything from general histories of printing, engraving, and composition, to illustrated exemplars of fine arts, new inventions and manufacturing. The monthly results 'will furnish material for a paper that shall not only be exceedingly desirable for all printers, publishers, and artists, but also a very welcome and cherished visitor in every family circle'.[17] Also included would be poetry, though not just any casual item. As the editor noted elsewhere in the issue when introducing a poem on printing ('The Press') by Captain G. W. Cutter, author of the 'Song of Steam', 'We do not design to fill the columns of *The Printer* with the ordinary poetry usually afloat; but an occasional piece of high order of merit, especially if devoted to the peculiar subjects appropriate to this journal, would doubtless be acceptable to our readers.'[18]

Its Scottish counterpart welcomed the new addition, praising its layout and content, and urging its readers to engage with the journal's contents. Noting its editorial commitment to 'the interests of the art preservative of all arts', the *Scottish Typographical Circular* editor gushed, 'It is really a superb specimen of the art it seeks to foster: and we have rarely seen so much taste displayed, or care and labour bestowed, in the getting up of any magazine.'[19] In May 1859, *The Printer* became the official news outlet of the National Typographical Union, a connection that lasted until 1866, when that role was taken on by the *Printers' Circular and Stationers' and Publishers' Gazette*.[20] *The Printer* continued publishing monthly until it closed down in 1875.

PRINTER LAUREATES

A feature of these early typographical journals was the use of in-house compositor-poets. Little has been said in the past of the creative compositors whose work proved such a mainstay of early print trade journals. Poetry was ubiquitous in the popular and periodical press of the nineteenth century, overflowing in fact through channels overlooked by past literary critics and historians. Only recently has this deficiency been addressed by scholars such as Kirstie Blair, Andrew Hobbs, Natalie Houston, Linda K. Hughes, and Kathryn Ledbetter.[21] It is worth reflecting on a recent data analysis of nineteenth-century local newspapers by Andrew Hobbs, who has estimated that there were between 4 to 6 million poems published in the

---

[16] Ibid.   [17] Ibid.   [18] 'The Press', *The Printer* 1, no. 1 (1858).
[19] 'The Printer', *Scottish Typographical Circular*, 1 October 1859.
[20] 'National Typographical Union. Official Report for "the Printer." Proceedings of the Eighth Annual Session, at Boston, Mass., May 2, 1859', *The Printer* 2, no. 1 (1859); Alfred McClung Lee, *The Daily Newspaper in America*, vol. 1 (London: Routledge and Thoemmes Press, 2000), p. 226.
[21] Kirstie Blair, ' "A Very Poetical Town": Newspaper Poetry and the Working Class Poet in Victorian Dundee', *Victorian Poetry* 52, no. 1 (2014); ' "Let the Nightingales Alone": Correspondence Columns, the Scottish Press, and the Making of the Working-Class Poet', *Victorian Periodicals Review* 47, no. Summer: 2 (2014); Natalie Houston, 'Newspaper Poems', *Victorian Studies* 50, no. 2 (2008); Andrew Hobbs, 'Five Million Poems, or the Local Press as Poetry Publisher, 1800–1900', *Victorian Periodicals Review* 45, no. 4 (2012); Linda K. Hughes, 'What the Wellesley Index Left Out: Why Poetry Matters to Periodical Studies', *Victorian Periodicals Review*, 40, no. 2 (2007); Kathryn Ledbetter, *Tennyson and Victorian Periodicals* (Farnham: Ashgate, 2007).

nineteenth-century English provincial press alone.[22] Print trade focused poetry fed into such textual bounty. While surveying six key UK and overseas typographical trade journals (*The Australian Typographical Circular, Compositors' Chronicle, The Printer, The Scottish Typographical Circular, The Typographical Circular*, and *The Printers' Journal and Typographical Magazine*), I have found over 200 poems published in the period 1840–70. There were also a significant number of short stories and memoirs featured in these and other related print trade publications. Such creative work appeared in a particularly enlightened phase of trade press management between 1850 and 1865. After 1870, as I note later in this chapter, there was a significant drop in creative material, due in large part to a reorientation and refocusing of typographical trade journals. However, a survey of the extant material, the background of creative compositors and printers, and the themes and topics they addressed, offers valuable insights into the way creativity was often harnessed to address trade specific social, cultural, and work-based themes and concerns.

Printer laureates of the print trade featured in practically every issue of relevant journals from the 1840s through to the early 1870s, either through their poetry, through reviews of their work, or in reports of their creative activities. Many have been unjustly neglected, with work that still stands out today for their vibrancy and creative flair. Scottish examples included Alexander Smart, James Smith, and Robert Brough, successive contributors to the *Scottish Typographical Circular* from its inception in 1857 and into the 1870s. English printer-poets included William Dorrington, Alfred Knott, John Lash Latey, and David Walkinshaw, active contributors to the *Compositors' Chronicle* (1840–3), the *Typographical Protection Circular* (1849–53) and its successors the *Typographical Circular* (1854–8), the *London Press Journal* (November 1858–January 1859)' and *The Printers' Journal and Typographical Magazine* (1865–7).

One of the most creative if tragic of such early compositor-poets was Alexander Smart. Born in 1798 in Montrose, near Dundee, Smart was based for much of his working life in Edinburgh. Smart, like his better-known and more lauded contemporary Hugh Miller, stonemason turned geologist and poet, created hymns and elegies to the working lives of the labouring classes, paralleling themes explored by the ultimate, iconic Scots 'lad of parts', the eighteenth-century poet Robert Burns. The printer-poet Smart found early success with verses featured in journals such as *Hogg's Weekly Instructor*, edited in Montrose by his friend James Hogg, the so-called Ettrick Shepherd. Smart's poem 'The Flight of Time' featured in the first volume of *Hogg's Weekly Instructor* in 1845, and was frequently reprinted in the 1850s and 1860s in US and Australian newspaper outlets.[23] Alexander would not be the only one in his family to involve himself in supporting labouring-class intellectual and creative aspirations: his brother James Smart (1800–1862), a compositor employed at the *Caledonian Mercury* for over forty years, was instrumental in founding the

---

[22] Hobbs. 'Five Million Poems, or the Local Press as Poetry Publisher, 1800–1900', p. 488.
[23] See for example Alexander Smart, 'The Flight of Time', *The Farmer and Mechanic*, 26 December 1850; 'The Flight of Time', *American Union*, 1 February 1851; 'The Flight of Time', *Boston Weekly Museum*, March 29 1851; 'The Flight of Time', *Christian Enquirer*, 4 January 1851; 'The Flight of Time', *American Union*, 1 May 1852; 'The Flight of Time', *Britannia and Trades' Advocate*, 3 February 1851; 'The Flight of Time', *Bacchus Marsh Express*, 2 March 1867.

Edinburgh Mechanics' Subscription Library in 1826, twice acting as its secretary, and avidly committed to its aims of providing 'plentiful and cheap reading for the working classes of Edinburgh'.[24] James Smith, referred to later in this piece, would become its librarian in 1869.

Throughout the 1840s and 1850s, Alexander Smart acquired a name for himself as a versifier of some talent, featured at public events and written about in newspapers and literary journals. When the eminent antiquarian Reverend Charles Rogers delivered a well-attended public lecture in Stirling on Scottish lyrical poets, he included Smart in a list of thirty important contemporary practitioners. The point was widely reported in papers throughout the region.[25] Similarly, when a grand day of celebrations was held in 1844 at the Alloway Kirk in Ayr on the Centenary of Robert Burns's birth, irate commentaries published in the *Dundee Courier* and *Scotch Reformers Gazette* lamented that the organizing committee had failed to give space at the celebration to poets like William Thom, William Miller, and Alexander Smart. These individuals were held up as exemplifying the continuing tradition of Scottish verse, 'kindred spirits of the great poet – the living personification, if we may so speak, of Burns himself'.[26] The editorials concluded scathingly, 'Would it have been any great stretch on the part of Messieurs Bone and Gray, the secretaries of this festival, to have invited these choice spirits to it, – these native bards, emulous, perhaps, of the fame of Burns, yet some of them struggling, perhaps, as he did, with adversity, but whose works are full of riches and sparkling gems.'[27] Smart did in the end attend the event, dedicating and delivering a forty-eight-line poem to Burns's three sons Robert Burns, Colonel William Nicol Burns, and Major James Glencairn Burns, who had been in attendance throughout the day's ceremonies.[28]

Though conscious that his public profile had been built on producing poetry in the vein of Burns, Smart focused much of his work in the late 1850s on labour, print trade, and domestic themes. Smart's poetry was a key element of the creative material featured in the *Scottish Typographical Circular* from its inception in 1857 through to late 1860. His trade press poetry offered commentary on labour themes, extolled the press and its honest print workers, and included reflective pieces centred on Scottish domestic scenes, often written in the Scots vernacular. His final collection of poems, *Songs of Labour and Domestic Life*, featured first in serial form in the *STC* between 1859 and 1860, was issued in book form in 1860. Reviews ranged from mildly excited to unremarkable in tone. Those on the positive side noted its range of subjects and pleasing poetic form. 'His poetry is genuine – vigorous, smooth and natural', remarked a critic for *The Stirling Observer*, 'while his subjects generally are well chosen, and treated in an intelligent and pleasing manner.'[29] A review in the *Elgin and Morayshire Courier* hailed Smart as a poet who wrote in a fine, healthy moral tone and elevated social feeling. 'With the patriotism of a genuine Scotchman', the

---

[24] 'Obituary', *Scottish Typographical Circular*, 2 August 1862.

[25] 'The Living Lyrical Poets of Scotland', *The Stirling Observer*, March 6 1856; 'The Living Lyrical Poets of Scotland', *The Fife Herald, Kinross, Strathearn and Clackmannan Advertiser*, 6 March 1856.

[26] 'The Burns' Festival', *Dundee Courier*, 6 August 1844.   [27] Ibid.

[28] 'The Burns Commemoration', *Caledonian Mercury*, 8 August 1844.

[29] 'Literature. Songs of Labour and Domestic Life; with Rhymes for Little Readers', *The Stirling Observer*, 14 October 1860.

reviewer exclaimed, 'he combines a love of the beautiful and true; and his muse is never more at home than in the liveliest scenes of domestic life.'[30]

Such praise seems not to have eased Smart's tortured lack of self-confidence, for it was said that the volume's indifferent critical reception led to the irreversible breakdown in health that confined him shortly after to Craighouse, a mental health sanatorium in the suburban hills of Morningside, Edinburgh. When news of Alexander Smith's commitment to an asylum in 1861 became public knowledge, a public subscription was launched to raise funds for his family. Over £40 was gathered, with contributions from print chapels in major publishing and printing houses such as William Blackwood & Sons, Oliver & Boyd, Blackie & Sons, and the *Scottish Press* and *Courant* newspaper offices.[31] He died five years later, on 18 October 1866, having never left the sanatorium grounds. Obituary notices were small but widespread, from Dundee, Glasgow and Edinburgh to Leeds, London, Wales, and the USA.[32] All stressed his dual vocation as compositor and poet, active in both from the 1830s onwards and highly celebrated by his fellow workers. 'The journeymen printers were all proud of him', a contemporary source acknowledged, 'and he, for his part, was always proud of the class to which he belonged, as his "Songs of Labour" and other poems abundantly testify.'[33] Despite early praise and commendation as a Scots lyrical poet, as labour poet he remained unsung and critically neglected in more general social terms, a fact pointedly remarked on in contemporary notices. 'It was not Mr Smart's fortune to secure any public recognition of his poetic efforts', commented the *Edinburgh Courant,* a point subsequently picked up and reprinted in the *Glasgow Herald*, the *Daily News,* and the *Brecon County Times,* for 'He shared the fate of nearly all "minor poets" – neglect.'[34]

James Smith (1824–1887), the next poet-laureate to occupy the pages of the *STC,* had more critical success, rising to prominence in the 1850s and 1860s as a working-class poet, children's versifier, and comic storyteller, and writing like Smart in the Scots vernacular. He was born in March 1824 in a crumbling Edinburgh tenement in St Mary's Wynd (now St Mary's Street), the son of a coach lace weaver. He began a printing apprenticeship aged eleven, and on completing it worked for thirty years in the print trade, 'tramping' in England and Ireland, then taking up positions as journeyman printer, reader and manager with the law printers Aikman, who produced the daily reports from the Scottish Court of Sessions. He also held positions as a reader for the *Scotsman* and the *Daily Review* newspapers. In 1869, when the board of the Edinburgh Mechanics' Subscription Library, based in Riddle's Court off Edinburgh's High Street, met to choose a new librarian from six

---

[30] 'Literature. Songs of Labour and Domestic Life; with Rhymes for Litttle Readers', *The Elgin and Morayshire Courier,* 21 September 1860.

[31] *Scottish Typographical Circular,* 6 July 1861, p. 337; 'The Case of Mr Alex. Smart and Family', *Scottish Typographical Circular,* 4 May 1861, p. 328.

[32] 'Death of a Scotch Poet', *Daily News,* 24 October 1866; 'Death of Alexander Smart, the Poet', *Dundee Courier,* 22 October 1866; 'Death of a Scotch Poet', *Leeds Mercury,* 24 October 1866; 'The Late Alex. Smart, Author of the "Songs of Labour"', *Glasgow Herald,* 23 October 1866; 'Death of a Scotch Poet', *Brecon County Times,* 3 November 1866; 'Pen, Pencil, and Scissors', *National Republican,* 16 November 1866.

[33] 'Death of Alexander Smart, the Poet'.

[34] 'The Late Alex. Smart, Author of the "Songs of Labour"'; 'Death of a Scotch Poet'.

shortlisted applicants, sixty-one to thirty-nine voted in favour of Smith. It was a position he held until his death of an acute attack of asthma and related disorders in December 1887.[35]

Smith distinguished himself as a comic storyteller, songwriter, and poet. During his lifetime, his poetry and comic work featured not just in the *Scottish Typographical Circular* but also in local newspapers and journals and in subsequent book form. Smith was held locally in great esteem and viewed with great fondness, a fact attested to in 1875, when Edinburgh citizens presented him with a silver salver and a purse of 200 guineas, raised by public subscription 'as a mark of their admiration of his genius and character'.[36] After his death in 1887, public donations were again forthcoming to fund installation in 1889 of a carved plinth over his grave in Edinburgh's Grange Cemetery, featuring a young child stretching to place a wreath around a bas-relief image of Smith (see Figure 3.8).

On assumption of his librarian duties in 1869, James Smith began to pull back from his work for the *STC*. In any case, his contributions as the *STC's* self-appointed poet-laureate had started tapering off throughout 1868 as a new, de-facto trade bard appeared alongside him in the journal's pages. This proved to be Robert Brough (1830–1903), whose first contribution to the *STC* dated back to 1861. Born in Wigtown, Brough had served as a compositor apprentice in Stranraer, possibly with Hugh Wylie, the main bookseller and printer based in Church Street, while living in the adjacent parish town of Leswalt.[37] He moved to Edinburgh with his family in 1860, and worked as a compositor first for Murray and Gibb, and then for Ballantyne and Co.[38] In August 1876 he shifted to Glasgow to take

---

[35] Anon, 'Edinburgh Mechanics' Library – Election of Librarian', *The Scotsman*, 18 November 1869. The library was founded in 1825 by members of the Mechanics Institute needing a place to study during the summer when the institute was closed. By 1830 the library had over 350 members, and by 1851 it boasted a catalogue of over 18,000 volumes and was issuing over 200,000 volumes per year. It closed in 1893 (Brian Burch, 'Libraries and Literacy in Popular Education', in *Libraries in Britain and Ireland*, vol. 2: *1640–1850*, ed. Giles Mandelbrote and K. A. Manley (Cambridge: Cambridge University Press, 2006), p. 381).

[36] Anon, 'The Late Mr James Smith', *The Scotsman*, 13 March 1887.

[37] Parish records show Robert was born in Wigtown on 5 October 1830, while the March 1851 census records him as working as a compositor apprentice and lodging in Leswat in a house headed by Jess Milright, whose half-sister Elizabeth Wyatt he would marry in November 1851. (See 'List of Baptisms in the Parish', Church Registers: Old Parish Register Records (1830), 5 October 1830; Census returns, 30 March 1851 Census 891/11/3; Church registers: Old Parish Register Records 891/20, p. 393, 24 November 1851.

[38] A membership register compiled for the Scottish Typographical Association in 1887 suggests Robert Brough joined the union in December 1860, while Edinburgh membership records show him paying dues fairly consistently between 1862 and 1874. See 'Edinburgh Typographical Society Contributor Records, 1861–1900'. Robert Brough is listed as one of the signatories of an 1861 Memorial Circular issue to the Edinburgh Master Printers by Compositors requesting an increase in wages, at which point he was working for Murray and Gibb. See 'Unto the Master Printers of Edinburgh, the Memorial of the Journeymen Compositors of That City', (Edinburgh). At some point in the late 1860s, Brough shifts employment to Ballantyne and Co., going on to feature as bard at many of their work-related events and outings through to the early 1870s. 1861 Edinburgh Census registers note him living in 19 India Place with his wife Elizabeth Wyatt, four children and sister-in-law Jess Milright, then in 1871 living in 37 India Place with a fifth child on the records. See 'Scotland Census Returns', (1861); 'Scotland Census Returns', (1871).

Figure 3.8. James Smith Plinth, Grange Cemetery, Edinburgh

up a position at Blackie & Co., then in 1878 joined the printers Anderson and Mackay. He would remain in Glasgow until his death in 1903.[39]

---

[39] Glasgow Typographical Society membership lists show Brough joining their branch in August 1876, when he took up a post at 'Blackie's Case', then shifting to Anderson and Mackay in January 1878. 'Glasgow Typographical Association Membership Lists'. The 1881 Glasgow Scotland Census

Brough specialized in trade-focused poetry, as well as material written in Scots. Early contributions to the *STC* were written in broad Scots, imitating the style and intonation of Robert Burns. His first submission, 'Coming Events Cast their *Shadows* Before', appeared in the January 1861 issue. A poem written in broad Scots with Burnsian phrasing, it took note of the contemporary movement of women into the printing world led and inspired by Emily Faithfull (such as the founding of the female only, London-based Victoria Press and its Edinburgh counterpart the Caledonian Press). The entry of women is portrayed tongue in cheek as an improvement in the print space: foul language would be moderated, brandy and snuff would be cast aside, and works would flow from the nimble fingers of independent women. As a result, Brough declaims:

> On every book we cast our e'en
> Some great improvement will be seen:
> A' coarse, vile words, and angry spleen,
> Changed to sublime:
> Woman will purge our language clean
> In little time.

> Then let ilk lassie raise a cheer,
> They'll a' be right before next year;
> A *Faithfull* friend, it would appear,
> Leads in the van.
> Wha sounds their praises far and near
> Throughout the lan'.

More to the point, men will quake and tremble before the newly empowered working woman:

> Already I can hear them speak,
> When they ha'e made a stunning week;
> It winna be the peevish squeak
> We used to hear;
> They'll mak the bluid dance to your cheek –
> You'll quake wi' fear.

> And this, nae doubt, is only right,
> For lang enough they've got the slight;
> But, noo when they stop wark at night,
> Aye fresh and nimble;
> Their stride o' independent might
> Will mak us tremble.[40]

records him as living in the Kelvinside area of Glasgow and employed as a compositor printer, though in the 1891 census he was recorded as unemployed. Death records from 1903 indicate he died of Bright's Disease (or chronic nephritis, a kidney disease) in Glasgow on 20 June 1903. See 'Scotland Census Returns', (1881); 'Scotland Census Returns', (1891). 'Statutory Registers, Deaths', ed. Crown Office (1903).

[40] Robert Brough, '"Coming Events Cast Their Shadows Before"', *Scottish Typographical Circular*, 5 January 1861.

From there, it's a short step from independence to emigration, and Brough ends the poem invoking the results and calling on young compositors to marry to stop such a calamitous exit to new lands:

> But, oh, if they should emigrate!
> We'll soon sink to a waefu' state;
> Then ye young chaps, ere its' ower late,
>   Rin, tak a wife!
> Implore the dears at hame to wait,
>   Save Briton's life![41]

It is difficult to tell whether Brough is openly sympathizing with the women's compositor movement or mocking their aspirations, but the poetic style is a standard rhyming couplet scheme seen also in the work of his *STC* printer-poet counterparts.

Brough's poetry featured sporadically in the *STC* between 1862 and 1867. He began contributing on a regular basis between 1868 and 1874, taking over as the *STC*'s key poetic commemorator of trade culture and events. He would write in standard English and also in broad Scots. A good example of the former can be found in a poem published in the May 1870 issue, which plays upon implied criticisms that the *STC* did not provide enough general news.[42] The answer: summarize the month's key events in verse! Brough's opening stanza lays out the arguments and urges all to pay heed to his news summary, so that it can be used to 'gabble like parrots':

> Some won't buy the *Circular* – making excuse
> That it seldom contains any General News;
> But that's quite absurd, for, in this very sheet,
> They'll find everything of importance complete;
> And, after this date, if men use such a plea,
> With their hair, ears, or nose, I'll be sure to make free.
> Look alive! Then, and get this rich stock in your garrets,
> Then on all public points you can gabble like parrots.[43]

Brough then cleverly works his way through political events, entertainingly fitting these in twenty-six rhyming couplets alongside crime, culture, and commerce items. Brough crams in references to Disraeli, Livingstone, members of the royalty, the Chancellor of the Exchequer, scientists, explorers, local events, and well-known advertisers.[44] (See appendix A for full poem.)

Brough comically chastises the skinflints who fail to buy their own copy of the *Circular*, for with just a penny they would thus receive all the news needed, mixed up like sausages bought from the local butchers:

> So there, that's the whole, even down to the locals,
> Well mixed, like those sausages purchased at Jockel's;
> Then, no more get-outs, for they're used by too many –
> For no other purpose than saving a Penny![45]

---

[41] Ibid.
[42] 'General News. By a Utilitarian Rhymer.', *Scottish Typographical Circular*, 1 May 1868.
[43] Ibid.   [44] See Appendix A for full poem.   [45] Ibid.

Brough would also play a part in the Edinburgh printers' strike of 1872–3 (events of which are detailed in Chapter 2, 'Striking Printers'), producing poetry for *Out on Strike,* the eight-page, octavo-sized weekly journal issued by workers during the union action. The 14 December 1872 issue featured one such contribution, a stirring call to arms in the wages struggle, 'Put Your Shoulder to the Wheel', which called on readers to fight for equality and justice. It began:

> Up, up! Arouse each honest man!
> There's danger I delay:
> Strive to be foremost in the van,
> And soon we'll gain the day.
> 'Tis not for class or rank we fight,
> But for the world's weal:
> Stand forth, then! Show that right is might:
> Put your shoulder to the wheel.

The poem continued with reminders to all that the fight was a just one, led by free men acting against tyranny, and resonated with a strident union rhetoric that had been absent from previous contributions from Brough. The concluding stanzas offered a vision of what could be the results of working towards a common purpose, namely victory, power and a liberty that would come from putting that shoulder to the wheel:

> Pull strength, and pull together all!
> Not distant is the hour
> When those who now are thought so small
> Will claim their share of power!
> When wealth does humble worth despite,
> And spurn each just appeal,
> There's something in each breast that cries –
> Put your shoulder to the wheel!
>
> Of half its jarring throughs and griefs
> This world might soon be free,
> If man to help his brother man
> In earnest would agree!
> Oh! could the great for one short hour,
> Feel what the lowly feel,
> Their pamper'd spirits soon would sour:
> Put your should to the wheel!
>
> See Victory from her lofty tower,
> In pride the battle scan:
> 'Fear not,' she shouts: 'the darkest hour
> Still comes before the dawn!'
> March on in triumph, loudly cheer,
> Till foes do backward reel,
> Then liberty bright smiles shall wear:
> Put your shoulder to the wheel![46]

---

[46] 'Original Poetry. Put Your Shoulder to the Wheel', *Out on Strike*, 14 December 1872.

Brough's contributions to the *STC* ceased on his move to Glasgow in 1876. There is no record of his doing further literary work, and by the turn of the century he had faded into obscurity and poverty, dying in a tenement section of the infamous and socially deprived Gorbals area of Glasgow in 1903.

Alfred Knott, a London-based printer, was the resident 'compositor-poet' of the monthly *Typographical Circular*, featuring in practically every issue from its inception in October 1854 through to its demise in September 1858, and appearing in its short-lived successor, the fortnightly *London Press Journal*, issued between 1 November 1858 and 1 January 1859. Alfred Knott, born in 1824, was connected for many years with the small London printing firm of Shaw and Danks, based in no. 9 Crane Court, Fleet Street. Little is known of his background, but he first appeared in the *Typographical Protection Circular* in September 1853 where, tucked into a short notice on the annual social outing of the printing firm Gilbert and Rivington, we find mention of the performance of a song entitled 'The Merry Days of Old', 'written for the occasion by Mr Alfred Knott, one of the gentlemen employed in the office'.[47] He achieved more prominence in the seventh issue (2 October 1854) of the *Protections Circular's* successor, the *Typographical Circular*, with a poetic call to printers for donations to the Almshouse Guarantee Fund. Declaring that the sum of £800 raised to date needed the help of 'Caxton's noble staff' to bring up to a more suitable £1,000, Knott appealed to the philanthropic side of print workers, reminding them of the social contract that bound all together:

> Who aideth others helps himself;
> And, should you aid so now
> The deed may tearful fruitage bear
> When age sits on your brow!
> Yes, though you ne'er may want such help,
> Yet choose the wiser part,
> For blessed is the merciful
> And philanthropic heart.[48]

Knott would become a ubiquitous presence in the *Typographical Circular*, with poems in almost every issue between November 1854 and May 1858 (just prior to its cessation). Knott's poems for the *Typographical Circular* were didactic, moralizing, and often themed to key events covered in the journal's main news section.

Similarly, there was the example of the Sheffield-based 'labour laureate' David Walkinshaw, a prime mover in founding the Provincial Typographical Association (PTA) as a breakaway union from the Northern Association in 1845, first chairman of the PTA, and chief versifier for the *Typographical Protection Circular* (1849–53). His poetry welcomed delegates to the Sheffield gathering in 1849 at which it was decided to form the PTA, and his long poem extolling the values of the PTA was sung at the conclusion of the organization's fiftieth anniversary celebrations in 1899, shortly before his death, and reproduced in its anniversary

---

[47] Alfred Knott, 'Wayzgoose', *Typographical Protection Circular*, September 1853.
[48] 'The Almshouse Guarantee Fund', *Typographical Circular*, 2 October 1854.

history.[49] He was actively involved in creative and educational initiatives in Sheffield, serving for example as a founding director of the combined Sheffield Athenaeum and Mechanics Institute, established in 1849.[50] In 1855 he demitted office, moved for a period to the Forest of Dean, and in 1857 shifted to Pontypool to found and edit the *Pontypool Free Press*. He would run this community-based paper until retiring in 1877, and then continue to publish poetry in the *Bristol Mercury* until shortly before his death in 1899.[51] A key unifier in social terms, he used his poetic contributions to satisfy local interests while offering creative satirical entertainment. As the *Bristol Mercury* observed in its obituary notice, he was fondly regarded for his unassuming erudition and refreshingly humorous poetic utterances. 'We need scarcely add', the notice concluded, 'that readers of the *Bristol Mercury* will deeply regret that they will never more have their interest excited and their love of genial wit and playful satire gratified with productions from the racy and ever ready pen of "D.W.".'[52]

EDUCATION AND KNOWLEDGE

Topics reflected upon by these printer-poets included reading, literacy, the art of printing, and union solidarity. Monthly reports in the *Typographical Circular* between January and October 1855 on progress in creating a printers' library in London, for example, were often succeeded by Alfred Knott poems extolling the benefits of such a move, or commenting on the library's cultural value. March and April 1855 issues featured Knott poems on the library, the first spelling out its potential for lifting printers 'upward and onward still', and the second calling on printers to donate books for the proposed opening. Knott's stanzas employed common tropes of the nineteenth-century self-improvement and trade union movements: books and educational self-improvement lifted individuals out of ignorance and darkness, and print trade unity was vital for aiding that educational process. In 'Books for the Library', Knott exhorted those who worked in the print trade to stand by their duty to enable themselves and others to benefit from print culture, and so donate freely of relevant material. Within this didactic call, there was also acknowledgement of the need for books of both educational and mass entertainment value within the Library stacks. As Knott trumpeted,

> Oh! Then, bring to the shrine of Wisdom divine
> Your gifts, as ye can, and are willing.

[49] 'News', *The British Printer* 1899; Richard Hackett and Henry Slatter, 'The Typographical Association: Fifty Years' Record, 1849–1899' (1899), p. 140.

[50] For more on the early history of the Sheffield Athenaeum and Mechanics Institute, see Alan White, 'Class, Culture and Control: The Sheffield Athenaeum Movement and the Middle Class', in *The Culture of Capital: Art, Power and the Nineteenth-Century Middle Class*, ed. Janet Wolff and John Seed (Manchester: Manchester University Press, 1988), pp. 95–8.

[51] 'Death of Mr D. Walkinshaw', *The Bristol Mercury and Daily Post*, 22 July 1899.

[52] Ibid.

> From the tome of great store of classical lore,
> To the "readable book" worth a shilling.

Knott rousingly concludes this call for contributions,

> For the Printer's the man who should in the van
> Of progress be guiding his brother,
> And this Library scheme is no fitful dream,
> If truly we stand by each other.[53]

Like Knott, Alexander Smart wrote feelingly about educational opportunities for the *Scottish Typographical Circular*. When the Edinburgh Typographical Society followed London in setting up a Printers Library, Smart was on hand to opine on its advantages. The opening of the Edinburgh Printers' Library on 20 November 1858 featured an Inaugural Address in verse delivered by Smart, subsequently reprinted on the front page of the December 1858 *STC*. The event saw Smart extolling the power of print and the right of Scottish printers to avail themselves of its riches:

> While radiant books leap from the press,
> Instinct with life and moral power,
> And master minds the world address
> Through winged sheets each morning hour;
> Shall Scottish printers lag behind,
> Nor seek, like free born men, to take
> Their station in the march of mind,
> When all the thinking world's awake!
>
> This evening, round the festive board,
> Our Library shall answer – No!
> And here, in brotherly accord,
> Its birth we hail with genial glow;
> This bantling, though of stature small,
> Of mental affluence the heir,
> Cradled with hope, and prized by all
> Will grow beneath our fostering care.[54]

LAUREATIONS

When key figures in the print movement passed away, commemorations and obituaries would be accompanied by poetic tributes, as in the case of William Cox, the Secretary of the London Society of Compositors, whose death at the age of twenty-eight was announced in the 15 January 1857 issue of the *Typographical Circular*. The two columned, black-edged obituary was followed by a specially

---

[53] Alfred Knott, 'Books for the Library', *Typographical Circular*, 1 April 1855.
[54] Anon, 'Edinburgh Printers' Library. Inaugural Soiree', *Scottish Typographical Circular*, 3 December 1858.

commissioned, one column poem in his honour. The death notice praised William for his commitment and energy, noting his role in shifting the Society's headquarters to new lodgings, and in establishing the Society's Library and News Room. His trade society commitments were reflected upon in verse penned by Alfred Knott, where members were asked to 'Whisper it low among the ranks, -/"Our brave Trade-Captain's dead!"' Knott then praised Cox as a 'brave soul worker', 'True as the trustiest weapon/ Toledo's fires anneal', and asked readers to remember Cox for his dedication to the print trade cause:

> Nay, for it was in our behalf
> He laboured long and well;
> God knoweth it, indeed, 'twere not
> In our cause he fell;
> And he has claims upon us
> To be remembered long;
> We fear we overburdened,
> The willing and the strong.[55]

The same honour was accorded Edward Ashmore, a London Society of Compositors committee member, whose short obituary in the 15 April 1857 issue of the *Typographical Circular* was preceded by 'In Memoriam', a Knott penned poetic tribute to both him and the departed William Cox.[56] Ashmore and Cox formed part of the quadrumvirate of committee members who had worked to secure new premises for the Society.[57] In his short three-verse poem lamenting the demise of Ashmore and Cox, Knott offered a rather morbid warning to the remaining members still extant to look after their health. As he mournfully exclaimed,

> Ah, how little we thought, when, with hearts full of hope,
> On our brotherly errand we wended,
> That soon two out of four should be coldly entombed,
> To their Maker their spirits ascended;
> May the twain that remain lay the warning to heart,
> For the shafts are still bright in Death's quiver,
> And we know not how soon we must render account
> For the talent of life to the Giver.[58]

In February 1869, the *Scottish Typographical Circular* notified its readers of the death of John Shand, 'so long the able and zealous assistant-secretary to the London Society of Compositors'.[59] Shand served his apprenticeship in Edinburgh before moving to London in 1840. He not only played a significant role in the London unions for many years, he also acted as London correspondent for the *Scottish Typographical Circular* between 1865 and 1869. The following month the *STC*

[55] Alfred Knott, 'In Memory of William Cox', *Typographical Circular*, 15 January 1857.
[56] 'In Memoriam', *Typographical Circular*, 15 April 1857.
[57] A footnote to the poem records that 'Messrs Ashmore, Hinds, and Knott formed the sub-committee for seeking a suitable building for the Society-house, and Mr Cox, the late secretary, co-operated with them.' Ibid.
[58] Ibid.   [59] 'Obituary', *Scottish Typographical Circular*, 1 February 1869.

published an accompanying valedictory poem sent in by a London contemporary, in which his honesty, lack of guile and proven worth in the arts was offered as a curious contrast to other Scottish expatriates whose worth had also been proven in the battlefield. The two verses and coda read:

> O Scotland! Thy stern teaching hath sent forth
> Those who are in arts and arms have prov'd their worth:
> 'Neath Afric sun, o'er Asia's parching ground,
> Wherever men may dare, thy sons are found,
> Shoulder to shoulder, bidding Fate defy,
> Teaching us how to live, and how to die.

> Tho' he whose loss we mourn in our own life
> But trod his way, guileless and free from strife
> Was his career, safe from such war as men
> Do bear adverse circumstances; hill or glen
> Southward ne'er sent a truer heart to cheer
> A comrade in distress: trace us his peer!

> One sigh doth 'scape us, bending o'er the churchyard sod:
> 'Here lies an honest man, the noblest work of God.'[60]

When Robert Chambers died on 18 March 1871, the *Scottish Typographical Circular* hurriedly dedicated two pages in its April issue to his memory, preceding an *In Memoriam* obituary with a short poem praising his work in spreading knowledge in quiet yet dedicated ways.[61] As the first stanza called out,

> A life so full of silent deeds
> Hath little need of utter'd praise;
> He scatter'd well the knowledge seeds
> That swell and bud for coming days.[62]

The obituary offered similar encomiums, while highlighting his work as editor, poet, prose writer, publishing innovator and 'considerate, liberal, and indulgent employer', all undertaken with the goal of meeting 'the requirements of an intelligent, cultivated, and progressive people'.[63]

Less significant if equally mourned compositors also had obituaries and verses contributed by friends or working acquaintances. When the Leeds-based compositor William Craven passed away in November 1844, a short notice was published in the December issue of *The Printer* commenting on the shattering effect on his health of a life spent tramping in search of work. His death had been 'in consequence of a general breaking up of the constitution, materially hastened by repeated journeys in search of employment, and more than ordinary privations.'[64] A sixteen-line stanza of commemorative verse accompanied the notice, sent in by 'A brother

---

[60] 'To the Memory of John Shand. Assistant Secretary, London Society of Compositors', *Scottish Typographical Circular*, 1 March 1869.
[61] 'In Memoriam', *Scottish Typographical Circular*, 1 April 1871.   [62] Ibid.
[63] Ibid.   [64] 'Death of Mr Craven, Compositor'.

typo, 27 years acquainted with the deceased.'[65] The poem, in general rhyming couplets, offered standard tropes of sorrow and farewell, at the same time counter-pointing the obituary's focus on the hard life spent tramping across regional trade networks, concluding,

> On earth, of troubles he'd his share, –
> Of tramping and a printer's care; –
> Of Blackstone Edge and drear Shap fell,
> His shattered frame remembered well;[66]

Robert Sutherland (1818–1880), an Edinburgh printer, received a similar eight-line poetic salute in the *Scottish Typographical Circular* when he died in December 1880. It offered a general reflection on his kind nature, though with little direct mention of his significance to the printing fraternity:

> From busy life he made his final bow;
> Few kinder spirits pass the doubtful bourne;
> True, honest purposes marked his open brow;
> All meanness had his sharp contempt and scorn.
> Quick to proclaim the right, condemn the wrong,
> But ever under Friendship's potent spell,
> He walked through life a man, erect and strong,
> Till called away by death's all-powerful knell.[67]

CIVIC CELEBRATIONS AND COMMUNITY SUPPORT

One feature stands out as an important aspect of labour poetry appearing in typographical journals of the period, namely the oral and bardic origins of such contributions. Many of the poems reproduced in typographical journals were originally performed in public for key events in the print trade, such as annual soirees, wayzgooses and trade dinners, launches, and unveilings of trade spaces and buildings, fundraisers for individuals or print related causes, and social gatherings to mark departures and retirements. In these circumstances, as the printed evidence makes clear, spoken and sung poetry and verse were vital parts of such public events, counterpointing key themes underpinning the commemorations proposed. Typographical trade journals reprinted such efforts wholesale, maintaining the original cadence and rhythm of the spoken texts as presented on the day.

Compositor-poets were treated as respected bards anchored in oral, local, and trade culture, and civic turns were expected of them. Alfred Knott was often called upon to perform commissioned works at print trade events, with some set to music and sung by local talent. Thus in the 1 May 1855 issue of the *Typographical Circular*, a note of a print trade cricket club evening dinner highlighted Knott's star turn with an original composition, which 'elicited much applause from the pointed

---

[65] Ibid.   [66] Ibid.   [67] 'In Memoriam', *Scottish Typographical Circular*, January 1881.

manner in which it was executed by Mr G. Fellowes, jun., who was accompanied by Mr Hartford on the pianoforte'.[68] Similarly, the 1 April 1856 issue of the *Typographical Circular* reported a benefit for the widow and children of Mr Green, recently deceased printer and society member, at which a Knott piece was performed with great success to an attentive evening audience.[69]

Alexander Smart's civic print trade turns were equally noted in the *Scottish Typographical Circular*. Smart, though, was accorded more prominence than his contemporary Knott, by featuring in the left-hand column of the front page of every issue from January 1858 through to late 1860. Like Alfred Knott, this Scottish 'labour's laureate' was in frequent demand to round off artisanal literary soirees, openings and social events with a poetic recitation or a specially commissioned piece set to music and sung by an invited entertainer. In November 1859, Smart appeared in public as the keynote speaker at the Edinburgh Letterpress Printers Soiree, where he recited his Scots dialect poem 'Madie's Schule', reprinted as the lead piece of the 3 December 1859 issue of the *STC*. Here, recalled for all was stern schoolteacher Madie, who ruled a garret school with discipline dispensed by way of a leather strap (a taws) or rewards of a penny and sweets for the top scholars:

> To the whir o' the wheel, while auld baudrons would sing,
> On stools, wee an' muckle, a' ranged in a ring
> Ilk idle bit urchin, wha glowered aff his book,
> Was caught in a twinkling by Madie's dread look.
> She ne'er spak' a word, but the taws she would fling!
> The sad leather whang up the culprit maun bring,
> While his sair bluthered face, as the palmies would fa',
> Proclaimed through the schule an example for a'.
>
> But though Madie could punish, she weel could reward,
> The gude and the eydant aye won her regard-
> A Saturday penny she freely would gi'e,
> And the second best scholar got aye a bawbee.[70]

Poets, versifiers, and singers were in demand at the opening of buildings, offices and public monuments. When the Ballantyne Press unveiled its new premises in Edinburgh's Causewayside area in November 1870, one of its employers, the *STC*'s poet in residence Robert Brough, composed a song especially for the occasion. The verses were reproduced in the December 1870 issue of the *STC*, along with a four-page summary of the premises and the celebrations accompanying its unveiling. The Ballantyne building covered 3,000 square yards and a full street length, stood two stories high with a roof 23 feet in height, and was buttressed by the latest in glass, steel and iron. The *STC* breathlessly extolled the firm's foresight in constructing one of the most progressive work spaces in Edinburgh, 'one of the most comprehensive, healthy, and cheerful-looking printing establishments, a model building in every respect, and in striking contrast to the many dark, dingy, and

---

[68] 'The United Cricketers', *Typographical Circular*, 1 May 1855.
[69] 'The Entertainment', *Typographical Circular*, 1 April 1856.
[70] Alexander Smart, 'Madie's Schule', *Scottish Typographical Circular*, 3 December 1859.

unwholesome erections usually devoted to the carrying on of the art in this and other great cities'.[71] Brough's verses etched out in Broad Scots the pleasures to be had in such new premises, where willing, nimble workers would flourish under generous hosts. The chorus, 'lustily' sung by all assembled at the grand opening, concluded in rousing fashion,

> In our bonnie, braw New House!
> Our gran', big roomy house;
> Our blythesome, cheery house.
> May peace and plenty aye attend
> Our bonnie, braw New House![72]

More tellingly, compositor-poets were ubiquitous voices in fundraising events for indigent printer families and trade-based social causes. The root cause of this attention to social welfare related to the legal restrictions on unions that existed until the 1871 Trade Union Act, which legitimized trade unions as lobbying bodies rather than as purely benevolent societies. Until then, employers, who when confronted with trade strike actions used legal devices to prosecute trade unions and their members for supposed political interference in the work place, closely watched union actions. The print trade press widely reported on socially responsive trade events, bearing witness, framing, and highlighting the social welfare mission upon which trade societies based themselves during the mid-century period of their organization.

Typographical trade journals were quick to note when poetry, song, and verse were pressed into the services of fundraising events. A good example can be found in the 5 April 1841 issue of the *Compositors' Chronicle*, which featured the printer-poet John Lash Latey, originally from Devon, later to gain acclaim as editor of the *Illustrated London News*. The *Chronicle* news item recorded the presence of Latey at a London fundraiser for the establishment of an 'Asylum for Aged and Infirm Printers', and printed in full the specially commissioned piece from him subsequently 'delivered with much point by Mr Darkin'.[73] Conjuring up a vision of a space where former compositors might live out their final years in pleasant company, the poet drops in trade specific jargon to enliven the rather pedestrian rhyme, calling on listeners to picture retirees puffing pipes and conversing in amicable typographical form:

> Of *solid digs* they talk – of *fat* and *lean*,
> And how some *proofs* were *foul*, and some so *clean*.
> (Thus do they chat, and puff away between.)
> Ah, happy souls! They have no further troubles
> With cursed *outs,* and eke as cursed *doubles;*
> And not a solitary fear have they
> Of *muckled* sheets, or *monks*, or *friars* grey;
> With making register they've nought to do –
> Their last *ret.* is *made ready* – smoothly on they go.[74]

---

[71] 'The Ballantyne Press: The Old House and the New', *Scottish Typographical Circular* (1 December 1870), p. 398.

[72] Ibid., p. 399.   [73] 'Printers' Almshouses', *Compositors Chronicle*, 5 April 1841, p. 64.

[74] Ibid.

Latey returned to the subject in 1844 in the March issue of *The Printer*, which printed a poem he had written for delivery by the union Secretary at a concert in December 1843 in aid of the Printers' Almhouse Fund.[75] Money was still needed to complete the project mooted three years before. Latey, having written poetic encomiums for the original scheme fundraiser, called on his printer compatriots to dig into their pockets once more, for

> Not humbly, cap in hand, come we to plead
> Our cause – the cause of suffering need;
> But face to face, as man to man should speak,
> Your kind co-operation now we seek
> In this our common cause.[76]

Noting the social benefits printers had already established for their working brethren, most notably a pension fund for retired printers, Latey requested that the concert attendees donate their sixpences, for as he concluded rousingly,

> Now, hark you, friends – to cut the matter shorter –
> *You raise* the funds, *we'll raise* the bricks and mortar![77]

The Scots printer-poet and comic writer James Smith offered similar succour to various union events, and the *Scottish Typographical Circular* records several instances of his presence at key fundraisers, such as a soiree announced for 4 April 1863 in aid of the Printers Library, which in addition to addresses by Edinburgh luminaries such as the publisher William Chambers, author William Aytoun and the *Courant* Editor James Hannay, featured James Smith, who was to 'enliven the evening with some of his humorous Scotch stories'.[78] The short notice urged readers to attend: 'The object is good; the ability of the speakers is of the very highest character; and, altogether, the entertainment promises to be one which the trade ought to feel privileged in having the opportunity of patronising.'[79] On another occasion, Smith appeared at an annual soiree and concert in Edinburgh's Waverley Hall sponsored by the printers W & R Chambers, where he 'kindly favoured the company with his inimitable representations of "Tibbieleeri on Scandal" and "Betty M'Clink," and succeeded, as he is wont, in putting his audience into thorough good humour'.[80]

DIALECT FORMS

A key feature of several poems and creative pieces published in regionally based trade journals was the use of regional and local dialect. Poetry and prose in the *STC*, for example, drew heavily on Scots dialect forms. It was not unique, as Scots

---

[75] 'Printers' Almhouse Fund', *The Printer*, 1 March 1844. My thanks to Helen Williams for bringing this item to my attention.
[76] Ibid.   [77] Ibid.
[78] 'Soiree in Aid of Library', *Scottish Typographical Circular*, 7 March 1864.   [79] Ibid.
[80] Anon, *Scottish Typographical Circular*, 1 April 1871.

dialect material permeated much of locally produced Scottish press material of the time, as William Donaldson has noted in his work on the subject.[81] Aimed at an audience with an ear for local spoken language, it bespoke a linguistic identity nestled within a broader trade and North Briton identity, evident in the English language pieces that enfolded Alexander Smart's Scots dialect poetry in the *STC*. Smart's work was highly valued by the *STC*'s editors and intended print trade audience: he was seen as one of their own exploring and invoking trade values in informal vernacular tone, while also offering sentimental rhymes on domestic and social topics. Themes of educational joy like those in 'Madie's Schule' were leavened by more reasoned expatiations on the benefit of self-help, clean living, and dignity in labour. They were part and parcel of Smart's output and reputation. 'He is a son of toil', noted one trade review of his collected *Songs of Labour*, 'and sings to the sons of toil. He sings of the blessing of labour, and inculcates the duties of self-culture, self-reliance, self-respect, and self-control . . . and he is ever ready, as "Labour's Laureate", to defend its honest claims, and to rebuke those capitalists who...would buy and sell his muscle and his brain in the same fashion as they would the most worthless article of merchandise.'[82] Others remarked that Smart's labour poetry 'vindicated his claims as the voice of the industrious poor'.[83]

Similar dialect forms featured in the work of James Smith, Smart's successor as *STC* poet in residence. Writing in Doric Scots as well as Metropolitan Scots, a dialect of the Old Town of Edinburgh, Smith was commended by contemporaries for verses that 'always glow with life', or in the case of his best-known children's poetry, displayed 'considerable powers of humorous expression'.[84] One such jaunty nursery piece, 'Baloo, My Bairnie, Fa' Asleep', featured in the *STC* in July 1864, sitting alongside correspondence on the dire health of printers and notices of union meetings. The first stanza gives an indication of the way in which Smith used Scots terminology to strong effect:

> My sonsy wean! My darlin' bairn!
> My bonnie sweet wee lammie!
> Cosy i' yer beddy-baw,
> Crawin' to yer mammy!
> Blessin's on yer cheekies red,
> An' wee bit lauchin' e'e.
> Sparklin' like the gowden lift,
> Wi' gladsome, sunny glee!
> Baloo, my bairnie, fa' asleep,
> O hushy, hushy baw![85]

---

[81] William Donaldson, *Popular Literature in Victorian Scotland: Language, Fiction and the Press* (Aberdeen: Aberdeen University Press, 1986).

[82] Anon, 'Review, Songs of Labour and Domestic Life', *Scottish Typographical Circular*, 6 October 1860.

[83] 'Review', *Glasgow Herald*, 23 October.

[84] 'Review', *The Scotsman*, 13 March 1874, 'The Late Mr James Smith'.

[85] James Smith, 'Baloo, My Bairnie, Fa' Asleep!', *The Scottish Typographical Circular*, 2 July 1864.

Subsequent generations of Scottish children grew up with a variation or other of his children's ditty 'Clap, Clap, Handies', which partially ran:

> Clap, clap handies
> Daddie's coming ben
> Wi' siller bells an' coral shells
> Three score an' ten;
>
> A' to gie his laddie –
> His bonnie wee bit laddie –
> Clap, clap, handies,
> Deddy's comin' ben![86]

These, and children's verses such as Smith's equally well-known composition 'Wee Joukydaidles', described by a contemporary as 'perfection of its kind', 'a graphic and life-like photograph of a steerin', dish-breakin', sugar-licking Scotch wean', were frequently reprinted in decades following. 'Wee Joukydaidles' in particular enjoyed a long afterlife, moving across newspaper and book formats and into popular culture. Originally featured in the 20 August 1864 issue of the *Scotsman*, it was quickly picked up by regional sources, and reprinted a few days later in both the *Dundee Courier and Argus* and the *Birmingham Daily Post*.[87] Subsequently reprinted in Smith's 1865 poetry collection *Poems, Songs and Ballads,* it became a perennial favourite internationally as poem, recited verse, and popular song. Over the next half century and through into the 1920s, the poem would feature in Scots ballad and children's verse collections, and reprints and notices of its public performance would appear in UK, US, Australian, and New Zealand press outlets.[88]

Smith's poetic contributions to the *STC* ranged from reflective to serio-comic in tone and language. Dialect forms were part of the mix, and over the years of association with the *STC*, Smith produced several pieces that drew on Broad Scots intonations and spelling. A typical example was his contribution to the front page of the 2 January 1864 issue, the eight-stanza poem 'The Three Wee Flowers'. The poem, ostensibly a rumination by a female narrator on three flowers blooming in her garden, turns quickly into a *memento mori*, revealing the sombre truth that the garden spoken of is a graveyard, and the three wee flowers are her children buried there. (One cannot help wondering why the editor chose such a downbeat piece to greet the New Year.) The phrasing, much like other Scots dialect examples featured in the *STC*, is complex and dependent on particular forms of Scots

---

[86] *Merry Bridal O' Firthmains and Other Poems and Songs*, 2nd ed. (Edinburgh: William P. Nimmo and Co., 1866), p. 26.

[87] 'Wee Joukydaidles', *The Dundee Courier and Argus*, 22 August 1864; 'Wee Joukydaidles', *Birmingham Daily Post*, 22 August 1864; 'Wee Joukydaidles', *The Scotsman*, August 20 1864.

[88] W. E. McAdam, 'Wee Joukydaidles', *The Ashburton Guardian*, 12 February 1903; 'Wee Joukydaidles', *Otago Daily Times*, 10 February 1903; 'Wee Joukydaidles', *Otago Witness*, 11 February 1903; 'James Smith, the Poet Printer', *Printers' Circular*, 1 December 1874; James Smith, 'A Children's Poet', *The Stark County Democrat*, 3 March 1881; Anon, 'A Children's Poet', *Stark County Democrat*, 3 March 1881; Alexander G. Murdoch, ed. *The Scottish Poets, Recent and Living* (Glasgow: Thomas D. Morison, 1883); 'Old Edinburgh Poets and Their Songs', *The Scotsman*, 14 January 1922; 'Glasgow Programme', *The Scotsman*, 12 August 1924; Jessie Mackay, 'Scottish Nursery Songs', *Otago Witness*, 3 July 1907.

spelling and pronunciation to ensure the rhyme scheme flows. It moves swiftly from wistful to tragic in the first two stanzas:

> Three flow'rets bloom'd i' my garden ha'.
> I' the blithe sweet days o' langsyne;
> An' bonny an' fair were the three wee flowers
> That ance were Willie and mine.
> But a blicht cam owre my puir wee flowers,
> I' the time o' the frost an' the snaw;
> For they nestl'd their heids i' my sorrowin' breast,
> An' they droopit an' dow'd awa.

The final stanza reveals where the narrator is declaiming this lament, namely the graveyard:

> An' leeze me lang on the core o' my heart,
> Whase fondness may I never tine;
> But it's low low doun i' yon eerie yird
> Lie the three wee flowers o' mine.[89]

Smith's Scots dialect contributions to the *STC* were not limited to poetry (sombre or otherwise). He also produced humorous prose and fiction in broad Scots. Typical was his piece in the October 1867 issue, 'The Scottish Londoners', a short tale of an Edinburgh printer encountering a group of compositor acquaintances on leave in between working stints in London. The piece has some barbed commentary on Scottish identity that also turns up in later pieces by other contributors. The narrator, 'Longprimer Three Nick', muses over reports of Scots printers moving to London and losing their Scottish identity, and worries over the truth or not of such loss of culture. 'This sets me thinking on the Caledonian youths o' the craft that are up there', opines the narrator, 'an' on the ither reports I had heard o' Scottish Londoners forgettin', whenever they got there, the auld mither country, the auld mither tongue, an' the guid auld familiar faces o' the chums o' their youthfu' days, wi' a' their kindly associations.' He concludes mournfully, '"It's a sair thocht," says I to mysel', "if it's true, and it made me grue to think that it micht be the case."'[90] The question of trade identity, wrapped up within questions of the permanence of Scottish cultural identity when relocated to other parts of the country, are decisively settled when Nick meets three London-based colleagues resting in Leith between work stints. (Leith was a separate harbour district adjoining Edinburgh that was not absorbed into the city boundaries until 1920.) They repair to the pub, drink, exchange anecdotes and toasts, and emerge wrapped up in a comradely glow of friendship and solidarity helped by the large amount of alcohol consumed during the encounter. London has not changed them, the narrator happily concludes, and the stories of Scots 'drappin auld friends, auld likings, and the auld tongue, after bein' a while in London, is a' a lee [lie].' Little chance, then, the narrator happily pronounces, of finding 'a douce, sensible Auld Reeekie callant

---

[89] James Smith, 'The Three Wee Flowers', *The Scottish Typographical Circular*, 2 January 1864.
[90] James Smith, 'The Scottish Londoners', *Scottish Typographical Circular* (1 October 1867), p. 603.

transmogrifyin' himsel' into what a real Londoner hates waur [more] than cauld water wi' his beef – an imitation Cockney.'[91]

Robert Brough picked up this theme a few years later in his broad Scots poem 'Address to the Printers of Auld Reekie Now in London', printed in the *Scottish Typographical Circular* in October 1870. In this case, however, the poem is not a consideration of Scots identity amongst London expatriates. Instead, it is a lament and a call to London-based Scots compositors to return to Edinburgh, 'Auld Reekie' being the affectionate term used by its residents to describe the city, with Reekie referring to Edinburgh's smoky atmosphere. The poet descries the loss of trade members to London, and asks what is wrong with the old city that prevents them returning. The language is complex and rooted in Scots terms and phonetic spelling, as the opening sequence demonstrates:

> Ye chaps wha toil at case and press in Lunnan's muckle toun,
> What's wrang wi' dear Auld Reekie now, that fient a ane comes doun?
> Your hearts are surely blunted sair, or something waur ta'en place,
> Since in the crowds by boat and rail we ne'er see ae kenn'd face.[92]

The poem goes on to list Edinburgh's many pleasures, its native air, comfortable streets, hills, and suburban pleasures, which are tongue-in-cheek compared to similar though less favourable London delights. It asks Scottish readers to recall the delights of walking in the Pentland Hills, or of strolling around Edinburgh's central landmark, the hilly outcrop of 'Arthur's Seat', 'Where Art and Nature ha'e combined to mak' the scene complete'. Do not forget your comrades, the poem concludes, return to Edinburgh before the summer passes, and you'll find a warm welcome, a bed, warm supper, and a friendly hand:

> Noo, then, I'm done! But to my words ye really maun tak' heed,
> And ne'er again let simmer pass unless ye cross the Tweed:
> For weel ye ken our clannish ways, -that, 'midst a' jeers and slurs,
> Auld honest cronies we respect, and stick to them like burs.
> What though your togs were no a' new, and wadna cut a dash?
> Or maybe – constant plague wi' me- ye werena rife o' cash;
> We'll a' be proud to see ye here; -and, hang me, but I'll vaunt-
> A dram, your supper, or a bed, I'll swear ye wadna want![93]

Trade-particular terminology and local dialect poetry and prose forms were not confined to Scottish titles. An unusual confluence of both was published in the *Compositors' Chronicle* between October 1842 and April 1843. Entitled 'Stray Chapters, from the Life of Wimble Flash, a Typographic Cosmopolite, collected by Himself', this fictional seven-part series detailed the experiences of a compositor from apprenticeship in a Dublin print shop through to travels across Ireland in search of work, replete with provincial and trade specific dialogue, poetry, Irish folk tales and 'song poems' spread liberally throughout the text.[94]

---

[91] Ibid. p. 604.   [92] Robert Brough, 'Address to the Printers of Auld Reekie Now in London'.
[93] Ibid.
[94] 'Stray Chapters from the Life of Wimble Flash, a Typographic Cosmopolite. Collected by Himself', *The Compositors' Chronicle*, October-April 1842–3.

The narrative prose is intertwined with poetry and verse of various lengths and focus. On his first day, Wimble has to dip his hand into his pocket to pay for refreshments for his new comrades, a social tradition imposed on all new recruits. Two quarts of whisky, some sugar, hard biscuits, and a bottle of beer are brought in and stored for dispersal after work ceases at seven pm. Several drinks and toasts later, songs and verses come spilling out of the company, with compositors taking it in turn to offer ballads and short verses on matters print-related. The soliloquies draw on common print trade poetic conventions, weaving print-related terms into the verses, and our attention is drawn to the print vernacular on the page through strategic use of italics. The longest of these verse recitals, 'The Editor's Hat', sets out in six stanzas a tale of an apprentice compositor and an overseer, the former anticipating what work he'd be assigned, the latter in charge of assignments stored in his 'Editor's Hat'. The poem's opening contrasts the two players in this scenario, highlighting as noted with italics the print terms rolled into the verses:

> One bleaky windy morning
> The *devil* set out,
> The chilly blast scorning,
> He held on his route;
> To a garret repairing,
> For *lean* or for *fat*;
> He knew he'd get either
> In *Th' Editor's Hat*.
>
> The man of the inkhorn
> Was seated upright
> On the pallet of straw
> Where he'd *rolled* thro' the night.
> His cloak was around him,
> His shoes on a mat –
> To a table beside him
> He stretched for his *Hat*.[95]

Contained within the hat are the contents of next day's news items and notices, and here we are treated to the panoply of topics that compositors might encounter over a day's work, from momentous political news to mundane comic fillers. On top of this, some items are also wrapped around the overseer's dinner, with humorous consequences:

> 'Twas chaotic confusion, –
> A *pie-box* to view.
> There were murders in plenty –
> A marriage or two;
> The last battle of Wellesley,
> French news and all that
> Were huddled together
> In the *Editor's Hat*.

---

[95] Ibid., p. 215.

> The late evening's play-bill
> Encircled a birth,
> While a loaf (price one penny)
> The 'Markets' did girth.
> A long strip of verses,
> The Foreign chit-chat,
> While some mouldy cheese lay
> In the *Editor's Hat*.
>
> The great speech of Grattan;
> Blow-up of a brig;
> A dog taught to whistle;
> The state whirligig;
> Dan O'Connell's preamble
> To civilize Pat,
> Were mixed humble-jumble
> In the *Editor's Hat*.[96]

After his stint in Dublin, the narrator embarks on a picaresque tramp through various parts of Ireland, stopping in Maynooth, Longford, Shannon, Jamestown, and Connaught. Along the way he encounters a mad young Irish man, pursued by an older woman (who is the man's mother). The encounter leads to an extraordinary section of Irish Gaelic conversation, in which the mother implores her son in Irish Gaelic, 'Padraig, my boy, go [and] lie down', to which he replies, 'I was going to, my mother.' The original text reads:

> The old woman was now some distance before him, and lingering a little, she beckoned to him, calling out at the same time, 'Paudrig, ma moughal, go lie.'
> 'Vhau me dhu, ma waugher', said he; and he began to lilt a wild song in his native tongue . . . [97]

The mad wanderer's 'wild song' is reproduced in English translation. Other traditional Irish tales and songs feature in later sections of the series, in what could be seen as incipient ethnographic studies of Irish customs. What is particularly striking about this inclusion in an English typographical trade journal is its attempt to ground the narrator's tramping experiences within Irish cultural contexts. The author makes clear he has an ulterior motive for this, for towards the end of the series, he launches into an *ad hominem* attack upon recent publications by English visitors purporting to offer authentic insights into Irish culture. He reserves particular scorn for the London-based authors Samuel Carter Hall and his wife Anna Maria, who between 1841 and 1843 published an extremely popular and influential

---

[96] Ibid.
[97] Ibid., p. 289. I am indebted to Regina Uí Chollatáin of University College, Dublin for translating this section of text. The three-stage translation from original print version to current Gaelic spelling, and then to English, reads as follows:

> 'Paudrig, ma moughal, go lie.' = 'Pádraig, mo bhuachaill, gabh a luí.' = 'Pádraig, my boy, go (and) lie down.'
> 'Vhau me dhul, ma waugher' = 'Bhá mé a dhul, mo mháthair' = 'I was going to, my mother'

three volume account of Irish tours undertaken between 1825 and 1840, *Ireland, its Scenery, Character etc.*[98] 'Let me indulge in an apostrophe', begins the narrator before venting his spleen in a forceful dissection of this and other studies of Irish character by English cultural tourists. 'When I take up the works of Mrs. Hall, and others, who *profess* to give the present generation true pictures of Ireland and the Irish, I cannot but grieve to see how superficial are their observations of the real manners and customs of the peasantry.'[99] The real issue for the irate narrator was the way that such colonial misrepresentations had become integrated into general views of the ruling classes overseeing Ireland's welfare, the absentee landlords and the members of English drawing room culture, who in general exhibited little interest in the Irish people except as part of an idealized scenery to be visited and exclaimed over. It comes as a bit of a shock to encounter the following splenetic articulation of nationalist rage in a narrative dedicated to tramping observations and typographical shenanigans:

> And when their works become standard, and are quoted as authorities, I am tempted to think that a full knowledge of those things *may* be learned in the drawing-room of high society, and that it only needs fine writing, well-rounded periods, and a laugh now and again at some provincial or localism (than which a more numerous list, and much more ridiculous, might be picked up *elsewhere*), to render a work *taking* in the present day, and have it stamped by a venal press with the title of 'The best Delineations of National Character extant'. In vain do I look for that faithful portraiture of Hibernian life that would create a feeling of shame in the breasts of absentee landlords and their haughty agents...[100]

The author concludes that far more authentic portrayals of Irish character could be found in the popular creative works of the recently deceased John Banim (1798–1842, labelled by some the Scott of Ireland), William Carleton (1794–1869) and Samuel Lover (1797–1868). Commendations of their work are made along with swipes (without mentioning her name) at his main cultural tourist target, Anna Maria Hall:

> But I am happy to say, that honest depictors of Irish scenery and manners have not passed away with Banim. While Carleton and Lover live, we have an antidote to the slip-slop ribaldry – the satire under a friendly mask, doled out to us on menstrual dishes; we have an anodyne to the ironical jests and washy descriptions – those libels perpetrated to create a simper on the curling lip of national antipathy, written with more attention to style than to truthfulness, and like the Yorkshireman's razors, less with a view to utility than sale.[101]

---

[98] For a recent study of the Halls' work and its conceptions of Ireland, see Amélie Dochy, 'Mr and Mrs Hall's Tour of Ireland in the 1840s, More Than a Unionist Guidebook, an Illustrated Definition of Ireland Made to Convince', *Miranda*, no. 9 (2014), http://miranda.revues.org/5917.

[99] 'Stray Chapters from the Life of Wimble Flash, a Typographic Cosmopolite. Collected by Himself', p. 262.

[100] Ibid.   [101] Ibid.

PROSE NARRATIVES

'Stray Chapters' was an unusual mixture of prose, verse, and literary commentary. It nevertheless was suggestive of the general range of creative material that featured in print trade journals in the early period of their development. Compositor written prose narratives and fiction like 'Stray Chapters' and Smith's 'The Scottish Londoners' appeared often in such journals throughout the 1840s to 1870s, offering affirmations of a world-view bounded by trade knowledge, shared skills, and traditions dating back centuries. The world-view was gendered (the print room in most cases was a male space for most of the century except in specified areas such as bookbinding and paper-folding) and overlaid with a need to adapt to nineteenth-century shifts in infrastructure, evolving technological innovations, and shifts in working conditions.

Paramount in these narratives was a vision of the workspace that in essence had not changed a great deal since the inception of printing. Though Linotype and later Monotype printing changed the skills required for tasks such as composing and laying out texts for printing, the general patterns of work and social interaction, and the spaces in which these took place, remained the same throughout the century: composing rooms took in manuscript material, composers stood at cases of type placing relevant letters into lines on composing sticks, that would then be laid into a large flat box or form. These lines were then shaped, hammered, and flattened into position and locked down in preparation for the pressmen to put through the inking and printing processes. Journeyman printers learned at the case through long apprenticeships of up to seven years. Good apprenticeships provided them with a background in grammar, syntax, sentence structure, and word alignment, typographical look and feel that many then took into the literary-cultural sphere as editors, poets, writers, and memoirists. Fiction and memoirs that fed from these experiences often drew attention to the visual and tactile nature of working with type and text.

Such direct interaction with hot metal not only shaped physical space within the periodical page, it also loomed large in the trade rituals noted in fiction and prose reflections. Typical is this description of a print room's celebration of the expiration of an apprentice's indentures and his entrance into the trade as fully fledged journeyman printer:

> Crowbars, sledge hammers, and steam hammers, seemed to be pounding away as though the order had been given to wreck the building; iron sidesticks, mallets, improvised gongs, the sound of which froze your blood and almost deafened you; clang! Clang! As to bring the police up the stairs; whilst the father banged till he perspired freely, and every man-jack, apprentice, and even the 'devil' himself joined in, the foreman raised his hands appealingly in the air as if imploring for a merciful deliverance from the pandemonium![102]

It was a skilled craft, for a period a dominant one in terms of working-class culture. Various tales in journals such as the *STC* play up this sense of eminence, at the

---

[102] J. W. Rounsfell, *On the Road: Journeys of a Tramping Printer* (Horsham: Caliban Books, 1982), p. 180.

same time enfolding such accounts within language and phraseology peculiar to the trade. An interesting example is James Smith's 'The Courtship o' Padie Cauldshouthers; or, the unco surprise', a three-part novella serialized between November 1861 and February 1862 in the *Scottish Typographical Circular* (see Figure 3.9). One of its striking features is its visual play with print traditions: at one point in the story a mockup of a printer's sign jumps out of the page in bold, boxed in type, satirizing the self-aggrandizing advertising spiels of contemporary print establishments.[103]

Another distinction of Smith's tale is its immersion in Scots dialect. The story of a Scottish printer who seeks and wins the hand of a sharp-eyed woman named Molly McTaggart, the narrative is replete with both dialect forms and print trade phraseology, as in this crucial, humorous moment when the hero attempts to impress the female love interest with his standing and his fame in the printing trade:

> 'I'm the heid manager o' the Toddrick's Wynd Ranter!' says he, 'an' Jock o' the Green's my richt-hand man! An' it was me that made' – an' here his buirdly form swelled wi' conscious greatness – 'it was me that made the heid-piece to Jock an his Mither!' . . . Then, wi' his hands still round her neck, he said, a' trummlin' frae heid to fit – 'If I'm spared to see the morn's morning, I'll send up the deevil to inquire for yer health, my petty!'
>
> 'The deevil!' says she, shrinking back, an' turnin' up the whites o' her e'en.
>
> 'Ay, my doo!' says he, 'I was yince a deevil mysel'!
>
> 'What!' cried she, throwin' aff his arm, 'does a deevil gang to the chapel!'
>
> 'Ou ay, an' the aul yin's whiles there tae', says Patie, wi' a lauch, 'but the deevil I mean's the youngest laddie i' the printing office. An' noo, my dear, what's yer name?'[104]

In 'Stray Chapters, from the life of Wimble Flash', strangely strangulated imitations of Scots dialect make their appearance in the early sections of the jaunty narrative, when the hero Wimble Flash meets the Scots foreman who takes charge of his apprenticeship in the Dublin newspaper the *Morning Fly*. The owner presents the recruit to 'Mr Scotchy', who begins the acquaintanceship in the following way:

> 'Hoo do ye loike the prentin?' asked the overseer, as soon as the proprietor had turned his back.
>
> Rather too soon by a little to ask, thought I; but alike disconcerted, I replied, 'Pretty well, sir.'
>
> 'Hoo auld are ye?' was his next query, after a short pause.
>
> 'Nearly fifteen,' replied I.
>
> 'Puir bairn!' said he, half comic, half pathetic, at the same time endeavouring to look important. 'Your trouble a' before ye, loike the young bears;' and he looked around him for a smile, in approval of his having committed a good thing.[105]

---

[103] James Smith, 'The Courtship O' Padie Cauldshouthers; or, the Unco Surprise', *Scottish Typographical Circular* (2 November 1861), p. 43.

[104] Ibid., p. 45.

[105] 'Stray Chapters from the Life of Wimble Flash, a Typographic Cosmopolite. Collected by Himself'.

THE SCOTTISH TYPOGRAPHICAL CIRCULAR.   43

THE COURTSHIP O' PATIE CAULDSHOUTHERS;

OR, THE UNCO SURPRISE.

IN THREE CHAPTERS.

CHAPTER I.—PRELIMINARY.

I'M jalousin' that the warst thing in a' this wide warld's to see twa folk 'gaun thegither, for better or waur, into the life-boat o' blessed matrimony, an' no rowin' the same way. An' to pit this to the proof, I'm jist gaun to tell ye a wee bit story about an auld freen o' mine ca'd Patie Cauldshouthers, a weel-faured, sonsy chield, but unco cauld i' the mornin's; an' as gude a ceveleesed cratur as ever broke the pairin-meal scones o' Christianity mixed wi' barley!—whase only faut was bein' a wee thing ower simple,—but that's often the case wi' the very best o' men. Noo ye maun ken Patie was the Heid Manager o' the great *Toddrick's Wynd Ranter,*—a post o' honour he had risen to by dint o' oncommon perseverance an' unwearied energy. He served his time wi' Cockledumdyte, the Janius, wha had a printin' office on a gigantic scale in Bull's Close, i' the Cowgate, first stair on the left hand as ye gang in, at the very tap flet. He printed sermons, sangs, an' drunken summonses by the hunder thoosand; an' every blessed thing he printed had a lion an' a unicorn at the tap o't, no to speak o' the grand sign-board out-side, that was the admiration o' a' the toon. An' this was the sign :—

BENJAMIN COCKLEDUMDYTE,

PRINTER TO THE KING'S MOST EXCELLENT MAJESTY.

Every defcription of Printing taken in and done for !

Bills of all kinds moft aftonifhingly cheap ; Songs and Ballads at Half-price; and Sermons printed for nothing !

Bread and Butter taken in exchange for Provision Merchants' Accounts, but Cafh indifpenfable from Druggifts !

Patronifed by the Earl of Fruchie, and the Earl of Fruchie's Father !

BULL'S CLOSE, COWGATE.

God fave the King and his Refpeĉable Grandmother !

Aweel, ye see, it wasna in the least to be wondert at, that under sic grand an' golden auspices, Patie cam on sae oncommonly weel. He was prime at makin' woodcuts for ballants, an' the famous heid-piece to *Jock an' his*

Figure 3.9 James Smith's 'The Courtship o' Padie Cauldshouthers; or, the unco surprise', *Scottish Typographical Circular*, 1861

The narrator continues with a close observation of the working day, the social dynamics at play in the workspace, and the odd characters inhabiting the print room. It is an unvarnished account offered in jocular tone, and interesting for its insights into workspace interactions. As an apprentice, Wimble begins his day at 6.30 a.m., opening the shop, sweeping the premises, cleaning printing tools and sorting type. Hour long meal breaks occur at 9 a.m. and 3 p.m., with final despatch of work by 7 p.m., followed by banter and general socializing over drinks. The intellectual leanings of the printers manifest themselves in unusual ways. Wimble describes several colleagues who pass the time in versifying, punning or declaiming at critical points in the composing process. Thus, we meet Patten, who 'sung a merry lilt after every meal', while in contrast, the apprentice 'Henry Bates indulged in his pun whenever he found an opportunity; and George Gregory (whom I have not before named, and whose taste was all in the histrionic line), laid down his composing-stick, upon meeting with an extract from a tragedy in his copy, in order to "take the floor", and rehearse the whole of the speech from which it was taken.'[106]

At one point a mock verbal battle ensues between Henry Bates and George Gregory, both compositors with theatrical leanings, in which commentary and Shakespearian verses are recast to feature heavy doses of print trade vernacular. Bates, despatched at times to deliver love letters for Gregory to his latest passion, is promised payment for this service, which is not forthcoming, as 'Gregory was not a master of a *sous*.'[107] Bates confronts him, at which point the two grandstand in a lengthy linguistic punning and versifying to-and-fro, much to the amusement of the assembled workers. In the section that follows, one can see the way in which the author cleverly mixes literary references and print terminology to great effect, with verbal puns that turn on shifts in pronunciation (pique pronounced as pica, for example), and soliloquies that draw on shared knowledge of Shakespearian verse. It is worth quoting at length.

> Gregory started and blushed. He did not wish to appear confused, and yet he could not help it. Regaining in some degree his self-possession, he looked his accuser in the face, while he replied, –
>   'Good name in man or woman
> Is the immediate jewel of our souls.
> Who steals my purse, steals trash; 'tis something, nothing, –
> 'Twas Mine, 'tis his, and has been slave to thousands;
> But he that filcheth from me my good name,
> Robs me of that which nought enricheth him,
> And makes me poor indeed.'
>
> 'True,' said Bates, smiling; 'but your purse never did much slavery, though you are doomed to be a *galley-slave* all your days. But, come, deliver, or –'
> 'Nothing extenuate, nor set down aught in malice,' chimed in Gregory.
> 'No, but I'll *set up* all in *pi-que*,' replied the punster, playing upon the word, which he pronounced as nearly as possible as if written *pica*.
>
> A little ticking, made by the fingers upon the cases at this juncture, proclaimed that the last sally was received with general approbation; when it subsided, the declaimer was soliloquizing –
>   'To pay, or not to pay, that is the question.
> Whether 'tis nobler in a man to suffer
> The affronts and slander of a whelp like this,
> Or to take out his purse and fork the blunt,

---

[106] Ibid., p. 222.   [107] Ibid., p. 230.

And, satisfying, stay his noisy tongue?
To pay; be out of debt, – no more – '
'Stop, stop!' cried the patience-worn apprentice, 'you had better down with the dust,
or I'll split the name of the lass I carried the note to.'[108]

TRADE PRINT CLASS AND CULTURAL DYNAMICS

That the printing fraternity in general, and the British print trade in particular, produced creative talents of various note, and developed outlets in which to feature such talent, was not as unusual as it would seem. Nineteenth-century working-class writing emanating from the printing trade was linked in key ways to a privileged sense of place in the social hierarchy of labour organization. Printers and compositors were at the forefront of nineteenth-century social and trade union movements, in terms of union organization, social support, establishing libraries and educational centres, and in organizing and actively engaging in literary and cultural events. One notable example linking several creatively inclined compositors was the formation in London in June 1853 of the Jerrold Dramatic Club. Formed as a means of providing entertainment to raise funds for print trade causes, its patron was Douglas Jerrold, noted elsewhere in this book for his place as a leading compositor turned dramatist of the period. Its secretary was William Dorrington, also noted for his poetic contributions and his later rise to editorial fame. Other trade members representing a range of firms formed the core organizational committee. A half-page prospectus for the new club was printed in the July 1853 issue of the *Typographical Protection Circular*, followed by a poem by William Dorrington delivered at Sadlers' Wells Theatre for a benefit in aid of the Compositors Emigration Aid Society.[109] The two items counterpointed the multiple ways in which the print trade drew on its creative membership to support social causes, and the prominence given to these activities in the trade press. Printing unions also hosted Burns nights in Scotland, celebrated 400 years of printing in 1850, ran literary soirees and fund raisers for bereaved printing families and widows, set up bereavement and funeral funds, retirement, and emigration schemes, and sponsored sick benefit and tramping or unemployment schemes. Newspapers, trade journals, and private members' publications were also subsidized. These allowed individuals the opportunity to reaffirm their interests and connections with cultural activity, through recitations of poetry and music, presentation of short plays, and the promotion of public readings.

Not all thought such literary miscellany material appropriate for a trade journal: as one reviewer sniffily commented in a piece comparing the *STC* with the newly launched *Australian Typographical Circular*, 'The Circular has had more of the

---

[108] Ibid., p. 230.
[109] 'Prospectus of the Jerrold Dramatic Club', *The Typographical Protection Circular*, July 1853; William Dorrington, 'An Address', *The Typographical Protection Circular*, July 1853.

literary mixed up with it than some might think desirable in a trade journal.'[110] In 1866, editors of the *Bookbinders' Trade Circular* found themselves defending the inclusion of poetry and a serialized history of bookbinding against charges that these were boring, with the latter likened to a funeral sermon.[111] Similarly, complaints were received from readers of typographical journals who saw no benefit in learning about literary matters. Responding to the launch in the December 1863 issue of the *Scottish Typographical Circular* of 'Recreations of a Reader', a column dedicated to literary topics and written anonymously by James Smith, one correspondent wrote indignantly protesting its inclusion. 'The "Reader" who is seeking to amuse and instruct us with his "Recreations", is obviously an egotist as well as a bookworm', the disgruntled correspondent exclaimed.[112] It was not helpful or wise encouraging printers to read widely, for a 'few good books ought to satisfy those whose time is principally given up to the earning of their bread by manual labour.'[113] Reflect deeply and observe the world, the correspondent chided, rather than skim books to cram oneself full of the ideas and words of others. 'Too much reading begets, or at least favours and fosters, indolent habits', the writer tartly concluded, 'and tends to indispose one for the rough work of every-day existence.'[114] Smith responded in the next issue by arguing that reading was a valuable recreation worthy of reflection and consideration. 'A man, surely, may recreate himself in many ways – each one of us has his own special traits or habits of mind; and what one may take great pleasure in, another may view with a feeling bordering on disgust.... and is not this spending of the evening over some favourite author, whose noiseless flow of living thought makes the longest night seem short, as truly "recreation" as any other and more material kind of pleasure?'[115]

Implicit in such comments were class-based tensions between expectations and aspirations. Printers and compositors were viewed as important accessories to literary and print communication, turning manuscripts and written text into printed form. But such practical knowledge seemed to militate in cultural terms against being taken seriously as creative producers. Such tensions manifested not just in views offered in the correspondence columns, but also in reviews of printer-poets.

A good example of this was brought out in a January 1865 *Scotsman* review of a volume of James Smith's poetry, a work that had been typeset and privately printed by Smith. Though generally admiring of his talent, and noting with some pleasure that several of the entries had originally appeared in the pages of the *Scotsman*, the reviewer suggested such creativity was not a common feature of the working man in general, and the compositor in particular. Quoting approvingly from remarks made by the contemporary historian John Hill Burton in his bibliographical study

[110] 'Book Notices'. The *Australian Typographical Circular*.

[111] Quoted in Melissa Score, 'Pioneers of Social Progress?: Gender and Technology in British Printing Trade Union Journals, 1840–65', *Victorian Periodicals Review* 47, no. 2 (2014), p. 276, footnote 6.

[112] Literatus, 'The "Reader" and His "Recreations"', *Scottish Typographical Circular*, 6 February 1864.

[113] Ibid.   [114] Ibid.

[115] James Smith, 'The Recreation of a Reader', *Scottish Typographical Circular* (5 March 1864), p. 492.

The Book Hunter on the perceived 'indifference of printers to literature save as it affects them in the shape of "copy"', the reviewer concurred with such estimations of the intellectual capacity of mere handlers of type. 'We have heard of printers being interested in a novel they were setting; we have now and then – to our wonderment from the rarity of such demonstration – heard a laugh from a reading-boy over one of *Punch's* jokelets; but as a rule Mr Burton is right; and the fact that few printers have become, in any but the literal sense, men of letters, bears out his implication of their general mediocrity of intellect; if, indeed, the blunders with which they vex authors' souls do not stamp then, in the mass, with deliberate dullness.'[116] It would have been interesting to know what the compositors of the *Scotsman* had made of this slur on their character as they went about typesetting the offending comments.

Two weeks later, the displeased editor of the *STC* made clear his own views, using the first three pages of the February issue to roundly castigate the reviewer for such fatuous remarks. 'Let us turn for a moment to the very important and remarkable discoveries he has made as to the intellectual darkness in which the members of the printing trade are at present enveloped', the *STC* editorial caustically noted, going on to quote the offending paragraph denigrating printing intellect, and then incredulously querying, 'Now, how are we, in the brief space of a single article, to meet these astounding assertions?'[117] The answer was to draw attention to prime exemplars of printers turned authors, journalists and editors, including the *Scotsman's* current editor, and to conclude scathingly that conceit and ignorant presumption might be attributes more potentially applicable to the reviewer himself.

Similar press prejudices were on view on the death of the author, dramatist, and journalist Douglas Jerrold in London in June 1857. Obituary notices were quick to point out his move from midshipman on a man-of-war to typesetting drudgery as a printer's apprentice, then to respected and talented author, propelled in part by self-discipline and auto-didactic efforts. As several notices commented, his move from sailor to apprentice was accompanied by a move to self-improvement and self-instruction. 'He became his own instructor after hours of labour', one obituary opined, and in doing so the dreariness of compositing was overcome, for 'it was not in the printing office that the mind of Douglas Jerrold was formed, although the aspirations of the boy might have thought that there was the home of literature.'[118] Dullness and mindless hack work was the lot of the compositor, as far as Jerrold's press contemporaries were concerned: 'The labours of a printer's apprentice are not ordinarily favourable to intellectual development', suggested one source, while another commentator concluded that in Jerrold's case, it was astonishing that he had emerged as a creative force 'after enduring years of drudgery at the mechanical duties of a compositor, which to one so imaginative and

---

[116] 'Literature', *The Scotsman*, 18 January 1865.
[117] Anon., 'The "Scotsman," Mr James Smith, and the Intellectual Mediocrity of Printers', *Scottish Typographical Circular* (1 February 1865), p. 86.
[118] 'Mr Douglas Jerrold', *The Gentleman's Magazine*, July 1857, p. 92.

powerful a mind must have been almost unbearable.'[119] Jerrold's breakout moment proved to be a review of the opera 'Der Freischutz', which Jerrold wrote overnight and submitted anonymously to the newspaper upon which he was employed as compositor. 'Mr Jerrold determined upon making his first essay as an author with this piece, and when it was accepted he had the pleasure of typesetting his own words for publication in the next issue.'[120] He would soon move into full time creative work as essayist, dramatist, and critic, lauded by contemporaries such as Charles Dickens and William Thackeray.[121]

The snide review to which James Smith's allies responded vigorously exemplified a standard class-based view of the artisanal nature of printing and typesetting, pronouncing sceptically on the ability of mechanics of print to engage meaningfully in creative endeavours. Similarly, obituary notices of Jerrold gestured towards the supposed dehumanizing effects of industrial print labour to counterpoint Jerrold's unusual rise above such mundane spaces to literary fame. Both made clear a social view that artisan typesetters were not suited to rise above mechanical labour into more rarefied literary labour. But as we have seen, Smith and Jerrold were just two of the many creative talents to emerge from the composing ranks, and typographical journals edited and written by trade members attested to the vigorous communicative abilities and self-expressive reflection of many within the trade fraternity.

Such value-laden views of creative compositors and printers were not confined to UK sources. Commenting on the short-lived *Australian Typographical Circular* (1858–60), mid-twentieth-century Australian labour historians steeped in classic Marxist views of class struggles and labour resistance saw little to commend in what they deemed as creative follies. As one study back-handedly commented, noting the lack of creative outlets for printers at the time, 'One of their compensations was to write letters to the *Australian Typographical Circular* in which Latin verse, Shakespearian quotations, Dickensian reference, and classical allusions all came tumbling out in a prose often grotesque but often curiously effective.'[122]

Twentieth-century Marxist historians and literary critics focused on the pulsing dynamism of the Chartist movement poets active between 1838 and 1848 have categorized compositors as members of the 'labour aristocracy', privileged skilled workers demarcated by their educational backgrounds and grounding in language usage.[123] Such categorizations also saw printers painted as conservative figures

---

[119] 'Death of Douglas Jerrold', *The Observer*, 14 June 1857; 'Mr Douglas Jerrold'.

[120] Ibid.

[121] For an in-depth study of Jerrold's life, see Michael Slater, *Douglas Jerrold, 1803–1857* (London: Gerard Duckworth & Co., Ltd, 2002).

[122] J. Hagan, *Printers and Politics: A History of the Australian Printing Unions, 1850–1950* (Canberra: Australian National University Press, 1966), p. 27.

[123] See for example Robert Q. Gray, *The Labour Aristocracy in Victorian Edinburgh* (Oxford: Clarendon Press, 1976), pp. 24–7; Patricia Hollis, *The Pauper Press: A Study in Working-Class Radicalism of the 1830s* (Oxford: Oxford University Press, 1970). Others ignore creative compositors completely, as for example Martha Vicinus, *The Industrial Muse: A Study of Nineteenth Century British Working-Class Literature* (London: Croom Helm, 1974); Brian Maidment, ed. *The Poorhouse Fugitives: Self-Taught Poets and Poetry in Victorian Britain* (Manchester: Carcanet Press Ltd, 1987).

standing to the side of class-based struggles, intent on protecting what in essence were trade guild privileges. Overlooked in such narrow perceptions of class, utilitarian processes, and human endeavour, were examples and models of creative compositors who utilized their skills to shift across class lines, becoming journalists, essayists, editors, press 'conductors' and proprietors, intent on advancing and improving educational and social conditions for all. Most of the typographical journals covered in this piece were launched sometime after the high tide of Chartism had dissipated. While not participants in the Chartist movement per se, the printers and compositors who contributed to these trade journals were sympathetic to the general tenets of the movement, which had sought universal male suffrage for the working classes and stronger parliamentary representation. The act of featuring creative work in trade press outlets was also political. As Kirstie Blair has noted, by championing the work of self-taught poets and writers, journals enacted a commitment to reformist, even radical, politics.

> In the common perception of the mid-Victorian period, writing poetry was a sign of aspirational culture and self improvement. It showed that working men and women were educated, thoughtful and intelligent, plus it indicated that they possessed 'right feeling'. Therefore, it constituted direct evidence that nothing was to be feared from extending the franchise in their favour.[124]

Later in the century, many compositors would play key parts in national union frameworks such as trade councils and the Trade Union Congress, seeking further political freedoms for the working classes. Of more immediate concern to the working-class printers who followed in the wake of the Chartist movement, though, were social reforms that enabled working-class advancement and encouraged personal independence, decent wages, and improved living standards. Those who made the most of their situations to shift across social borders were applauded by fellow print workers.

Typographical journals and local newspapers were quick to note such advancements, recording the taking up of ownership, journalistic and editorial roles by former typographical union members, with celebrations or announcements published in relevant press sections. When news of overseas successes reached colleagues, these were also celebrated. 'We learn with pleasure that two old friends and fellow-comps, – Mr D Stark and Mr Henry Mackintosh', ran one example in the *Scottish Typographical Circular* in June 1869, 'both of Edinburgh, and at one time of the *North British Advertiser* – have started a newspaper in Otago, New Zealand under the title of the *Independent*.'[125] Celebrated individuals closer to home included John Lash Latey (1808–1891), Tiverton-born compositor printer and verse contributor to the *Compositors' Chronicle* (1840–3). He began writing for the *Illustrated London News* on its inception in 1842, worked his way into the literary editor's seat in 1858, then went on to serve with distinction as general

---

[124] Kirstie Blair, ed., *The Poets of the People's Journal: Newspaper Poetry in Victorian Scotland* (Glasgow: The Association for Scottish Literary Studies, 2016), p. xvi.
[125] 'News', *Scottish Typographical Circular*, 1 June 1869.

editor from 1863 until 1890.[126] Equally prolific and significant in trade press history terms was William Dorrington (1816–1894) who, as already noted, appeared often in the pages of the *Typographical Circular* and its predecessors. As compositor in Bradbury and Evans, he was ever present and involved in the 1840s and 1850s in producing *Punch* and then *Household Words*. He also led a parallel career as dramatist, writing plays and farces for London venues, as poet, publishing verse and reciting at printers' outings and events, and as journalist, moving into press work by founding, editing and producing a significant percentage of material for over twenty-five years for the *London, Provincial, and Colonial Press*, from 1866 until 1893.[127]

Such exemplars demonstrated an upward mobility in terms of skills and employment opportunities, with individuals building upon their experiences as compositors to advance creatively, drawing on their understanding of language, composition and writing which were key aspects of print trade work. The spaces offered by typographical journals also enabled aspiring contributors to craft identities that extended beyond the compositor space, and complicated notions of rigid class and professional identity. The elasticity of movement of skilled compositors into creative and editorial work was not confined to Britain. Mid-century US trade journals featured and noted with pride similar high achieving printer compatriots. Among luminaries to emerge from compositor ranks were Horace Greeley (1811–1872), larger than life founder and first editor of the *New York Tribune*; Franklin J. Ottarson, also known as 'Bayard' (1816–1884), New York compositor, editor and printer who published print trade related poetry, was a key founder of the National (later International) Typographical Union, then moved into journalism as editor of the *New York Tribune* and later the *New York Times*; and the writers Bret Harte and Samuel L. Clemens (Mark Twain).

But as the century progressed, more rigid views about the utilitarian and political value of such news spaces, and the abilities of printers to engage creatively given the artisanal nature of their work, began increasingly to shape the direction and content of typographical journals. Over the last quarter of the nineteenth century, print unions started new journals both locally and overseas which drew on different print dynamics to shape content and editorial approach. The 1870s through to the

---

[126] Latey's time with the *Illustrated London News* has been the subject of some confusion for later commentators. See for example the short biography of his son John Latey, in John Sutherland, *Stanford Companion to Victorian Fiction*, 2nd ed. (Stanford, CA: Stanford University Press, 1989), pp. 363–4, where Lash Latey is said to have been editor of the *Illustrated London News* from 1858 to 1890. More precise if still somewhat confusing summaries of his *Illustrated London News* career are to be found in 'The Late Mr J.L. Latey', *Illustrated London News*, 10 January 1891; 'Mr. John Lash Latey', *Illustrated London News*, 14 May 1892. Here, distinctions are made between his role initially as literary editor, which lasted from 1858–1863, and general editor, which began in 1863 and lasted until 1890. Latey's editorial role is also mentioned in Patrick Leary's valuable introductory history to the Gale Cengage digitized archive of the *Illustrated London News*. See Patrick Leary, 'A Brief History of the *Illustrated London News*', (2014), http://gale.cengage.co.uk/images/PatrickLeary.pdf.

[127] Dorrington's recollections of working for Bradbury and Evans feature in William Dorrington, 'Incidents of My Life', *London, Provincial, and Colonial Print News* (1886). For context on Dorrington's involvement in *Punch*, see Patrick Leary, *The Punch Brotherhood: Table Talk and Print Culture in Mid-Victorian London* (London: The British Library, 2010), pp. 19, 48, 136, 138.

1890s saw journals founded in South Africa, Australia, and New Zealand, as well as monthly journals in London (serving the London Society of Compositors), Manchester, and Leeds.

Striking was the increasing move away from the miscellany format. When the newly formed South African Typographical Union launched an accompanying monthly journal in March 1898, it declared its focus to be twofold: to represent the trade and to provide South African trade related information. As its leader editorial declared, 'One great complaint hitherto existing has been that no definite information was to be readily obtained as to the state of the printing trade and other details in the towns of South Africa. The Conference felt that the time was ripe for the issue of a thoroughly representative Trade Journal, and decided to issue the same monthly. Today therefore sees our first issue.'[128]

The Leeds Typographical Society launched its quarterly *Leeds Typographical Circular* in May 1888, with a solemn promise to run a journal 'in the interests of our venerable and incomparable profession', whose primary aim was 'the insertion from time to time of a brief account of the proceedings of our Society, notably those efforts which are put forward and achieved for the present, as well as the permanent welfare of our profession as such, and our fellow-craftsmen as a body.'[129] Material published included trade notices, correspondence, and 'Intelligence relating to kindred and other Trade Societies'. Creative material was not included in the list, and featured extremely infrequently, notably as small poetic fillers in between more serious trade discussions.

Though the occasional poem and comic tale pops up in such venues, the general tenor of these new journals was increasingly trade focused, information driven, and politically and professionally engaged in a manner demonstrative of the contemporary shift of print trade unions to more activist stances. Notable exceptions occur, such as memoirs of trade personnel such as J. W. Rounsfell, whose recollections of being a migrant printer in the 1880s and 1890s were serialized in thirty-three parts under the title *On the Road: Journeys of a Tramping Printer* in the *Typographical Circular* between 1899 and 1904.

SCISSOR AND PASTE/EXCHANGE JOURNALISM

What nineteenth-century typographical trade journals throughout the decades did share was a standard approach to circulating material. Such journals, as Sydney Shep has pointed out, acted as 'intersecting points in a sophisticated global communication network mediated and sustained through print'.[130] As part of such information network systems, typographical journals, much like general press outlets, engaged in standard press practices of scissor and paste or exchange journalism: that is, the

[128] Anon, 'The New Union', *South African Typographical Journal* 1, no. 1 (1898).
[129] 'To Our Readers', *Leeds Typographical Circular*, May 1888.
[130] Sydney J. Shep, 'Culture of Print: Materiality, Memory, and the Rituals of Transmission', *Journal of New Zealand Literature* 28, no. 2 (2010), p. 184.

recirculation and wholesale reproduction of relevant information and material culled from other newspapers and journals. This could take the form of reproducing poetry, prose and news items on related typographical subjects from partner publications across the US, Australasia, Canada, and Great Britain.

Transnational exchanges saw journals borrowing material across international boundaries. *The Australian Typographical Circular* borrowed freely from the *Scottish Typographical Circular* for news and poetry. Among the items it reprinted in August and September 1859 were poems by the *STC*'s laureate in residence Alexander Smart, one of which ('A Song of the Press') had featured in the first issue of the *STC*'s relaunch in March 1858.[131] Other items included trade news and long reports of printers' soirees held in Glasgow and Edinburgh.[132] When the *STC* reported on the demise of the Edinburgh women's printing cooperative, *The Caledonian Press*, in its July 1865 issue, its New York counterpart *The Printer* reproduced the news item a few weeks later with full acknowledgement of the original source.[133] The *STC* also proved the source of another particularly wonderful example of transnational recirculation, occurring over the space of seven months and linking Edinburgh, New York, and London print centres. A poem by Robert Brough, 'The Vacant Frame', featured in the August 1867 issue of the *Scottish Typographical Circular*. A lament for a dead compositor companion, the poem offered a bleak vision of the comrade's deserted composition space going to rack and ruin, its galley broken, its type drawers shattered, and the frame upon which the dead compositor had set his type now empty and vacant. The poem was subsequently reprinted in the New York-based *Typographic Messenger*, and in turn picked up and reprinted by the London-based *Printer's Journal and Typographical Magazine* in February 1868 which due acknowledgement of its US source.[134]

The pages of *The Printers' Journal and Typographical Magazine* offered other examples of cross-border scissoring and pasting, such as reproducing poetry by Robert Brough directly from the *Scottish Typographical Circular,* and dedicating six pages across its 18 June and 2 July 1866 issues to reproducing a paper on medieval printing by the esteemed printer and typographical authority Theodore L. De Vinne (1828–1914), which had been read before the New York Typographical Society and published in its US counterpart *The Printer*.[135] Other items scissored

---

[131] Alexander Smart, 'The Republic of "Letters"', *The Australian Typographical Circular.*, no. 20 (1859); 'The Republic of "Letters"', *Scottish Typographical Circular*, January 1859. 'A Song of the Press', *Scottish Typographical Circular*, March 1858; 'A Song of the Press', *Australian Typographical Circular*, no. 21 (1859).

[132] 'Review'; 'Glasgow Letterpress Printers' Soiree', *Scottish Typographical Circular*, 4 February 1860; Anon, 'Edinburgh Printers' Library. Inaugural Soiree', *Scottish Typographical Circular*, 3 December 1858; 'Edinburgh Printers' Library-Inaugural Soiree', *Australian Typographical Circular*, no. 15 (1859).

[133] 'The Caledonian Press', *Scottish Typographical Circular*, 1 July 1865; 'The Caledonian Press', *The Printer* 6, no. 6 (1865).

[134] Robert Brough, 'The Vacant Frame', *Scottish Typographical Circular*, no. 72 (1867); 'The Vacant Frame', *Printer's Journal and Typographical Magazine* 1, New Series, no. 78 (1868).

[135] Robert Brough, 'A Youthful Enquirer', *Printer's Journal and Typographical Magazine* 2, New Series, no. 118 (1868); 'A Youthful Enquirer', *Scottish Typographical Circular*, 7 December 1868. 'A Noble Example', *The Printers' Journal and Typographical Magazine* May 21 1866. 'A Noble Example',

and pasted into the pages of *The Printers' Journal and Typographical Magazine* included profiles of key trade people, such as one on the publisher Charles Knight, lifted wholesale from the monthly *Good Words* in 1867, and interestingly, a long extract printed over two issues of a story entitled 'On the Tramp', written by the popular novelist George Manville Fenn and reprinted from the *Evening Star*.[136] In introducing the latter item, the editor highlighted its entertaining take on trade matters, while nudging readers to overlook its naïve portrayal of print trade skills. 'Some very entertaining and characteristic sketches have recently appeared in the *Evening Star*, under the heading "Readings by Starlight", and one of the best of the series is entitled "On the Tramp", the author of which is evidently not a novice in the case-room.'[137]

Trade press editors were aware of the way such transnational exchanges could lead to corrupted information. In 1867, *The Printers' Journal and Typographical Magazine* printed an amusing account of the ease with which a news item could be reformulated, mistranslated and re-circulated across space and time, in this case journeying from London to Paris, to New York and then back to London, high-lighting the way unchecked material could 'go round the press' with little difficulty. In 'The Life and Adventures of a Newspaper Paragraph', the launch of the *Aldgate Magazine* becomes the subject of ever expanding mistranslations and adjustments of text and meaning as it moves from journal to journal. Launched in London, with ads from various British merchants featuring alongside fiction and other lit-erary postings, the journal falls into the hands of a French hack journalist, who mistranslates the contents to suggest the journal's stories cleverly incorporate prod-uct placement complete with prices. 'On opening the magazine, one is astonished at the singular mixture of literature and arithmetic which strike the eye. While the reader is deeply absorbed in reading "The Unexpected Legacy," his eyes fall sud-denly on the prices of Mills & Co's Goods', notes the slightly confused commen-tator, adding with some approval of this marketing novelty, 'Is it not ingenious? These prices of clothing are cleverly intermixed with the text of the novel.'[138] The piece gets cut and pasted by other French editors, then picked up and rewritten by a London-based correspondent for the *New York Times*. The news sails to the USA, then back to London, where the revised version is featured in an evening paper seeking filler for its short news section, before being sharply debunked by another local newspaper, who acerbically conclude that English journalistic standards have yet to drop so low as to fully merge commerce and literature in such dubious man-ner. 'It is doubtless a pleasing sensation to our American cousins to think that

Scottish Typographical Circular, October 1 1866. Theodore L. De Vinne, 'Medieval Printing', *The Printers' Journal and Typographical Magazine* 1, nos. 36–37 (1866). A useful survey of De Vinne's life, work and influence on the development of typographical arts in the U.S. can be found in Michael Koenig, 'De Vinne and the De Vinne Press', *The Library Quarterly: Information, Community, Policy* 41, no. 1 (1971).

[136] 'Charles Knight', *The Printers' Journal and Typographical Magazine*, 16 September 1867.

[137] George Manville Fenn, 'On the Tramp', *The Printers' Journal and Typographical Magazine*, 21 May; 4 June 1866, p. 112.

[138] 'The Life and Adventures of a Newspaper Paragraph', *The Printers' Journal and Typographical Magazine*, 15 April 1867, p. 182.

English literature is gradually sinking to the low level of American writers', the debunker concludes with a sly kick at US literary pretensions, 'but it is well that they should know that here not even a professedly trade magazine has as yet reached the depth of degradation.'[139] The story ends by mockingly noting how fame and publicity could accrue to a journal through such inadvertent and unintended means, though at a cost to journalistic truthfulness. 'Though the Newspaper Paragraph was conceived by ignorance, enlarged with spite, born of laziness and travelled through blind belief, it accomplished a great end – the extension of the fame of the *Aldgate Magazine*.'[140]

Sometimes such information exchanges could go awry. In 1865 one such series of borrowings led to heated words and accusations of theft. Plagiarism had been committed, declared the editor of the *Printers' Journal and Typographical Magazine* on reading through offending sections of the May 1865 edition of the *Scottish Typographical Circular*. The editor concluded that the *STC* had lifted three pieces wholesale from their own issue of 17 April without due acknowledgement. This was not a comradely act. It had to be brought out into the open. The subsequent debate, carried out through editorials and commentary throughout June 1865, reveals a great deal about general approaches to the recirculation of trade news across regional trade publications.

The *Printers' Journal* editor wrote an irate editorial in the June issue chastising the *Scottish Typographical Circular* editor for appropriating such material without due acknowledgement. 'Neither ourselves nor "throes of our readers who may have seen the last issue" of our Scottish contemporary', he fulminated, 'are in the least astonished at the flippant manner in which the editor of that print treats our complaint against piracy of these pages.'[141] The *STC* editor responded robustly to the charges, pointing out that journalistic conventions encouraged fair use and recirculation of important news items. 'Nothing appears in our columns but what is written either by or for ourselves, or is acknowledged as the production of some one else', the *STC* editor pronounced.[142]

The issue here was that the material in question had not been lifted so much as 'condensed'—'not given as an original report but as a paragraph.'[143] Such summaries did not constitute appropriation. Rather, it was standard journalistic practice, 'done every day in almost every newspaper office in the kingdom.'[144] The *STC* editor slyly pointed the finger back at the *Printers' Journal* by noting remarkable similarities between the *Printers' Journal* report of a presentation to a leading Sheffield compositor (Josephus Speak) in its 15 May issue and a *Sheffield Telegraph* report of the event published on 8 May.[145] The *STC* fully acknowledged repackaging the Sheffield material in its June issue, but the *Printers' Journal* had not. As the *STC* pointed out, this recirculation 'word for word the same' across regional

[139] Ibid., p. 183.   [140] Ibid., p. 184.

[141] 'Notice', *Printers' Journal and Typographical Magazine*, 19 June 1865.

[142] 'Those of Our Readers', *Scottish Typographical Circular*, 1 June 1865.

[143] Ibid.   [144] Ibid.

[145] For the original item in the *Sheffield Daily Telegraph*, see 'Munificent Present to a Compositor', *Sheffield Daily Telegraph*, 8 May 1865.

journals, was part of a common news information narrative shared by all. Otherwise, it was hypocritical to claim theft, given the reuse of such material in the *Printers' Journal* itself. 'It would appear that our contemporary has been eating out of the same dish as ourselves', noted the *STC* with some asperity.[146]

The *Printers' Journal* team were having none of this, responding that the Sheffield piece had been constructed from Sheffield sources who had either been at the meeting or had given speeches on the day: 'We have never seen a copy of the "Sheffield Daily Telegraph"; and...our report was partly furnished by a valued correspondent in Sheffield and partly by the gentlemen themselves who made the leading speeches on the occasion.'[147] The spat concluded with the *Printers' Journal* declaring it would take measures to prevent further unacknowledged incursions into its material: 'In future, however, should occasion require, we shall take such steps as will effectively secure to us our own.'[148]

CONCLUSION

Sydney Shep has argued that the typographical press functioned as guardians of historical memory, playing 'a critical role in manufacturing, disseminating, and sustaining the trade identity and socio-cultural memory practices of printers'.[149] Commemorations, celebrations, and notes of trade traditions featured as part of the makeup of such journals. Such material could be seen as functioning to remind printers of their shared trade heritage and history, as well as using shared traditions within which to enfold and contextualize new ideas and trade innovations. But the creative material featured in the early years of the typographical trade press complicates and nuances this argument. Creative poetry and prose, as we have seen in the striking examples discussed in this piece, sat alongside news and trade event reports, counterpointing, commenting, commemorating, and critiquing. Such material was used not just to reflect on and shape trade identity, but also to engage with the contemporary realities of the print workspace, and the political, social, and cultural concerns of print trade workers. Creative work published in these journals addressed readers through shared trade language, offered poems, verses and stories grounded in oral and bardic traditions, featured locally recognized trade 'labour laureates', and drew on regional dialects to connect directly to intended audiences. Equally significant was the way the layout, content and editorial direction of early typographical trade journals linked directly to literary miscellanies of the period. The typographical trade press of the 1840s to the 1870s aligned their practices to literary miscellany counterparts, using creative work to counterpoint reportage documenting social, cultural, and trade issues (a model exemplified most famously by Charles Dickens's editorial 'conducting' of *Household Words* between 1850 and 1859).

---

[146] 'Those of Our Readers'.   [147] 'Notice'.   [148] Ibid.
[149] Shep, 'Culture of Print: Materiality, Memory, and the Rituals of Transmission', pp. 184, 187.

Printers' creative work after the 1870s was given less space in typographical journals as such outlets became more focused on labour relations, industrial concerns, and battles over issues such as women entrants to the trade, working hours, emigration and shifts in working conditions and wages. The high tide of creative self-expression soon passed, leaving behind a significant record of unacknowledged engagement in literary endeavour. What is clear is that early typographical journals offered valuable spaces for creative experimentation. Compositor-poets and writers had their place in such textual spaces, and as can be seen, were honoured, supported, and given freedom to publish work of social interest which better enables us to interpret and engage contextually with nineteenth-century print trade culture.

Afterword

Recent work by Gary Magee and Andrew Thompson on British colonial systems has argued persuasively for the need to incorporate culture into the analysis of Victorian economies and trade developments.[1] 'Economies operate within cultural contexts,' they note, and in the Victorian world both culture and economies became increasingly transnational in nature as the century progressed. 'Cultural economy', to borrow their term, depends on networks built up across time and space, underpinned by a 'moral aspect of culture', that is, networks of trust built up via such means as religious, family, and organizational ties.[2] The printing world I have sketched out in the preceding pages maps onto such a 'cultural economy', though as I've argued it was more overtly a 'print economy', based on a moral community of printers bound together by a shared trade identity. In arguing this, I have approached the issues in interdisciplinary fashion, focusing on individuals and events traversing space and time, and arguing for a socially engaged analysis of cultural factors informing print culture developments and geographical movement. The print economies and print diasporas of the Victorian world were expansive in nature, encompassing links and activity across an English-speaking world that drew together Australasia, the British Isles, North America, and South Africa, with India and other sections of South-East Asia also involved but not chronicled in this study. Future research might profitably follow such connections into India, the Caribbean and South-East Asia, for example exploring how European and North American transnational missionary print networks of the Victorian era bound together similar moral communities.

During much of the nineteenth and early twentieth centuries, skilled print workers drew on communal trade and union networks to participate in a global exportation and insertion of print skills and knowledge into new territories. They acted as ambassadors for trade values, imbued with a staunch belief in social organization. They founded businesses that were central to emerging print economies in new and developing communities and towns. They parlayed and passed on their knowledge and expertise to others they encountered in their travels. They drew on communal support structures to advance demands for improved wages and working conditions, and in doing so developed complex information networks in response to worker movement and the need for informed knowledge exchange. Movement

---

[1] Gary B. and Andrew S. Thompson Magee, *Empire and Globalisation: Networks of People, Goods and Capital in the British World, c. 1850–1914* (Cambridge: Cambridge University Press, 2010), p. 14.
[2] Ibid., p. 15.

of people and ideas through union led migration networks established a global typographical knowledge and skills exchange system across the anglophone world that cut across national boundaries. As this volume suggests, the tramping and migration narratives discussed, the strike actions taken, and the creative material developed by the print community over the course of the Victorian and Edwardian era paint a clear picture of culture influencing print trade outlooks and values. Print trade workers understood themselves to be participants in a moral community of artisans, with a duty to support others like them when required, to work together to achieve changes in the workplace, and to bear testimony where possible as to the results.

We have seen in earlier sections of this book how unions established information flow systems that transcended national borders. Print union branches depended on efficient and timely handling and receipt of information, as for example when scrutinizing the credentials of incoming print workers, or when seeking aid for labour activity. During strike actions, information networks were vital in securing funds and help from allied organizations and print colleagues. Likewise, much use was made of trade informants to gather intelligence on employers, and effective information flows between regional networks were key to providing financial, moral, and trade backing when needed. Notable was the similarity of narrative arcs in 1870s' strike actions that took place in four separate cities. How the actions were fought, information was circulated, and trade help was petitioned for and received, reflected strongly the influence of trade union cohesion and common structures, and the way print union organizers collaborated in sharing information about people, tactics, and actions.

Trade information was also circulated in transnational print trade journals founded or supported by unions from the 1840s and 1850s onwards. As noted, these publications played 'a critical role in manufacturing, disseminating, and sustaining the trade identity and socio-cultural memory practices of printers'.[3] Creative material featured heavily in the early decades of the journals' operations, counterpointing, commenting, commemorating, and critiquing. Many trade journals were modelled on contemporary literary miscellanies, using similar layouts, and offering space to a similar mix of creative material, news and general information. Such material reflected on and shaped trade identity, as well as engaged with the contemporary realities of the print workspace, and the political, social, and cultural concerns of print trade workers.

The period under discussion, 1830–1914, saw tremendous technological change in printing, which towards the end of the century would feed into changes in work demands and skills. The introduction of the linotype machine in the 1880s, for example, added a new range of skills that began superseding the hand held, typesetting methods that had dominated print rooms until then. The use of keyboards to produce moulded lines of type, ready for insertion into the print form or boxed layout from which page imprints were cast, offered potential entry into the workspace for women trained in secretarial skills, though such

---

[3] Shep, 'Culture of Print: Materiality, Memory, and the Rituals of Transmission', pp. 184, 187.

incursions were strongly resisted across the anglophone world until after 1914, when this volume concludes. What my volume does suggest, however, is that until then, a strong shared identity, based around common printing skills training and codes of conduct, enabled highly literate and culturally engaged men to be extremely mobile, mobilized, and creative in ways previously unacknowledged or not fully understood.

APPENDIX A

Robert Brough, 'General News. By a Utilitarian Rhymer.'
Scottish Typographical Circular, 1 May 1868, p. 28.

> Some won't buy the *Circular* – making excuse
> That it seldom contains any General News;
> But that's quite absurd, for, in this very sheet,
> They'll find everything of importance complete;
> And, after this date, if men use such a plea,
> With their hair, ears, or nose, I'll be sure to make free.
> Look alive! Then, and get this rich stock in your garrets,
> Then on all public points you can gabble like parrots.
> In fact, if you'd only watch what you're about,
> You might get Dizzy's [Disraeli] seat, *when* the Tories come out.
>   Now, to exhibit how all classes thrive,
> Yesterday evening the Queen took a drive,
> While another good woman (I saw this, with sorrow)
> Got her evening's drive on the policeman's barrow.
> Then, next, that vagabond called O'Farrel
> At the Duke of Edinburgh fired a barrel;
> But never a shot will he fire more –
> He's dead – and so is King Theodore.
>   The Vegetable Markets at Waverley Station
> Are filling the *Scotsman* with argumentation.
> But Ballantyne's tea, though ever so good,
> Is not the Lentil Revalenta foo;
> This and the Littre Wine together
> Are really grand in the summer weather.
>   The Spanish prime-minister now, you must know-
> Since Narvaez is dead – is Gonzales Bravo!
> And the very best dye you can use for your hair
> Is the Melanogene of Dicquemare.
>   We're done with the Water of Leith pollutions;
> But then there's Gladstone's resolutions,
> And those strange tales of the spiritu'list Home,
> And the Empress Eugenie going to Rome.
>   Brave Livingstone's as safe with savages
> As caterpillars are 'mongst cabbages.
> I'll tell you, too – but it's not worth much –
> That Lockyer's determined to go to the North;
> And, seeing he's one of the human race,
> 'Tis well he goes to no warmer place.
>   The trial of Johnson goes on at New York,
> And the Lancashire colliers prefer not to work.
> Bus'ness is dull at the Cape of Good Hope,

And Barrett, the Fenian, gets off – by a rope.
Though B. Hyam's Tweeds are the cheapest of all,
Yet they're not in request at the Suez Canal;
And the Tyne fishers think it a shade beyond gammon
That the Chapter of Durham should claim their best salmon.
Scarce one hundred members heard Mr Ward Hunt,
When he read the details of the Exchequer blunt.
The tax comes away from the poor shepherd's dogs
The moment the cabmen dispense with their clogs.
So there, that's the whole, even down to the locals,
Well mixed, like those sausages purchased at Jockel's;
Then, no more get-outs, for they're used by too many –
For no other purpose than saving a Penny!

Glossary of Terms

Apprentice: Young person serving a specified period in a print establishment to gain trade experience and knowledge.

Bastard fonts: Non-standard-sized typographical fonts.

Bed: Part of a press where the block, type or plate is fixed in preparation for inking and impressing pages.

Case: Divided cabinet holding type used in hand composition.

Caseroom: Room in which cases of type are held.

Casting: The process of forcing molten metal into a mould to create a character, letter, or an individual slug of type.

Chapel: Worker-run unit within a print establishment, charged with managing work spaces, work distribution, and work discipline.

Comp: To compose; abbreviated form of compositor.

Compositor: Individual responsible for making up type into lines used for printing.

Copy: Manuscript or written text used in preparing typeset material for printing.

Devil: Youngest apprentice in a print establishment.

Distribution: The act of returning letterpress type into cases after printing use.

Edition: All copies of a printed work produced from the same run of printed plates.

Em: Standard unit of print measurement, calculated using the width of lower-case letter m in any typeface.

En: Standard unit of print measurement, calculated using the width of lower-case letter n in any typeface.

Father of the Chapel: Democratically elected chairperson of a chapel.

Fat or phat material: Items for typesetting, such as advertisements, containing more blank spaces than regular typeset work, and thus easier to complete.

Fonts: Differently styled typefaces used in composing rooms.

Flatbed press: Printing press with a flat printing surface.

Form or forme: Printing surface featuring lines of type mounted, imposed, and ready for printing.

Frame: Sloped stand for holding cases of type.

Furniture: Letterpress spacing material, usually in form of blank slugs or wooden dowels of varying sizes.

Jobbing printing: General printing work including production of bills, pamphlets, labels, newspapers, posters, and other print ephemera.

Journeyman: Individual printer who has served and completed an apprenticeship.

Letterpress: Printing from images with a raised surface from which impressions are made onto paper.

Letterpress printer: Person who prints using letterpress printing techniques.

Linotype: Metallic lines of type produced using a linotype machine.

Linotype machine: Popular line-casting machine developed by the Linotype company.

Litho: Abbreviation for lithographer or lithography, depending on context.

Lithography: Printing where image is chemically treated to attract oiled litho ink and repel water.

Make ready: Prepare typeset material for printing.

Monotype: Popular 'hot metal' typecasting machine that produced individual character and letter slugs, superseded by the Linotype machine from the 1880s onwards.

Orphan: First line of a new paragraph or a subheading that appears on its own at the foot of a page.

Pica system: Standard unit of print measurement measuring approximately $\frac{1}{6}$ inch, and equal to 12 leads or brass rules.

Pie box: Container holding used type for distribution into cases.

Pressman: Individual involved in the more mechanical production side of printing.

Proof: A test printed sheet made before final production, used to check for corrections and amendments needed.

Rats: Blacklisted compositors and printers who crossed picket lines and/or agreed to work below union agreed wage rates.

Reader: Individual who checks proofs for accuracy.

Rotary press: Printing press producing print with plates mounted on a cylinder.

Shop floor: Generic term for main production spaces of print establishments.

Stab wages: Weekly wage rates offered to contracted print workers, in contrast to piece work rates offered to temporary workers.

Stone: Surface on which pages of metal type are assembled and smoothed down.

Tails: Bottom margins of pages.

Tramp: Itinerant journeyman printer.

Travelling Cards: Cards issued to union members attesting to their bona fide status, enabling them to claim travel stipends from union branches while in search of work.

Typeface: Generic term for specifically designed styles of type.

Typographer: Another term used for an individual specializing as a compositor.

Vigilance committees: Union-backed groups set up during strikes, with the purpose of monitoring and hindering strike breaking activities of print trade owners.

Wayzgoose: Annual day outings or events for workers organized by Chapels or print establishments.

Widow: Short line of a paragraph on its own at the top of a printed page, contrasting with an orphan.

Working cards: Union cards issued to members noting details of membership and dues paid.

Bibliography

Addams, W. E. *Memoirs of a Social Atom*. 2 vols. London: Hutchinson & Co., 1903.

'Address'. *The Printers' Journal and Typographical Magazine*, 2 January 1865, 1.

'Address'. *Typographical Circular* 1, New Series (1 April 1854), 1.

'Address'. *Compositors' Chronicle*, 7 September 1840, 1.

Alloway, Ross. 'Appendix A: Personnel in the Print and Allied Trades'. In *Edinburgh History of the Book in Scotland*, vol. 3: *Ambition and Industry, 1800–1880*, ed. Bill Bell, 476–85. Edinburgh: Edinburgh University Press, 2007.

Amory, Hugh and David D. Hall, eds. *A History of the Book in America*, vol. 1: *The Colonial Book in the Atlantic World*. Chapel Hill: University of North Carolina Press, 2007.

Anderson, Benedict. *Imagined Communities: Reflections on the Origins and Spread of Nationalism*. London: Verso, 1991.

'Another Alleged Outrage by a Printer on Strike'. *The Scotsman*, 4 February 1873, 4.

'The Arrest'. *Ontario Workman*, 18 April 1872, 5.

The Australian Typographical Circular, January 1858, 1.

Babcock, Robert H. and T. J. Ryan. 'A Newfoundland Printer on the Tramp'. *Labour/Le Travail* 8/9 (1981–1982), 261–7.

'Bailie Paris. Edinburgh Magistrate's Death'. *The Scotsman*, 29 December 1938.

Baines, Dudley. *Emigration from Europe, 1815–1930*. Basingstoke: Palgrave Macmillan, 1991.

Baines, Dudley. 'European Emigration, 1815–1930: Looking at the Emigration Decision Again'. *Economic History Review* New Series 47, no. 3 (August) (1994), 19.

Ballantine, Tony. 'Empire, Knowledge and Culture: From Proto-Globalization to Modern Globalization'. In *Globalization in Modern History*, ed. A. G. Hopkins, 115–40. London: Pimlico, 2002.

'The Ballantyne Press: The Old House and the New'. *Scottish Typographical Circular*, 1 December 1870, 397–400.

Barnard, John and D. F. McKenzie, eds. *The Cambridge History of the Book in Britain*, vol. 4: *1557–1695*. Cambridge: Cambridge University Press, 2002.

Barnett, George E. 'The Printers: A Study in American Trade Unionism'. *American Economic Association Quarterly* 10, no. 3 (1909), 3–379.

Battye, John. 'The Nine Hour Pioneers: The Genesis of the Canadian Labour Movement'. *Labour/Le Travail* 4 (1979), 25–56.

Bell, Bill, ed. *The Edinburgh History of the Book in Scotland*, vol. 3: *Ambition and Industry 1800–1880*. Edinburgh: Edinburgh University Press, 2007.

Benson, Charles. 'The Dublin Book Trade 1801–1850, 4 Volumes'. PhD thesis, Trinity College, Dublin, 2000.

Benson, Charles and C. J. Falkiner. 'Thom, Alexander (1801–1879)'. In *Oxford Dictionary of National Biography*. Oxford: Oxford University Press, 2004. http://www.oxforddnb.com/view/article/27189, accessed 14 May 2015.

'Better Than Speeches. The Army of Subscribers to Relieve the Sufferers'. *The New York Herald*, 12 October 1871.

'"Big Six" Honor Roll, 50 Year Membership I.T.U.' *American Labor World*, 1941.

Blair, Kirstie. ' "Let the Nightingales Alone": Correspondence Columns, the Scottish Press, and the Making of the Working-Class Poet'. *Victorian Periodicals Review* 47, no. 2, summer (2014), 188–207.

Blair, Kirstie. ' "A Very Poetical Town": Newspaper Poetry and the Working Class Poet in Victorian Dundee'. *Victorian Poetry* 52, no. 1 (2014), 89–109.

Blair, Kirstie, ed. *The Poets of the People's Journal: Newspaper Poetry in Victorian Scotland*. Glasgow: The Association for Scottish Literary Studies, 2016.

'The Board of Works Report: Criminal Information against Saunders Irish Daily News'. *Irish Times*, 29 July 1878.

'The Board of Works Report: Criminal Information against Saunders Irish Daily News'. *The Irish Times*, 5 August 1878, 5.

'Book Notices. The Australian Typographical Circular'. *Scottish Typographical Circular*, June 1858, 31.

Bradby, L. Barbara. 'Edinburgh Compositors and Women's Work'. *The Women's Industrial News*, New Series, no. 6 (December 1898), 73–7.

Brevier, Linafont. *Trampography: Reminiscences of a Rovin' Printer, 1913–1917*. Glendale, CA: n.p., 1954.

Brough, Robert. ' "Coming Events Cast Their Shadows Before" '. *Scottish Typographical Circular*, 5 January 1861, 295–6.

Brough, Robert. 'The Vacant Frame'. *Scottish Typographical Circular*, 1 August 1867, 576.

Brough, Robert. 'General News. By a Utilitarian Rhymer'. *Scottish Typographical Circular*, 1 May 1868, 28.

Brough, Robert. 'A Noble Example'. *The Printers' Journal and Typographical Magazine*, 21 May 1866, 235.

Brough, Robert. 'A Noble Example'. *Scottish Typographical Circular*, 1 October 1866, 417–18.

Brough, Robert. 'The Vacant Frame'. *Printer's Journal and Typographical Magazine* New Series, 1, no. 78 (8 February 1868), 90.

Brough, Robert. 'A Youthful Enquirer'. *Printer's Journal and Typographical Magazine* New Series, 2, no. 118 (7 December 1868), 234–5.

Brough, Robert. 'A Youthful Enquirer'. *Scottish Typographical Circular*, 2 November 1868, 99.

Brough, Robert. 'Address to the Printers of Auld Reekie Now in London'. *Scottish Typographical Circular*, 1 October 1870, 383.

Brough, Robert. 'Original Poetry. Put Your Shoulder to the Wheel'. *Out on Strike*, 14 December 1872, 4.

Brown, Stephen and Warren McDougall, eds. *The Edinburgh History of the Book in Scotland*, vol. 2: *Enlightenment and Expansion, 1707–1800*. Edinburgh: Edinburgh University Press, 2011.

'Building Society Meeting'. *Tuapeka Times*, 11 September 1875, 2.

Burch, Brian. 'Libraries and Literacy in Popular Education'. In *Libraries in Britain and Ireland*, vol. 2: *1640–1850*, ed. Giles Mandelbrote and K. A. Manley, 371–87. Cambridge: Cambridge University Press, 2006.

'The Burns Commemoration'. *Caledonian Mercury*, 8 August 1844.

'The Burns' Festival'. *Dundee Courier*, 6 August 1844.

Burr, Christina. 'Class and Gender in the Toronto Printing Trade, 1870–1914'. PhD thesis, Memorial University of Newfoundland, 1992.

'The Caledonian Press'. *The Printer* 6, no. 6 (July 1865), 86.

'The Caledonian Press'. *Scottish Typographical Circular*, 1 July 1865, 165–6.

'Canada. Correspondence Relating to the Complaint of Certain Printers Who Were Induced to Emigrate to Canada by False Representations', ed. House of Parliament, 27. London: His Majesty's Stationery Office, 1906.

Cannon, I. C. *The Compositor in London: The Rise and Fall of a Labour Aristocracy*. London: St Bride Library, 2011.

Careless, J. M. S. *Brown of the Globe*, vol. 2: *Statesman of Confederation, 1860–1880*. Toronto: The Macmillan Company of Canada, Ltd, 1963.

Carroll, M. J. 'The Tramp Printer'. *The Inland Printer* 6 (April 1889), 583.

'The Case of Mr Alex. Smart and Family'. *Scottish Typographical Circular*, 4 May 1861, 328.

Casper, Scott E. 'Introduction'. In *A History of the Book in America*, vol. 3: *The Industrial Book, 1840–1880*, ed. Scott E. Casper, Jeffrey D. Groves, Stephen W. Nissenbaum, and Michael Winship, 1–39. Chapel Hill: The University of North Carolina Press, 2007.

Casper, Scott E., Jeffrey D. Groves, Stephen W. Nissenbaum, and Michael Winship, eds. *A History of the Book in America*, vol. 3: *The Industrial Book, 1840–1880*. Chapel Hill: University of North Carolina Press, 2007.

'Charles Knight'. *The Printers' Journal and Typographical Magazine*, 16 September 1867, 423–7.

Chartrand, Mark. 'The First Canadian Trade Union Legislation: An Historical Perspective'. *Ottawa Law Review* 16 (1984), 267–96.

Child, John. *Industrial Relations in the British Printing Industry: The Quest for Security*. London: Allen and Unwin, 1967.

'A Children's Poet'. *Stark County Democrat*, 3 March 1881, 7.

'Classified Ad 25'. *The Scotsman*, 8 February 1873.

'Classified Ad 1'. *The Scotsman*, 6 June 1873, 1.

'Classified Ad 5'. *The Scotsman*, 20 October 1873.

'Classified Ad 66'. *The Scotsman*, 23 May 1861, 1.

'Classified Ad 94'. *The Scotsman*, 27 March 1861, 1.

'Classified Ad 139'. *The Scotsman*, 9 November 1861, 6.

Coleman, Lipset, Seymour Martin, Martin A. Trow, and James S. Coleman. *Union Democracy: The Internal Politics of the International Typographical Union*. New York and London: Free Press; Collier-Macmillan, 1956.

'Compositors, Pressmen, Machine-Minders (Journeymen and Apprentices), and Female Compositors, in Edinburgh, Sept 1875'. In *Edinburgh Typographical Society Records*: National Library of Scotland.

'Correspondence'. In *Blackwood Papers*: National Library of Scotland.

'Correspondence 1871–1880'. In *Oliver and Boyd Papers*: National Library of Scotland.

Craven, Paul. 'Workers' Conspiracies in Toronto, 1854–1872'. *Labour/Le Travail* 14 (1984), 49–72.

Creighton, D. F. 'George Brown, Sir John Macdonald, and the "Workingman": An Episode in the History of the Canadian Labour Movement'. *Canadian Historical Review* 24, no. 4 (1943), 362–76.

Creighton, D. F. *John A. Macdonald: The Young Politician, the Old Chieftain*. Toronto: University of Toronto Press, 1998.

Darnton, Robert. *The Great Cat Massacre and Other Episodes in French Cultural History*. New York: Viking, 1984.

Darnton, Robert. *The Literary Underground of the Old Regime*. Cambridge, MA: Harvard University Press, 1985.

De Vinne, Theodore L. 'Medieval Printing'. *The Printers' Journal and Typographical Magazine* 1, no. 36–37 (18 June; 2 July 1866), 138–40; 49–51.

'Death of a Scotch Poet'. *Leeds Mercury*, 24 October 1866.

'Death of a Scotch Poet'. *Daily News*, 24 October 1866.

'Death of a Scotch Poet'. *Brecon County Times*, 3 November 1866, 3.

'Death of Alexander Smart, the Poet'. *Dundee Courier*, 22 October 1866.

'Death of Douglas Jerrold'. *The Observer*, 14 June 1857, 7.

'Death of Mr Craven, Compositor'. *The Printer*, no. 2 (1 December 1844), 25.

'Death of Mr E. T. Lefroy'. *Irish Times*, 1 September 1879, 6.

'Death of Mr D. Walkinshaw'. *The Bristol Mercury and Daily Post*, 22 July 1899.

'Death of Mr John Hancock, M.L.A.'. *South African Typographical Circular* 1, no. 17 (January 1900), 16.

'Deaths'. *The New York Herald*, 22 September 1894.

'Deaths'. *The Sydney Morning Herald*, 17 June 1946, 12.

Denoon, Donald. *Settler Capitalism: The Dynamics of Dependent Development in the Southern Hemisphere*. Oxford: Clarendon Press, 1983.

'Desertion of Service by Compositors'. *The Scotsman*, 23 August 1872, 6.

'Dispute in the Scotsman'. *The Scotsman*, 10 August 1872, 4.

'Dissolution of Partnership'. *Tuapeka Times*, 28 December 1871, 4.

'Dissolution of Partnership'. *Tuapeka Times*, 23 June 1870, 4.

Dochy, Amélie. 'Mr and Mrs Hall's Tour of Ireland in the 1840s, More Than a Unionist Guidebook, an Illustrated Definition of Ireland Made to Convince'. *Miranda*, no. 9 (2014), 1–27. Published electronically 3 March 2014. doi:10.4000/miranda.5917, http://miranda.revues.org/5917.

'Dominion of Canada'. *The Scotsman*, 11 May 1872, 8.

'Dominion of Canada'. *The Scotsman*, 23 April 1872, 3.

Donaldson, William. *Popular Literature in Victorian Scotland: Language, Fiction and the Press*. Aberdeen: Aberdeen University Press, 1986.

Dorrington, William. 'An Address'. *The Typographical Protection Circular*, July 1853, 258.

Dorrington, William. 'Incidents of My Life'. *London, Provincial, and Colonial Print News* (December 1886), 17–19.

Downes, A. J. *Printers' Saga, Being a History of the South African Typographical Union*. Johannesburg: South African Typographical Union, 1952.

Dublin Typographical Provident Society (Dublin). *Constitution of the Dublin Typographical Provident Society. Revised and Amended up to M.Dccc.Lxxxvi*. Dublin, 1887.

'Dublin Typographical Provident Society Committee Minute Books'. In *Dublin Typographical Provident Society Records*: Trinity College, Dublin.

'Dublin Typographical Provident Society Council Minutes'. In *Dublin Typographical Provident Society Records*: Trinity College, Dublin.

Duffy, Patrick. *The Skilled Compositor, 1850–1914*. Aldershot: Ashgate Publishing, 2000.

'Dundee Typographical Society Minute Books, 1858–1877'. In *Dundee Typographical Society Records*: Dundee City Archives.

'Edinburgh Mechanics' Library – Election of Librarian'. *The Scotsman*, 18 November 1869, 2.

'Edinburgh Printers' Library. Inaugural Soiree'. *Scottish Typographical Circular*, 3 December 1858, 82–4.

'Edinburgh Printers' Library – Inaugural Soiree'. *The Australian Typographical Circular*, no. 15 (March 1859), 116–17.

'Edinburgh Typographical Society Contributor Records, 1861–1900'. In *Edinburgh Typographical Society Records*: National Library of Scotland.

'Edinburgh Typographical Society Income and Expenditure Account, 1 July 1846–2 Jan 1879'. In *Edinburgh Typographical Society*: National Library of Scotland.

'Edinburgh Typographical Society Index to Members of the Society, 1871–1880'. In *Edinburgh Typographical Society Records*: National Library of Scotland.

'Edinburgh Typographical Society Minute Books'. In *Edinburgh Typographical Society Records*: National Library of Scotland.

'Edinburgh Typographical Society Outgoing Letter Books'. In *Edinburgh Typographical Society Records*: National Library of Scotland.

Faithfull, Emily. 'Women and Work'. *Women and Work*, no. 19 (10 October 1874), 5.

Fenn, George Manville. 'On the Tramp'. *The Printers' Journal and Typographical Magazine*, 21 May; 4 June 1866, 112–13; 24–6.

Finkelstein, David. 'Nineteenth-Century Print on the Move: A Perilous Study of Translocal Migration and Print Skills Transfer'. In *Theory and Practice in Book, Print and Publishing History*, ed. Jason McElligott and Eve Patten, 150–66. Basingstoke: Palgrave Macmillan, 2014.

Finkelstein, David and A. McCleery. *The Edinburgh History of the Book in Scotland: Professionalisation and Diversity, 1880–2000*. Edinburgh: Edinburgh University Press, Vol. 4, 2007.

Fisher, Paul. *An Uncommon Gentry*. Columbia: University of Missouri, 1952.

Fitzgerald, R. T. *The Printers of Melbourne: The History of a Union*. Melbourne: Sir Isaac Pitman and Sons, Ltd, 1967.

Fleming, Patricia Lockhart, Gilles Gallichan, and Yvan Lamonde, eds. *History of the Book in Canada*, vol. 1: *Beginnings to 1840*. Toronto: University of Toronto Press, 2004.

'The Following Appeared in the October Issue of the *Australian Typographical Journal*'. *London Typographical Journal* 1, no. 2 (February 1906), 6.

'Forty Years Ago'. *London Typographical Journal*, October 1907, 10.

Franks, Peter. *Print & Politics: A History of Trade Unions in the New Zealand Printing Industry, 1865–1995*. Wellington: Victoria University Press, 2001.

Fredeman, William E. 'Emily Faithfull and the Victoria Press: An Experiment in Sociological Bibliography'. *The Library* 29, no. 2 (1974), 139–64.

'From Our Own Correspondent'. *The Scotsman*, 19 September 1872, 3.

'Funeral of Mr E. T. Lefroy'. *Irish Times*, 3 September 1879.

Fyfe, Aileen. 'Steam and the Landscape of Knowledge: W & R Chambers in the 1830s–1850s'. In *Geographies of the Book*, ed. M. Ogborn and C. Withers, 51–78. Farnham: Ashgate Press, 2010.

Gennard, John. *Mechanical to Digital Printing in Scotland: The Print Employers' Organisation*. Edinburgh: Scottish Printing Archival Trust, 2010.

Gennard, John and Peter Bain. *A History of the Society of Graphical and Allied Trades*. London: Routledge, 1995.

Gillespie, Sarah C. *A Hundred Years of Progress. The Record of the Scottish Typographical Association, 1853 to 1952*. Printed for the Scottish Typographical Association by Robert Maclehose & Co.: Glasgow, 1953.

'Glasgow Letterpress Printers' Soiree'. *Scottish Typographical Circular*, 4 February 1860, 197–8.

'Glasgow Programme'. *The Scotsman*, 12 August 1924, 6.

'Glasgow Typographical Association Membership Lists'. In *Glasgow Typographical Association Records*: Strathclyde University Archives.

Gorman, John. *Images of Labour*. London: Scorpion Publishing Ltd, 1985.

Goutor, David. *Guarding the Gates: The Canadian Labour Movement and Immigration, 1872–1934*. Vancouver: UBC Press, 2007.

Gray, Robert Q. *The Labour Aristocracy in Victorian Edinburgh*. Oxford: Clarendon Press, 1976.

Gross, Robert A. 'Introduction'. In *A History of the Book in America*, vol. 2: *An Extensive Republic, Print, Culture, and Society in the New Nation, 1790–1840*, ed. Robert A. Gross and Mary Kelley, 1–50. Chapel Hill: University of North Carolina Press, 2010.

Gross, Robert A. and Mary Kelley, eds. *A History of the Book in America*, vol. 2: *An Extensive Republic, Print, Culture, and Society in the New Nation, 1790–1840*. Chapel Hill: University of North Carolina Press, 2010.

Hackett, Richard and Henry Slatter. 'The Typographical Association: a Fifty Years' Record, 1849–1899'. Manchester: Printed for the Typographical Association by the Labour Press Limited, 1899.

Hagan, J. *Printers and Politics: A History of the Australian Printing Unions, 1850–1950*. Canberra: Australian National University Press, 1966.

Hammond, Joseph W. 'The Founder of "Thom's Directory"'. *Dublin Historical Record* 8, no. 2 (1946), 41–56.

'Hansard House of Commons Debates'. London, 1878.

Hicks, John Edward. *Adventures of a Tramp Printer, 1880–1890*. Kansas City, MO: Midamericana Press, 1950.

Hobbs, Andrew. 'Five Million Poems, or the Local Press as Poetry Publisher, 1800–1900'. *Victorian Periodicals Review* 45, no. 4 (2012), 488–92.

Hobsbawm, E. J. 'The Tramping Artisan'. *The Economic History Review* 3, no. 3 (1951), 299–320.

Hofmeyr, Isabel. *Gandhi's Printing Press: Experiments in Slow Reading*. Cambridge, MA: Harvard University Press, 2013.

Hollis, Patricia. *The Pauper Press: A Study in Working-Class Radicalism of the 1830s*. Oxford: Oxford University Press, 1970.

Holtzberg-Call, Maggie. *The Lost World of the Craft Printer*. Urbana and Chicago: University of Illinois Press, 1992.

Hossack, 'Correspondence'. In *Labour Party Archives*: Labour History Archive and Study Centre, People's History Museum/University of Central Lancashire, 1906.

Houston, Natalie. 'Newspaper Poems'. *Victorian Studies* 50, no. 2 (2008), 233–42.

Howe, Ellic and Bibliographical Society (Great Britain). *The London Compositor: Documents Relating to Wages, Working Conditions and Customs of the London Printing Trade, 1785–1900*. Small Quarto Series/Bibliographical Society. London: Bibliographical Society, 1947.

Howe, Ellic and Harold Waite. *The London Society of Compositors (Re-Established 1848): A Centenary History*. London: Cassell and Company, 1948.

Hughes, Linda K. 'What the Wellesley Index Left Out: Why Poetry Matters to Periodical Studies'. *Victorian Periodicals Review* 40, no. 2 (2007), 91–125.

'If the System of Tramping'. *The Typographical Protection Circular*, May 1849, 19–20.

'In Memoriam'. *Scottish Typographical Circular*, 1 April 1871, 448–9.

'In Memoriam'. *Scottish Typographical Circular*, January 1881.

Ingram, J. P. 'At the Cape'. *Pacific Union Printer* (September 1893).

International Typographical Union. *A Study of the History of the International Typographical Union, 1852–1963*. 2 vols. Colorado Springs, Colorado: International Typographical Union Executive Council, 1964.

'J. Farrell, First President S.A.T.U.'. *South African Typographical Journal* 4, no. 39 (January 1902), 13–14.

'J. P. Farrell'. *South African Typographical Journal* 1, no. 20 (June 1900), 10.

'James Smith, the Poet Printer'. *Printers' Circular*, 1 December 1874, 308–9.

Jennings, Margaret Allen. 'The History of Lawrence, Otago, New Zealand, from Earliest Times to 1921, Including a Review of Its Future Prospects'. MA thesis, Canterbury University College, 1921.

'John Wilson Dead'. *Cambridge Tribune* 26, no. 11 (16 May 1903), 7.

Johns, Adrian. *The Nature of the Book: Print and Knowledge in the Making*. Chicago: University of Chicago Press, 1998.

Johnston, Alastair M., ed. *Typographical Tourists: Tales of Tramping Printers*. Berkeley, CA: Poltroon Press, 2012.

Jones, Aled. *Press, Politics and Society: A History of Journalism in Wales*. Cardiff: University of Wales Press, 1993.

Jones, Ifano. *A History of Printing and Printers in Wales to 1810, and of Successive and Related Printers to 1923. Also, a History of Printing and Printers in Monmouthshire to 1923*. Cardiff: William Lewis (Printers), Ltd, 1925.

'Jottings from Lawrence'. *Lake Wakatip Mail*, 4 August 1874, 3.

Kaestle, Carl F. and Janice Radway, eds. *A History of the Book in America*, vol. 4: *Print in Motion: The Expansion of Publishing and Reading in the United States, 1880–1940*. Chapel Hill: University of North Carolina Press, 2009.

Katz, Elaine N. *A Trade Union Aristocracy: A History of the White Workers in the Transvaal and the General Strike of 1913*. Johannesburg: University of Witwatersrand, 1976.

Kealey, Gregory S. '"The Honest Workingman" and Workers' Control: The Experience of Toronto Skilled Workers, 1860–1892'. *Labour/Le Travail* 1 (1976), 32–68.

Kealey, Gregory S. *Toronto Workers Respond to Industrial Capitalism, 1867–1892*. Toronto, Buffalo, NY, and London: University of Toronto Press, 1991.

Kelly's Directory of Stationers, Printers, Booksellers and Publishers of England, Scotland, Wales and Ireland. London: Kelly and Co., 1880.

Kinane, Vincent. 'Irish Booklore: A Galley of Pie: Women in the Irish Book Trades'. *The Linen Hall Review* 8, no. 4 (1991): 10–13.

Kinane, Vincent. 'Printers' Apprentices in 18th- and 19th-Century Dublin'. *The Linen Hall Review* 10, no. 1 (1993), 11–14.

Kinane, Vincent. *A History of the Dublin University Press, 1734–1976*. Dublin: Gill and Macmillan, 1994.

Kirk, Neville. *Comrades and Cousins: Globalization, Workers and Labour Movements in Britain, the USA and Australia from the 1880s to 1914*. London: The Merlin Press, 2003.

Knott, Alfred. 'Wayzgoose'. *Typographical Protection Circular*, September 1853.

Knott, Alfred. 'The Almshouse Guarantee Fund'. *Typographical Circular*, 2 October 1854, 55.

Knott, Alfred. 'Books for the Library'. *Typographical Circular*, 1 April 1855, 103.

Knott, Alfred. 'The United Cricketers'. *Typographical Circular*, 1 May 1855, 108–9.

Knott, Alfred. 'The Entertainment'. *Typographical Circular*, 1 April 1856, 202.

Knott, Alfred. 'In Memoriam'. *Typographical Circular*, 15 April 1857, 326.

Knott, Alfred. 'In Memory of William Cox'. *Typographical Circular*, 15 January 1857, 301.

Koenig, Michael. 'De Vinne and the De Vinne Press'. *The Library Quarterly: Information, Community, Policy* 41, no. 1 (January 1971), 1–24.

'The Labourers' "Sweet Voices"'. *New York Herald*, 7 August 1872, 8.

Lamonde, Yvan, Patricia Lockhart Fleming, and Fiona A. Black, eds. *History of the Book in Canada*, vol. 2: *1840–1918*. Toronto: University of Toronto Press, 2005.

Larkin, Jack. '"Printing Is Something Every Village Has in It": Rural Printing and Publishing'. In *A History of the Book in America*, vol. 2: *An Extensive Republic, Print,*

Culture, and Society in the New Nation, 1790–1840, ed. Robert A. Gross and Mary Kelley, 145–60. Chapel Hill: University of North Carolina Press, 2010.

'The Late Alex. Smart, Author of the "Songs of Labour"'. *Glasgow Herald*, 23 October 1866.

'The Late George Mackay'. *Scottish Typographical Circular*, November 1869, 241.

'The Late Mr James Smith'. *The Scotsman*, 13 March 1887, 4.

'The Late Mr J. L. Latey'. *Illustrated London News*, 10 January 1891.

'Lawrence Revisited, after an Absence of Thirty Five Years'. *Tuapeka Times*, 8 December 1917, 3.

Leary, Patrick. *The Punch Brotherhood: Table Talk and Print Culture in Mid-Victorian London*. London: The British Library, 2010.

Leary, Patrick. 'A Brief History of the *Illustrated London News*' (2014). http://gale.cengage.co.uk/images/PatrickLeary.pdf, accessed 16 January 2018.

Ledbetter, Kathryn. *Tennyson and Victorian Periodicals*. Farnham: Ashgate, 2007.

Lee, Alfred McClung. *The Daily Newspaper in America*, vol. 1. London: Routledge and Thoemmes Press, 2000.

Leeson, R. A. *Travelling Brothers*. St Albans: Granada Publishing Ltd, 1979.

Leroux, Eric. 'Trades, Labour, and Design'. In *History of the Book in Canada*, vol. 2: *1840–1918*, ed. Yvan Lamonde, Patricia Lockhart Fleming, and Fiona A. Black, 75–87. Toronto: University of Toronto Press, 2005.

'The Life and Adventures of a Newspaper Paragraph'. *The Printers' Journal and Typographical Magazine*, 15 April 1867, 182–4.

'List of Baptisms in the Parish', Church Registers: Old Parish Register Records, National Archives of Scotland, 1830.

'Literature'. *The Scotsman*, 18 January 1865.

'Literature. Songs of Labour and Domestic Life; with Rhymes for Little Readers'. *The Stirling Observer*, 14 October 1860, 2.

'Literature. Songs of Labour and Domestic Life; with Rhymes for Litttle Readers'. *The Elgin and Morayshire Courier*, 21 September 1860, 3.

Literatus. 'The "Reader" and His "Recreations"'. *Scottish Typographical Circular*, 6 February 1864, 479.

'The Living Lyrical Poets of Scotland'. *The Fife Herald, Kinross, Strathearn and Clackmannan Advertiser*, 6 March 1856, 2.

'The Living Lyrical Poets of Scotland'. *The Stirling Observer*, 6 March 1856, 3.

'Local Intelligence'. *Tuapeka Times*, 4 March 1874, 2.

'LSC Membership Card Competition'. *The British Printer* 20, no. 119 (October–November 1907), 226–8.

Lumley, J. 'The Printer'. *The Printer* 6 (October 1866), 177.

'The M.T.S. Organiser'. *The Australasian Typographical Journal*, 7 October 1909, 10.

McAdam, W. E. 'Wee Joukydaidles'. *The Ashburton Guardian*, 12 February 1903, 1.

McAdam, W. E. 'Wee Joukydaidles'. *Otago Daily Times*, 10 February 1903, 6.

McAdam, W. E. 'Wee Joukydaidles'. *Otago Witness*, 11 February 1903, 30.

McGrath, Nicholas. 'Meandering through the Past'. In *Dublin Typographical Provident Society Records*: Trinity College Dublin.

Mackay, Jessie. 'Scottish Nursery Songs'. *Otago Witness*, 3 July 1907, 82.

McKitterick, David, ed. *The Cambridge History of the Book in Britain*, vol. 6: *1830–1914*. Cambridge: Cambridge University Press, 2009.

Magee, Gary B. and Andrew S. Thompson. *Empire and Globalisation: Networks of People, Goods and Capital in the British World, c. 1850–1914*. Cambridge: Cambridge University Press, 2010.

Maidment, Brian, ed. *The Poorhouse Fugitives: Self-Taught Poets and Poetry in Victorian Britain*. Manchester: Carcanet Press Ltd, 1987.

Marks, Gary. *Union in Politics: Britain, Germany, and the United States in the Nineteenth and Early Twentieth Centuries*. Princeton, NJ: Princeton University Press, 1989.

Marks, Gary. 'Variations in Union Political Activity in the United States, Britain, and Germany from the Nineteenth Century'. *Comparative Politics* 22, no. 1 (1989), 83–104.

Marsh, Arthur and John B. Smethurst. *Historical Directory of Trade Unions. Vol 5: Including Unions in Printing and Published Local Government, Retail and Distribution, Domestic Services, General Employment, Financial Services, Agriculture*. Aldershot: Ashgate, 2006.

'Memories of the Tuapeka Times'. *Tuapeka Times*, 4 February 1905.

'Minutes of Scotsman Chapel'. In *Edinburgh Typographical Society Records*: National Library of Scotland.

'Mr Douglas Jerrold'. *The Gentleman's Magazine*, July 1857, 91–4.

'Mr William Epps. Presentation by Hospital Staff'. *The Sydney Morning Herald*, 16 June 1932, 8.

'Mr. John Lash Latey'. *Illustrated London News*, 14 May 1892.

'Munificent Present to a Compositor'. *Sheffield Daily Telegraph*, 8 May 1865.

Murdoch, Alexander G., ed. *The Scottish Poets, Recent and Living*. Glasgow: Thomas D. Morison, 1883.

Musson, A. E. *The Typographical Association: Origins and History up to 1949*. London: Oxford University Press, 1954.

'National Typographical Union. Official Report for "the Printer." Proceedings of the Eighth Annual Session, at Boston, Mass., May 2, 1859'. *The Printer* 2, no. 1 (May 1859), 7.

'The New Union'. *South African Typographical Journal* 1, no. 1 (March 1898), 1.

'New Zealand'. *Scottish Typographical Circular*, 1 October 1866, 415–16.

'The New Zealand Gazette'. *Otago Daily Times*, 21 June 1879, 3.

'News'. *Scottish Typographical Circular*, 1 June 1869, 183.

'News'. *The British Printer*, 1899, 208.

'News'. *Scottish Typographical Circular*, 3 November 1860, 275.

The Newspaper Press, 1 February 1872, 58.

Nord, David Paul, Joan Shelley Rubin, and Michael Schudson, eds. *A History of the Book in America*, vol. 5: *The Enduring Book: Print Culture in Postwar America*. Chapel Hill: University of North Carolina Press, 2009.

'Notice'. *Printers' Journal and Typographical Magazine*, 19 June 1865, 114.

'Obituary'. *Scottish Typographical Circular*, 1 August 1888, 676.

'Obituary'. *Scottish Typographical Circular*, 1 February 1869, 135.

'Obituary'. *Scottish Typographical Circular*, 2 August 1862, 200.

'Obituary: John Carbery'. *Scottish Typographical Circular*, 2 March 1868, 684–5.

'Obituary. Welsh Newspaper Proprietor. Mr G. J. Jacobs, Rhymney'. *Cardiff Times and New South Wales Weekly*, 17 October 1908, 7.

Ogborn, Miles and Charles W. J. Withers, eds. *Geographies of the Book*. Farnham: Ashgate Press, 2010.

'Old Edinburgh Poets and Their Songs'. *The Scotsman*, 14 January 1922, 11.

Olsson, Lars. 'Tramping Typographers – National and Trans-National Labour Migration at the Break Through of Industrial Capitalism in Northern Europe'. In *Eighth European Social Science History Conference*. Ghent, Belgium, 2010.

Ostry, Bernard. 'Conservatives, Liberals, and Labour in the 1870s'. *Canadian Historical Review* 41, no. 2 (1960), 93–127.

'Our Mission'. *Ontario Workman*, 18 April 1872, 4.

'Our Own Correspondent'. *The Scotsman*, 19 September 1872, 3.

'Our Views and Intentions'. *Scottish Typographical Circular*, 1 September 1857, 1.
'Ourselves and Our New Enterprise. A Few First Words'. *The Printer* 1, no. 1 (May 1858), 8.
'Outgoing Correspondence'. In *Blackwood Papers*: National Library of Scotland.
'The Outrage by a Unionist Printer'. *The Scotsman*, 6 February 1873, 3.
'Pen, Pencil, and Scissors'. *National Republican*, 16 November 1866.
'Pension Application Disapproved'. *The Typographical Journal*, July 1935.
'Perth Typographical Society Minute Books'. In *Perth Typographical Society Records*: AK Bell Library.
Pike, William, ed. *A Dictionary of Edwardian Biography: Edinburgh and the Lothians*. Edinburgh: Peter Bell, 1983.
Pinkerton, Allan. *Strikers, Communists, Tramps, and Detectives*. New York: G. W. Carleton, 1878.
Pollard, Mary. *A Dictionary of the Members of the Dublin Book Trade, 1550–1800*. London: Bibliographical Society, 2000.
Post-Office Edinburgh and Leith Directory, 1887–88. Edinburgh: Morrison and Gibb, 1887.
'Presentation to Retiring Hospital Secretary'. *The Sydney Morning Herald*, 16 June 1932, 12.
'The Press'. *The Printer* 1, no. 1 (May 1858): 5.
Pretzer, William S. 'Tramp Printers: Craft Culture, Trade Unions, and Technology'. *Printing History: The Journal of the American Printing History Association* 6, no. 2 (November 1984), 3–16.
Pretzer, William S. ' "Of the Paper Cap and Inky Apron": Journeymen Printers'. In *A History of the Book in America*, vol. 2: *An Extensive Republic, Print, Culture and Society in the New Nation, 1790–1840*, ed. Robert A. Gross and Mary Kelley, 160–74. Chapel Hill: University of North Carolina Press, 2010.
The Printer 2 (February 1844), 56.
'The Printer'. *Scottish Typographical Circular*, 1 October 1859, 158.
'Printers' Almhouse Fund'. *The Printer*, 1 March 1844, 78.
'Printers' Almshouses'. *Compositors Chronicle*, 5 April 1841, 64.
'The Printers' Strike. Alleged Intimidation'. *The Scotsman*, 4 January 1873, 6.
The Printers' International Specimen Exchange. Vol. 10, London: The British Printer, 1889.
'Prospectus of the Jerrold Dramatic Club'. *The Typographical Protection Circular*, July 1853, 258.
Reith, Reinhold. *Lohn Und Leistung. Lohnformen Im Gewerbe 1450–1900*. Stuttgart: Franz Steiner Verlag, 1999.
Remoortel, Marianne van. *Women, Work and the Victorian Periodical: Living by the Press*. Basingstoke: Palgrave Macmillan, 2015.
'Review'. *Glasgow Herald*, 23 October 1860.
'Review'. *The Scotsman*, 13 March 1874, 4.
'Review, Songs of Labour and Domestic Life'. *Scottish Typographical Circular*, 6 October 1860, 262.
Reynolds, Sian. *Britannica's Typesetters*. Edinburgh Education & Society Series. Edinburgh: Edinburgh University Press, 1989.
Richards, J. H. 'Social and Economic Aspects of Combination in the Printing Trade before 1875'. MA thesis, University of Liverpool, 1957.
Rose, Jonathan. '[Review of] Duffy, Patrick: The Skilled Compositor, 1850–1914: An Aristocrat among Working Men'. *Victorian Studies* 45, no. 1 (2002), 173.
Rounsfell, J. W. *On the Road: Journeys of a Tramping Printer*. Horsham: Caliban Books, 1982.

Rowles, George E. *The 'Line' Is On: A Centenary Souvenir of the London Society of Compositors 1848–1948*. London: Co-Operative Printing Society, Ltd, 1948.

Rumble, Walker. 'A Showdown of "Swifts": Women Compositors, Dime Museums, and the Boston Typesetting Races of 1886'. *The New England Quarterly* 71, no. 4 (1998), 615–28.

Rumble, Walker. *The Swifts: Printers in the Age of Typesetting Races*. Charlottesville and London: University of Virginia Press, 2003.

Score, Melissa. 'Pioneers of Social Progress?: Gender and Technology in British Printing Trade Union Journals, 1840–65'. *Victorian Periodicals Review* 47, no. 2 (2014), 274–95.

'Scotland Census Returns'. 16, 1891.

'Scotland Census Returns'. 23, 1881.

'Scotland Census Returns'. 1, 1871.

'Scotland Census Returns'. 11, 1861.

The Scotsman, 4 January 1873, 4.

'Scotsman Office: Action by a Compositor for Dismissal without Notice'. *The Scotsman*, 29 August 1872, 6.

'The "Scotsman," Mr James Smith, and the Intellectual Mediocrity of Printers'. *Scottish Typographical Circular*, 1 February 1865, 85–7.

'The "Scotsman" and Its Compositors'. *Daily News*, 29 August 1872.

'The "Scotsman" and Its Late Compositors'. *The Scotsman*, 10 August 1872, 4.

'The "Scotsman" and Its Late Compositors'. *The Scotsman*, 21 August 1872, 4.

'The "Scotsman" and Its Late Compositors'. *Birmingham Daily Post*, 13 August 1872.

'The "Scotsman" Strike of 1872: Reason for Non-Union Basis'. *The Scotsman*, 13 May 1926, 6.

Scottish Typographical Association: A Fifty Years' Record, 1853–1903. Glasgow: Scottish Typographical Association, 1903.

'Scottish Typographical Association (Aberdeen Branch) Minute Books'. Aberdeen University Library.

Scottish Typographical Circular, 6 July 1861, 337.

Scottish Typographical Circular, 1 April 1871, 451.

Sharma, Rajendra Kumar. *Social Disorganisation*. New Delhi: Atlantic Publishers and Distributors, 1998.

Shep, Sydney J. 'Culture of Print: Materiality, Memory, and the Rituals of Transmission'. *Journal of New Zealand Literature* 28, no. 2 (2010), 183–210.

Shep, Sydney J. 'The Printer's Web: New Tools to Crack Old Chestnuts'. In *Advancing Digital Humanities: Research, Methods, Theories*, ed. Paul Longley and Katherine Bode Arthur, 68–82. Basingstoke: Palgrave Macmillan, 2014.

Shepperson, Wilbur S. 'Industrial Emigration in Early Victorian Britain'. *The Journal of Economic History* 13, no. 2 (1953), 179–92.

Slater, Michael. *Douglas Jerrold, 1803–1857*. London: Gerard Duckworth & Co., Ltd, 2002.

Smart, Alexander. 'The Flight of Time'. *The Farmer and Mechanic*, 26 December 1850, 619.

Smart, Alexander. 'The Flight of Time'. *American Union*, 1 February 1851, 4.

Smart, Alexander. 'The Flight of Time'. *American Union*, 1 May 1852, 4.

Smart, Alexander. 'The Flight of Time'. *Bacchus Marsh Express*, 2 March 1867, 4.

Smart, Alexander. 'The Flight of Time'. *Bell's Life in Sydney and Sporting Reviewer*, 4 January 1851, 1.

Smart, Alexander. 'The Flight of Time'. *Boston Weekly Museum*, 29 March 1851, 335.

Smart, Alexander. 'The Flight of Time'. *Britannia and Trades' Advocate*, 3 February 1851, 4.

Smart, Alexander. 'The Flight of Time'. *Christian Enquirer*, 4 January 1851, 4.

Smart, Alexander. 'A Song of the Press'. *Scottish Typographical Circular*, 5 March 1858, 1.

Smart, Alexander. 'Madie's Schule'. *Scottish Typographical Circular*, 3 December 1859.

Smart, Alexander. 'The Republic of "Letters"'. *The Australian Typographical Circular*, no. 20 (August 1859), 160.

Smart, Alexander. 'The Republic of "Letters"'. *Scottish Typographical Circular*, January 1859, 85.

Smart, Alexander. 'A Song of the Press'. *The Australian Typographical Circular*, no. 21 (September 1859), 168.

Smith, James. 'The Courtship O' Padie Cauldshouthers; or, the Unco Surprise', *Scottish Typographical Circular*, 2 November 1861, 43–6.

Smith, James. 'Baloo, My Bairnie, Fa' Asleep!' *Scottish Typographical Circular*, 2 July 1864, 567.

Smith, James. 'The Recreation of a Reader'. *Scottish Typographical Circular*, 5 March 1864, 492–5.

Smith, James. 'The Three Wee Flowers'. *Scottish Typographical Circular*, 2 January 1864, 457.

Smith, James. 'Wee Joukydaidles'. *Birmingham Daily Post*, 22 August 1864.

Smith, James. 'Wee Joukydaidles'. *The Dundee Courier and Argus*, 22 August 1864.

Smith, James. 'Wee Joukydaidles'. *The Scotsman*, 20 August 1864, 3.

Smith, James. *Merry Bridal O' Firthmains and Other Poems and Songs*. 2nd ed. Edinburgh: William P. Nimmo and Co., 1866.

Smith, James. 'The Scottish Londoners'. *Scottish Typographical Circular*, 1 October 1867, 603–4.

Smith, James. 'A Children's Poet'. *The Stark County Democrat*, 3 March 1881, 7.

'Social Gathering'. *Tuapeka Times*, 22 February 1882, 3.

'Soiree in Aid of Library'. *Scottish Typographical Circular*, 7 March 1864, 305.

'Statutory Registers, Deaths'. ed. Crown Office, 61. Edinburgh: National Records of Scotland, 1914.

'Statutory Registers, Deaths'. ed. Crown Office, 135. Edinburgh: National Records of Scotland, 1903.

Steinberg, Mark D. 'Culture and Class in a Russian Industry: The Printers of St. Petersburg, 1860–1905'. *Journal of Social History* 23, no. 3 (1990), 513–33.

Steinberg, Mark D. *Moral Communities: The Culture of Class Relations in the Russian Printing Industry, 1867–1907*. Berkeley: University of California Press, 1992.

Stevens, G. A. *New York Typographical Union No. 6; Study of a Modern Trade Union and Its Predecessors*. Albany, NY: J. B. Lyon Co., State printers, 1913.

'Stray Chapters from the Life of Wimble Flash, a Typographic Cosmopolite. Collected by Himself'. *The Compositors' Chronicle*, October–April 1842–1843, 214–15; 22–3; 30–2; 38–40; 42–3; 54–5; 62–4.

'The Strike at the "Scotsman" Office'. *The Manchester Guardian*, 29 August 1872, 8.

'Strike of Printers at Winnipeg'. *The Labour Gazette*, 6 February 1906, 920.

'Strike of the Journeymen Printers'. *Philadelphia Inquirer*, 26 March 1872, 1.

Suarez, Michael F. and Michael L. Turner, eds. *The Cambridge History of the Book in Britain*, vol. 5: *1695–1830*. Cambridge: Cambridge University Press, 2009.

Suarez, Michael F. and H. R. Woudhuysen. *The Oxford Companion to the Book*. 2 vols. Oxford: Oxford University Press, 2010.

'Supreme Court. -in Banco'. *Tuapeka Times*, 13 April 1878, 7.

Sutherland, John. *Stanford Companion to Victorian Fiction*. 2nd ed. Stanford, CA: Stanford University Press, 1989.

'Telegrams'. *Clutha Leader*, 23 July 1874, 3.

'Telegraph Item'. *Hartford Daily Courant*, 26 March 1872, 3.

Thom, Colin W. *Bervie and Beyond*. N.p.: Xlibris Corporation, 2013.

'Those of Our Readers'. *Scottish Typographical Circular*, 1 June 1865, 161.

'Threatened Typographical Strike in Canada'. *New York Herald*, 23 March 1872, 3.

'Through Our Exchanges'. *Bruce Herald*, 1 August 1882.

'To Our Readers'. *Leeds Typographical Circular*, May 1888, 1.

Toronto Typographical Union. 'Account Books, 1908–1909, Toronto Typographical Union (Local 91)'. ed. Archives of Ontario. Toronto: Archives of Ontario, 1978.

Toronto Typographical Union. 'Minute Books, 1859–1871, Toronto Typographical Union (Local 91)'. ed. Archives of Ontario. Toronto: Archives of Ontario, 1978.

'To the Memory of John Shand. Assistant Secretary, London Society of Compositors'. *Scottish Typographical Circular*, 1 March 1869, 148.

'The Toronto Printers' Strike: Arresting the Malcontents'. *New York Herald*, 18 April 1872, 9.

'Trade Disputes: Edinburgh Printers' Strike'. *The Scotsman*, 11 February 1873, 6.

'Trade Disputes: Edinburgh Printers' Strike and the Non-Society Hands'. *The Scotsman*, 5 December 1872, 5.

'Trade Disputes: The Edinburgh Printers' Strike'. *The Scotsman*, 13 December 1872, 5.

'Trade Disputes. Great Strike of Printers in Edinburgh'. *The Sheffield Daily Telegraph*, 16 November 1872, 3.

'Trade Movements. Edinburgh Printers' Strike and the Non-Society Hands'. *Dundee Courier & Argus*, 6 December 1872.

'Trade News: Glasgow'. *Scottish Typographical Circular*, 1 September 1868, 72.

'The Trade Tramp'. *Leisure Hours*, 1 June 1868.

'Tramping'. *Scottish Typographical Circular*, 5 July 1862, 169–72.

'Try to Live to 150 Ends at 83'. *Sunday Mail*, 14 July 1946, 3.

'The Tuapeka Times'. *The Tuapeka Times*, 15 February 1868.

'Tuapeka Times' General Printing Office'. *Tuapeka Times*, 15 February 1868, 1.

Tucker, Eric. ' "That Indefinite Area of Toleration": Criminal Conspiracy and Trade Unions in Ontario, 1837–77'. *Labour/Le Travail* 27 (1991), 15–54.

'A Typographical Dispute'. *South African Typographical Journal* 5, no. 49 (November 1902), 14–15.

'A Typographical Dispute'. *South African Typographical Journal* 4, no. 50 (December 1902), 14.

Ulman, Lloyd. *The Rise of the National Trade Union*. Cambridge, MA: Harvard University Press, 1955.

'A Unionist Sent to Prison'. *The Sheffield Daily Telegraph*, 6 February 1873, 3.

'Unto the Master Printers of Edinburgh, the Memorial of the Journeymen Compositors of That City'. Edinburgh, 1861.

'A Veteran Treasurer'. *Typographical Circular*, March 1918, 5.

Vicinus, Martha. *The Industrial Muse: A Study of Nineteenth Century British Working-Class Literature*. London: Croom Helm, 1974.

Webb, Sidney and Beatrice Webb. *Industrial Democracy*. New ed. London: Longman, Green and Co., 1897.

Webb, Sidney and Beatrice Webb. *The History of Trade Unionism, 1666–1920*. London: Self published for the Trade Unionists of the United Kingdom, 1919.

White, Alan. 'Class, Culture and Control: The Sheffield Athenaeum Movement and the Middle Class'. In *The Culture of Capital: Art, Power and the Nineteenth-Century Middle Class*, ed. Janet Wolff and John Seed, 83–115. Manchester: Manchester University Press, 1988.

Williams, Helen. 'Regional Print Economies in 19th-Century Scotland'. PhD thesis, Edinburgh Napier University, 2018.

Wolman, Leo. *The Growth of American Trade Unions, 1880–1923.* New York: National Bureau of Economic Research, 1924.

Zerker, Sally F. 'A History of the Toronto Typographical Union, 1832–1925'. Ph.D. thesis, University of Toronto, 1972.

Zerker, Sally F. 'The Development of Collective Bargaining in the Toronto Printing Industry in the Nineteenth Century'. *Relations industrielles/Industrial Relations* 30, no. 1 (1975), 83–97.

Zerker, Sally F. 'George Brown and the Printers' Union'. *Journal of Canadian Studies/Revue d'etudes canadiennes* 10, no. 1 (1975), 42–8.

Zerker, Sally F. *The Rise and Fall of the Toronto Typographical Union, 1832–1972: A Case Study of Foreign Domination.* Toronto and Buffalo, NY: University of Toronto Press, 1982.

Index

Page numbers in *italics* refer to captions, those suffixed '(n)' refer to notes

Index